# Workbook – Institutional economics and economic organisation theory

# Workbook

# Institutional economics and economic organisation theory

## *an integrated approach*

**Dr. Louis H.G. Slangen**

**Pieter W. Heringa**

*Wageningen Academic*
P u b l i s h e r s

ISBN: 978-90-8686-120-0

First published, 2009

© Wageningen Academic Publishers
The Netherlands, 2009

# Table of contents

# Preface

This Workbook accompanies the textbook 'Institutional Economics and Economic organisation Theory; an integrated approach'. The book IE & EOT is the first textbook to integrate the various theoretical aspects of New Institutional Economics and economic organisation theory into one analytical framework. The structure of this book is designed to introduce the theoretical aspects of institutional economics and economic organisation theory in a step-by-step manner. Each chapter focuses on a specific topic that is integral to institutional or economic organisation analysis. In addition, as the main topic is introduced, the reader is also introduced to the links between the concepts and theories discussed in the different chapters. As the chapters progress, these related theories are developed in more depth.

The goal of this book is not only to introduce the theory of institutional economics and economic organisation, but also to give examples of how the different theoretical perspectives can be applied. Some chapters contain additional questions on, for example, the calculation of the quasi-rents and the application of the principal-agent theory. However, to make sure that students are able to understand the different theoretical perspectives and their applications, more exercises could be needed. For that reason we have developed a workbook with questions and exercises. This workbook is intended to complement the concepts and study material with real-world examples and exercises. The workbook consists of 11 chapters, just as the textbook. For most of the questions in the workbook, the answers are given and explained. A selected number of examination questions from the last 10 years are included. We are grateful for the contribution of dr. Laura Loucks to earlier versions of this workbook.

*Dr. Louis H.G. Slangen*
Associate professor, Agricultural Economics and Rural Policy, Wageningen University.
louis.slangen@wur.nl

*Pieter W. Heringa*
Student assistant, Agricultural Economics and Rural Policy, Wageningen University.
pieter.heringa@wur.nl

# 1. Introduction and overview

## 1.1 The growing role of institutions
a. Why is there a growing interest in the role of institutions?
b. Which recent political developments have accelerated and increased the relevance and importance of new institutional economics?
c. What problems can arise if we as consumers have to conclude contracts?
d. For which types of problems is the new institutional economic theory important and why?
e. Some years ago, the Dutch government concluded performance contracts with the police force. Why is it import to know the effects of these contracts?

## Answer 1.1 The growing role of institutions
a. Both from a **societal** and from an **economic** point of view it becoms more and more clear that institutions are important for economic growth and development. In the textbook in Section 1.1, some examples are given.
b. A first important development is the fall of the wall separating East and West Germany in 1989. This event marked a new era; the collapse of the communist system. At the time, many people, including famous economists and policy makers, expected rapid economic growth in Central and Eastern European countries. However, this did not happen. Rather, it became clear that a sound institutional setting is a pre-condition for well-functioning markets.

   A second important development is the privatisation of state enterprises. In the last 25 years, thousands of state firms in Africa, Asia, Latin America, and Western and Eastern Europe have gone private. Government firms supplying resources and services such as gas, water, electricity, railways etc. were transformed from public to private firms. At the same time, markets were liberalised. This also raises the question of how the provision or supply of goods and services should be organised.
c. The provision of goods, like gas, forces us into entering into contracts with large and powerful corporations. This creates problems such as: What are the effects of these contracts? Can we easily switch from one service provider to another? Do we have enough information to compare costs and benefits? Are there hold-up and lock-in effects that force us to remain with one company? Who is able to capture the residual income of these contracts, or more in general, of the privatisation and liberalisation processes? Is it the consumer or the producer who benefits?
d. The theory of new institutional economics is very important for analysing questions such as: (1) what and (2) how to organise transactions in our daily lives, in our households, firms, organisations (like the government) or between them. Which governance structure can be used? The market and the government are often seen as the only solution. However, not only can both fail, but the approach is too simplistic. Many transactions (or activities) are coordinated by other governance structures, often called hybrids, such as clubs and contracts. More attention is needed to other governance structures.
e. It is important to know the effects of these types of contracts. For example, what are the effects of performance contracts on the behaviour of the police force? How will these contracts influence the behaviour of the individual policeman? Will they result in more fines or in more safety? Which type of crimes will be solved: the easiest ones?

### 1.2 Neo-classical economic theory and new institutional economics
a. Why is there, within economics, a growing interest in institutions?
b. What does the standard economic theory assume about information?
c. How is the firm perceived in the standard economic theory and what is the role of the producer?
d. Are the assumptions of the standard economic theory realistic? Explain your answer.
e. How important is the market as a governance structure?
f. Why is it useful to go beyond the view of the firm as a 'black box'?

### Answer 1.2 Neo-classical economic theory and new institutional economics
a. Within economics there is a growing interest in the role of governance structures, social embeddedness and the institutional environment. These developments are partly a reaction to the limitations of standard economic theory concerning, for example, perfect competition with completely functioning markets, and the firm as an economic agent with a single identity.
b. Under perfect competition, all the necessary information is included in the prices and the involved parties have all the relevant information.
c. A firm is seen as a production function, with clear links between the input and output, and in a position to produce a variety of products by using different amounts and combinations of inputs. In its simplest form, the firm is regarded as a 'black box' or production function, without any internal structure but able to produce a large variety of output(s) using different combinations of inputs. Every economic agent is assumed to have perfect information; that is, all agents know all technically feasible production and consumption plans and all prices in every market. The role of the producer is relatively simple, given the existence of prices for all goods and perfectly functioning markets and complete information.
d. The assumptions of traditional neo-classical economic theory do not always correspond to the reality. For example, the conditions of perfect competition (numerous buyers and sellers, homogeneous products, complete and symmetric information, etc.) are often not met in practice. Often, the price cannot incorporate all the dimensions of a product or service. Sometimes there is no market price at all (think of environmental goods, such as nature and biodiversity).
e. Not everything is co-ordinated via the invisible hand of the market. On the contrary, other governance structures are often more important. In addition to markets, other organisational forms such as firms, contracts, clubs, and households can also function as a governance structure. For example, within firms, we see that the decision-making process and the transaction mechanism 'the market' are replaced by another structure or decision-making mechanism which ensures co-ordination.
f. To understand how firms and other organisations function, we have to open the 'black box' firm as a single unit with a single identity). Within a firm, different parties (or stakeholders) are working together. A firm can also be seen as a 'nexus of contracts' where each of the concerned parties is driven by self-interests, which can be different and may be contradictory. This view makes clear that it is not only differences in external organisation but also in internal organisation that can have consequences for the results of a firm.

### 1.3 Markets
a. What is a pre-condition for well-functioning markets?

b. What four basic conditions characterise a competitive market?
c. Are the assumptions of the traditional neo-classical economic theory always in line with reality?

### Answer 1.3 Markets

a. A sound institutional setting is a pre-condition for well-functioning markets. A good international indicator for the institutional setting is the yearly *Transparency International Corruption index* (http://www.infoplease.com/ipa/A0781359.html).
b. Four basic conditions characterising competitive markets are:
   - A large number of either actual or potential buyers and sellers.
   - Product homogeneity.
   - Rapid dissemination of accurate information at low costs.
   - Free entry and exit in the market.
c. The conditions of perfect competition (numerous buyers and sellers, homogeneous products, complete and symmetric information, etc.) are often not met in practice.

### 1.4 Firms

a. What is a firm?
b. How do you explain the existence of firms if markets are so useful for managing economic transactions?

### Answer 1.4 Firms

a. Economists have developed several different definitions of a firm. The idea has generally been given up that a firm is a production function and should be viewed as a black box. Firms and other organisations do not function as a single unit with a single identity. A more modern approach is to view a firm as a cooperation of different parties (or stakeholders). This view can reveal the workings of the black box. The firm can also be seen as a 'nexus of contracts" where each of the concerned parties is driven by self-interests, which can be different and may be contradictory. This course focuses on a more modern view of the firm, including the firm as a focal point for a set of contracts.
b. Firms exist because of the costs associated with the use of markets. For example, the presence of firms can reduce the number of transactions between consumers and owners of factors of production from $n \times m$ to $n + m$. Another example is the contracting cost associated with firm-specific assets. Outsourcing of activities can be preferable to reduce hold-up costs and lock-in effects, given the asset specificity of certain firm investments. Another example is a firm that has a long-term contract with a supplier of tyres, of chairs, of windows, etc. That is much easier (and may also be cheaper) than if a market transaction had to be organised for the purchase of such parts for every case separately.

### 1.5 Theory of the state and theory of the firm

a. Please give a brief and stylised description of the modern theory of the firm.
b. What is motivating for the principal and what does it mean for the internal institutions and the relationship with the agents?
c. Please give a brief and stylised description of the theory of the state.

d. What would a 'wise' ruler do? Is there a mechanism that can exert pressure on the ruler to design efficient institutions?

e. How do the principal and ruler ensure that everyone follows the rules of the firm or State?

**Answer 1.5 Theory of the state and theory of the firm**

a. A principal recognises an opportunity to increase the return that can be achieved when individuals are potentially involved in an interdependent relationship. The entrepreneur (we will call him the principal) then negotiates a series of contracts with various participants that specify how they are to act in a coordinated, rather than independent, fashion. Each participant voluntarily chooses whether or not to join the firm, but allows the principal to choose across some range of choices. The participants become agents of the principal. After paying each of the agents, the principal retains the residual income (or absorbs losses).

b. Due to residual income, the principal is highly motivated to organise the activities as efficiently as possible. When a firm is located in an open market, one can presume that external competition will pressure the principal towards developing efficient internal institutions.
The principal attempts to design contracts with agents that will induce them to act so as to increase the return of the principal, and the principal monitors the agents' performances. Because agents freely decide whether or not to accept the terms of the principal's contract, the organisation is considered private and voluntary. Furthermore, agents are driven by different types of incentives.

c. A ruler recognises that substantial benefits can be obtained by organising some activities. If a ruler gains a monopoly on the use of force, the ruler can use coercion as the fundamental mechanism to organise a range of human activities that will produce collective benefits. The ruler obtains taxes, labour or other resources from subjects by threatening them with severe sanctions if they do not provide the resources.

d. A 'wise' ruler would use the resources obtained to increase the general level of economic well-being of the subjects to such a degree that the ruler can increase tax revenues while being able to reduce the more oppressive uses of coercions. Rulers, like the principals, keep the residuals. Subjects, like agents, may be substantially better off as a result of subjecting themselves to the coercion exercised by the rulers. No mechanism exists, such as a competitive market, that would exert pressure on the ruler to design efficient institutions.

e. In both the theory of the firm and the theory of the state, the principal or the ruler make credible commitments to punish anyone who does not follow the rules of the firm or the state. Because they gain the residuals, it is in their interests to punish non-conformance to their rules if they are confronted with non-conformance. It is also in their interest to monitor the action of agents and subjects to be sure they conform to the prior agreement. Both theories thus address how a new institutional arrangement can be created, how credible commitment can be made, and why monitoring must be supplied.

**1.6 Free markets**

Evaluate the following statement:

Using free markets and the price system always results in a more efficient resource allocation than central planning. Just look at what happened in Eastern Europe in the past.

**Answer 1.6 Free markets**

The demise of many centrally-planned economies suggests that central government planning in a large economy is likely to be inefficient. Nevertheless, the observation does not suggest that all central planning is bad. Sometimes it can reduce transaction costs relative to the use of markets. This argument provides an explanation for the existence of firms where there is often central economic planning (but in a market economy, these firms constantly face competition from markets and other firms as alternative methods of organising production; this ongoing competition provides powerful incentives to maintain efficient markets).

In the last twenty years, thousands of government-owned firms in Africa, Asia, Latin America, and Western and Eastern Europe have been privatised. Government-owned firms supplying resources and services such as gas, water, electricity, railways, etc. were transformed from public to private firms. At the same time, markets were liberalised. In the Netherlands, the provision of gas, water, electricity, and railways has been split up into network activities and the delivering of gas, water, electricity, or taking care of the transportation of people and goods. The government is still the legal owner of the network facilities of gas, water electricity and railways. However, the way it is organised is not always simple and we need new institutional arrangements such as long-term contracts and conflict-resolving mechanisms.

For example, the Dutch government has delegated the maintenance and management of the railway network on a contractual basis to one private company, called ProRail. The income of ProRail comes from subsidies from the government (currently 80%) and from the user of the railway (currently 20%). The user of the railway is Dutch Railway (NS) which is a private company, but all the shares are owned by the government. The relationship between ProRail and NS has been contractually laid down. NS has to pay ProRail a 'user compensation'. The performance criteria of NS concerning its transportation function have been defined in a contract with the government.

A way to increase the income of ProRail is to increase the 'user compensation'. Recently, ProRail wanted to increase the tariffs for the use of the railways by 17% (April 2009). Apparently, ProRail behaves as a monopolist, it determines the tariffs and also who uses the railways and when (Volkskrant, 27 April 2009). The question is: What can NS do? NS can also be considered a monopolist. Does it have to accept the higher tariffs? In this case it can go to the Netherlands Competition Authority (NMa). Because both ProRail and NS can be considered as being monopolists, we have a situation of bilateral monopoly.

This case makes clear that the alternatives of government-owned enterprises for the provision of gas, water, electricity, railways are not without problems. Long-term contracts have to be developed, conflict-resolving mechanisms such as the NMa have to be implemented, monitoring is necessary, sanctions should be possible, etc. This creates transaction costs. For analysing such phenomena, the standard neoclassical economics have to be complemented with the transaction cost and contract theory. To encourage investments in networks (pipes or railways) and in e.g. trains, hold-up and lock-in effects of the investing parties should be taken into account. Last but not least, exclusive contracts as described above create monopoly power involving negative welfare effects.

# 2. Background, origin and positioning

## 2.1 New Institutional Economics (NIE) and Economic Organisation Theory (EOT)
a. What do these theories have in common?
b. What is a transaction?
c. What is the focus of the economic analysis of transactions?
d. What are the differences between New Institutional Economics and Economic Organisation Theory?

## Answer 2.1 New Institutional Economics (NIE) and Economic Organisation Theory (EOT)
a. Both theories deviate in some parts from the neo-classical economics. In both theories the fundamental unit of analysis is the transaction.
b. Transaction is synonymous with the economic concept of exchange. It is a two-sided mechanism: the transfer of goods or services from one individual to another or the trade-off between performance and counter performance, *quid pro quo,* and the transfer of property rights. Transactions can be organised by markets, firms or by so-called hybrid forms.
c. The economic analysis of the transaction focuses on:
   - *co-ordination* – i.e. what needs to be co-ordinated, how co-ordination is achieved in markets, inside organisations and in hybrid forms (such as contracts), which alternatives can be used for achieving co-ordination between units, and how does each part of a system fit together;
   - *motivation* – i.e. what and who needs to be motivated, which incentives are needed, what alternative kinds of incentive systems there are, and what needs to be done to make incentive systems effective and efficient (in short, inducing persons or organisations to do what you want them to do);
   - *demonstrating* that these aspects of organisation matter.
d. The scope of NIE is somewhat broader than that of EOT. NIE explicitly focuses on institutions; i.e. the rules of the game as laid down in the formal and informal rules of society. The scope of NIE is:
   - the role and meaning of the social embeddedness, including social capital and the informal rules;
   - the formal rules of the game as included in the formal rules of society and property rights;
   - public choice processes including rent seeking and activities of shifting coalitions, and principal/agent relationships between politicians and government bureaucrats;
   - the areas common to NIE and EOT, regarding the fundamental question about the reason for the existence and the functioning of institutional arrangements (like firms, organisations, contracts). Both make use of information and behavioural economics, principal/agent, transactions cost, and contract theory.

## 2.2 Industrial organisation theory and the SCP approach
a. Which approach dominated the theory of industrial organisation until the 1970s? Give a description of this theory
b. Which elements belong to the structure, conduct and performance of a branch of industry?
c. What was the effect of the influence of the behaviourists on the use of the SCP approach, and how does it influence the current use of the SCP approach?

d.  What was the main problem with the original SCP approach?

e.  How can the modern variant of industrial organisation theory be characterised?

**Answer 2.2 Industrial organisation theory and the SCP approach**

a.  Until the 1970s, the theory of industrial organisation was dominated by the old Structure-Conduct-Performance (SCP) approach. The emphasis was on empirical research about how well the various branches of industry were functioning. This approach assumed that structure determines conduct and performance.
    Following this approach, a number of empirical studies were conducted, initially neglecting the *conduct link* in the SCP framework. This was based on the argument that the conduct of firms can only be analysed in the context of market results. Representatives of the structuralist school, such as the founder Bain (1968), assume a relatively permanent structure in which both conduct and performance are determined.

b.  The elements of structure include: the size and number of sellers/producers in the branch or sector, market concentration ratio, market power, the degree of product differentiation, the cost structure, the barriers to entry, the degree of vertical integration with suppliers, etc. Conduct refers to the price, research and development, investments, advertising, etc., and conduct yields performance. Performance is reflected by efficiency, the ratio of prices to marginal costs, product variety, innovation rate and distribution.

c.  Under the influence of the behaviourists, including one of the most important representatives, Scherer (1980), greater attention has been gradually devoted to the *conduct variables*. According to the behaviourists, the inter-relationships between firms and their strategy determine the performance. If oligopolies by means of cartels, collusion or price leadership can co-ordinate their actions, then their resulting interdependence can lead to collective profit maximisation.

d.  The main problem with the original SCP approach was that the relationships were formulated as mono-causal. New theoretical insights indicate that SCP relationships are fundamentally multi-causal in nature. The structure of a branch of industry or sector is not given exogenously, but is determined by the conduct of the firms. Firms select the degree of product differentiation, their cost structure, degree of vertical integration, etc. It means there is not only a path from *structure to behaviour/conduct* but also from *behaviour/conduct to structure*.

e.  The modern variant, called Modern Organisation Theory, is characterised by the importance of the functioning of markets and the strategic behaviour of firms which operate in these markets, analysed using models such as game theory models. In these models, the economic agents or firms, whether new entrants or established firms, are all considered to be rational. Everyone takes the action of everyone else into account: the so-called strategic interaction. The level of aggregation is not the branch of industry but the agent who makes decisions. In

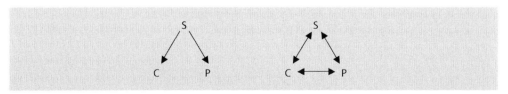

*Figure 2.1. Old (left) and modern Structure Conduct Performance approach (right).*

the case of a monopoly (a product or service is sold by only one firm) or perfect competition (all actors are price takers), the nature and magnitude of strategic interaction is too small for a formal use of game theory.

### 2.3 Long-run decisions, sunk costs and sunk investments
a. What is the difference between long-run decisions and short-run decisions?
b. What are sunk costs?
c. What are sunk investments?
d. What is the relationship between sunk investment and asset specificity?
e. What is the consequence for the governance structure of sunk costs and sunk investments?

### Answer 2.3 Long-run decisions, sunk costs and sunk investment
a. Long-run decisions are generally taken only once in a while. The construction of a new factory, building an office, a cowshed, a barn, or a greenhouse are examples of such decisions. Once the decision is made, it is not possible to reverse it easily, and a reversal of the decision entails costs that cannot be recovered. These are known as *sunk costs*. Short-run decisions are made regularly, and can be reversed or changed without incurring major costs. In this view, long-run decisions are decisive for short-run decisions.
b. *Sunk costs* are non-recoverable costs. *Sunk costs* means that once a decision is made, it is not possible to reverse it easily, and a reversal of the decision entails costs that cannot be recovered. These costs are called sunk costs. *Sunk costs* are strongly related to *sunk investments*.
c. Sunk investments are investments that generate profits in the case of a particular application but have little value in another application.
d. *Sunk costs* and *sunk investments* are related to the concepts of fixed assets and asset specificity. The use of fixed assets and investments with a high level of asset specificity result in sunk investments and sunk costs.
e. Sunk costs and sunk investments influence the choice of the best *governance structure*. It has consequences for the question: How to organise? What is, given the circumstances, the best or most suitable governance structure? Are spot markets, contracts, vertical integration or in-house production the best governance structure? This question deals with feasible organisational alternatives. The problem of sunk costs can be reduced by concluding long-term contracts or vertical integration (also called in-house production). For example, if a farmer wants to build a new greenhouse, he could first conclude a long-term contract with a retailer. That way, he is better assured of a return on the investment of the greenhouse. This reduces the problem of sunk costs.

### 2.4 Contestable markets
a. What is a perfectly contestable market?
b. Which three conditions should be fulfilled for markets to be contestable?
c. What type of costs will not arise in a contestable market?
d. Do contestable markets occur frequently? Please give some examples.

### Answer 2.4 Contestable markets
a. A perfectly contestable market is one where entry and exit is free and without costs. Sunk costs and sunk investments do not arise in this case.

b.  A perfectly contestable market requires three conditions. **First**, there are no sunk costs. **Second**, potential new firms should have no disadvantage compared to existing firms concerning entry to production technology and product quality. **Third**, firms that enter should be able to apply *hit and run* tactics.

c.  Sunk costs and sunk investments do not arise in contestable markets. Switching costs to another market or producer are negligible.

d.  Contestable markets will not often occur. Some examples of contestable markets are selling via Internet and a free site for selling products for private individuals, for example, on the Queen's Birthday in the Netherlands (but even in such cases, there are often some costs involved, e.g. searching costs).

## 2.5 Evolutionary theory
a.  What are the sources of inspiration of the evolutionary theory?
b.  Which Darwinian concepts are used for explaining economic phenomena such as economic change and adaptation?

## Answer 2.5 Evolutionary theory
a.  The sources of inspiration of the evolutionary theory are: (1) *Darwinian evolutionary theory* and (2) the *criticism of neo-classical theory.*
b.  Supporters of evolutionary theory believe that economic phenomena such as **economic change and adaptation** can be adequately described and explained by using Darwinian concepts such as (1) heredity; (2) natural selection (= survival of the fittest); and (3) variation, including mutation (= new variation). The analogous economic concepts are routines, selection mechanisms and innovations.

## 2.6 Routines
a.  What does the term 'routines' mean?
b.  What are the functions of routines?
c.  What could the consequences of routines be?

## Answer 2.6 Routines
a.  Routines or rules of thumb refer to all regular and predictable behaviour patterns. In general, the behaviour of firms is stable and routine, because in a world of uncertainty (resulting from incomplete information) we rely as far as possible on our own existing knowledge and experience when making decisions. It means that firms and individuals often fall back on routines for decision-making.
b.  Routines fulfil two functions in organisations. First, they function as the memory of the organisation. Organisations remember largely by doing. Routines that are not used for some time tend to disappear. Second, routines can be seen as stabilising forces in the organisation. They keep possible conflict within an organisation under control; in that sense they present a truce in an interorganisational conflict.
c.  Routines have often been incorporated in specific and irreversible investments, which involve high sunk costs and because of that they often have a stable character. Changing routines requires enormous investments (switching costs) and the effect on the competitiveness of the firm is often uncertain. The higher the switching costs, the less quickly a firm will change.

## 2.7 Selection

a. What is the view of evolutionary theory about selection?
b. What do selection mechanisms consist of?

## Answer 2.7 Selection

a. **Selection** is viewed as an enormous evolutionary mechanism that investigates the pattern of organisations at every point of time as it were, and tests their ability to fulfil their role. The evolution of institutions and their performance implications are affected strongly by their path-dependency nature. Path dependency means the direction and scope of institutional change cannot be divorced from its early course or past history. Because of their path-dependency characteristics, institutions are the *carriers of history*, reproducing themselves well beyond the time of their usefulness.

b. In evolutionary economics, the forces influencing competition processes are called selection mechanisms. These selection mechanisms consist of markets, institutions and the spatial environment. They function as a kind of filter, through which adapted firms can survive, and the less well adapted will disappear. These selection forces form the explanation framework of Evolutionary economics, because they take care of a certain level of continuity (in addition to routines). Selection mechanisms determine which routines and innovations will survive and which will not.

## 2.8 Innovations

a. According to evolutionary theory, what is the role of innovations in the economy?
b. According to evolutionary theory, why do firms persist with innovations?

## Answer 2.8 Innovations

a. Mutations in evolutionary biology lead to new variations in the population. According to the theory of evolutionary economics, innovations are sources of new variations in the economy. Innovations in firms make it possible for them to survive in the market.

b. Firms persist in a world of persistent routines and strong competition with innovations because they are threatened in their existing routines: search is failure-induced. Innovations are broadly defined as 'changes in routines'. They can be changes in products, in production technologies, in organisational forms and in markets, etc.

## 2.9 Criticism of neo-classical economics

a. On which criticism of neo-classical economics does the evolutionary theory focus?
b. What does the evolutionary theory say about rationality, reversibility, homogeneity and static equilibrium?

## Answer 2.9 Criticism of neo-classical economics

a. The criticism of evolutionary economics of neo-classical economy focuses on the assumptions of rationality, reversibility, the homogeneity of economic agents (the firm as black box), and the static equilibrium concept.

b. Evolutionary economics supposes and emphasises bounded rationality, irreversibility and path dependency, heterogeneity (variation), change and dynamics instead of static equilibrium.

### 2.10 Bounded rationality
a. What does bounded rationality mean?
b. What are the consequences of bounded rationality?

### Answer 2.10 Bounded rationality
a. *Bounded rationality* is said to arise when the cognitive ability of people is insufficient to deal with the complexity of the world. People are not in a position to take all circumstances into account when making a decision. As a result, human behaviour is: '… intendedly rational, but only limited so[1]'. Think for example of subscriptions to mobile telephones: even if you possessed all relevant information on all the options available, it would be very difficult, if not impossible, to make a rational choice.
b. One of the consequences of bounded rationality could be that people make use of rules of thumb, or routine behaviour. Routine behaviour is regular and relatively predictable, conservative and risk averse.

### 2.11 Reversibility, technical lock-in and path dependence
a. What is the view according to evolutionary economics on reversibility?
b. What is the relationship between technical lock-in and path dependency?
c. What is an important reason for path dependency for a firm or economy?

### Answer 2.11 Reversibility, technical lock-in and path dependency
a. Evolutionary economics is characterised by the analysis of irreversible historical processes. This is an important difference with neo-classical economics in which reversibility is the key factor.
b. The notion of technical lock-in is similar to the broader concept of path dependency. As a result of technological adaptation, the related sunk implementation and learning costs involved, a firm or an economy can be pushed in the direction of a particular situation.
c. An important reason for path dependency for a firm or an economy is the technology applied.

### 2.12 Heterogeneity
a. How do neo-classical and evolutionary economics differ in their assumptions about the economic agents?
b. Name one reason for heterogeneity?

### Answer 2.12 Heterogeneity
a. Neo-classical economics supposes that economic agents are homogeneous and have rational behaviour. In evolutionary economics, heterogeneity (variation) is the key principle.
b. This heterogeneity has to do with bounded rationality. For example, firms are not always completely informed about new innovations. There is mostly information asymmetry and firms could have different expectations about the technological route or innovation, because of bounded rationality. If information about new knowledge becomes directly public for everyone at the same time, it would make no sense for firms to develop new innovations or knowledge. This is also known as the *fundamental paradox of information*: the value of

---

[1] Simon, A.H., 1961. Administrative behaviour. 2nd edition. MacMillan Company, New York, NY, USA, p. xxiv.

information can only be revealed to another party by disclosing that information, while such disclosure destroys the value of the information. To illustrate this, imagine an engineer who has an excellent idea for a new machine, and wants to sell it to a firm. In order to do so, he must first reveal quite some information on his idea, decreasing the value of the information he would like to sell.

## 2.13 Change and dynamics
a. What explains economic changes according to evolutionary economics?
b. What is the view of evolutionary economics about the initial birth, evolution, selection and performances of institutions?

## Answer 2.13 Change and dynamics
a. The explanation of change (new variation) of evolutionary economics consists of coincidence, inventions, and selection elements. It considers technological change as the most important determinant of economic growth.
b. Evolutionary theory also deals with institutions. The emphasis is less on the emergence of institutions, but more on the function performed and the contribution of the institution to the welfare or success of a social unit. For explaining an institution, we first have to know its contribution to the survival of society or an organisation (like a firm). The **initial birth** (development) of an institution does not require to be explained. Institutions may arise due to coincidence, unexpected events, or as a result of the standard process of the *invisible hand* (i.e. the market), or even as a result of a conscious objective. An important view here is that the **selection process** is *'non-man made'* and is the result of the environment.
   **Selection** of institutions is viewed as an enormous evolutionary mechanism testing the ability of organisations to fulfil their role. The evolution of institutions and their **performance** implications are affected strongly by path dependency: the direction and scope of institutional change cannot be divorced from its early course or past history.

## 2.14 Sunk costs
Discuss the following statement: 'Sunk costs matter. People who pay €20,000 to join a golf club play golf more frequently than people who play on public golf courses'.

## Answer 2.14 Sunk costs
People who pay € 20,000 to join a golf club are likely to have a greater than average interest in playing golf. Once they have paid, they may consider only the marginal costs (e.g. travel time) and benefits in choosing how much to play. However, given their interest in golf (marginal benefits are high) they will tend to play frequently. Thus, the observation is more likely to reflect 'self-selection' than sunk costs.

## 2.15 Economic Darwinism
Briefly describe *Economic Darwinism.*

### Answer 2.15 Economic Darwinism

Economic Darwinism is the economic counterpart of 'natural selection' in biology. Competition in the market place weeds out those organisations that are less efficient and fail to adapt to the environment. The result is the 'survival of the fittest'.

### 2.16 Common elements of New Institutional Economics (NIE), Economics Organisation Theory (EOT) and Evolutionary Theory (ET)

a. Which assumptions of the standard neo-classical economics are criticised?
b. What is the criticism of the black box approach to firms and households?
c. What is the role of institutions in standard neo-classical economics?

### Answer 2.16 Common elements of NIE, EOT, and ET

a. These theories share the following doubts about a number of standard assumptions in traditional neo-classical economics: (1) the behaviour of economic subjects, concerning rationality, utility-maximisation by households and profit maximisation by firms; (2) the availability of complete (and/or free or costless) information; (3) completely defined and enforceable private property rights; (4) unlimited market transactions; (5) absence of transaction costs; (6) completely divisible inputs and outputs.
b. In standard neo-classical economics, households and firms are usually perceived as a 'black box', within which everything works perfectly and everyone acts as they are supposed to act. Firms were assumed to strive for profit maximisation and to produce at the lowest cost. The neo-classical economics says nothing about the internal structure of firms, their hierarchical structure, how decisions are delegated, and who has authority for making decisions. Problems arise like: *who has the power of control and who is able to capture the quasi-rent or the residual income?* People in a firm or organisation do not have the same interests. What can we do about this? The standard neo-classical theory also neglected incentive problems within the firm. These incentives can be based on rewards (carrot), punishment (stick), building-up reputation, credible commitment, and career concern.
c. The standard neo-classical economics neglects the role of institutions. This is a basic argument for applying NIE. In the last few decades, there has been increased interest among economists in the role played by institutions in the working of economic systems. Institutions consist of both informal constraints (sanctions, taboos, customs, traditions, and codes of conduct), and formal rules (constitutions, laws and property rights). Such institutions have important economic consequences.

### 2.17 Behaviour of the firm

a. Name at least two major arguments for criticising of the traditional profit-maximising theory.
b. Why do firms often adopt simple 'rules of thumb', e.g. for pricing?
c. What does profits 'satisfying behaviour' often mean in a large company with shareholders?
d. What is the focus of the behavioural theories of the firm?

### Answer 2.17 Behaviour of the firm

a. Two reasons are: (1) firms may not have the information to maximise profits; (2) they may not even want to maximise profits, e.g. as results of satisfying behaviour.

b. Firms often adopt simple 'rules of thumb' because of lack of information on demand and costs, and on the actions and reaction of rivals, and a lack of use of opportunity costs concepts.
c. Managers aim to achieve sufficient profit to keep the shareholders happy, this is a secondary aim to one or more alternatives.
d. Behavioural theories of the firm examine how managers and other interest groups actually behave. Managers may seek to maximise their own utility. Shareholders, workers, customers, suppliers and creditors may have their own aims. A conflict between the different aims is likely to arise.

## 2.18 Quasi-rent

Suppose an entrepreneur has invented a new machine that makes special widgets. The machine costs € 950,000 to build. To learn how to operate the new technology, workers with appropriate initial qualifications require training and experience for one year. Their alternative wage or opportunity costs is $W_{alt}$ = 20,000 Euros per year. In this novel situation, it may be necessary for the entrepreneur to pay them for the specialised training. If she hires five workers, the total cost of training them, or human capital investment (leading to human asset specificity) will be € 50,000, H = 50,000. The total investment of the entrepreneur is thus 1 million Euros, I = 1,000,000.

- the machine with the team of five trained workers produce 10,000 widgets per year;
- the market price of widgets is P = 50;
- the sales revenues are S = 500,000 Euros;
- to stimulate the worker to work hard, to take care of the machine and not to shirk, the entrepreneur pays the workers a wage of € 40,000 per year;
- the borrowing rate for the investment of I = 1,000,000 is 5%;
- the variable costs are € 5 per widget;
- The depreciation term of investment in the machine is 10 years, i.e. the yearly depreciation costs are € 95,000.

a. Calculate the results for the first year.
b. Next, we suppose that after one year the widget market collapses and the price falls to P = 35.
c. Analyse the alternatives after the price fall. What criteria can be used to investigate what is the preferred solution: close down the business or continuation?
d. What does the outcome mean for the mode of organisation? Would a partnership be a better solution?

## Answer 2.18 Quasi-rent

a. Table 2.1 presents the results for the first year. The total surplus is € 105,000. Notice that the workers have a quasi-rent of $W_0 - W_{alt}$ = 40,000 – 20,000 = 20,000 Euros per person. The entrepreneur has a surplus or profit of € 105,000.
b. After the market collapse, the resale value or salvage value of the machine is, say € 180,000. The entrepreneur could close down the business and try to fire the five workers. There are some objections to this solution. Firing the workers can be difficult. The entrepreneur has to pay back the loan; but can she do this? What kind of sources of income does she have?
   An alternative could be that she starts to renegotiate the wage contract with the workers and to settle for a new wage, for example, $W_1$ = 35,000 Euros. For the workers this is more than their opportunity costs $W_{alt}$ = 20,000 Euros per year. This renegotiation process involves transaction costs. However, staying in the firm still means a quasi-rent of € 15,000 for workers, compared

Table 2.1. The results in the first year in Euros.

|  | Yearly return in € | Yearly costs in € | Surplus in € |
| --- | --- | --- | --- |
| Return 10,000 x 50 | 500,000 |  |  |
| Wage 5 x 40,000 |  | 200,000 |  |
| Variable costs 10,000 x 5 |  | 50,000 |  |
| Depreciation costs |  | 95,000 |  |
| Interest 5% of 1,000,000 |  | 50,000 |  |
| Total | 500,000 | 395,000 | 105,000 |

to being fired. Depending on the bargaining power of both parties (the entrepreneur and the workers) a lower wage for workers could be possible, given their alternatives.

Given the salvage value of the machine of € 180,000 the depreciation can be based on this amount. With a life span of 9, years the yearly depreciation can be €20,000. The sunk costs of the machine are:

€950,000 – €95,000 (depreciation costs of the first year) – €180,000 (salvage value) = € 675,000. The total quasi-rent consists of € 55,000 + € 75,000 = € 130,000. This can be split up into € 55,000 for the entrepreneur and € 75,000 for the workers. Table 2.2 gives the results.

Table 2.2. The results after the market collapse.

|  | Yearly return in € | Yearly costs in € | Quasi-rent in € |
| --- | --- | --- | --- |
| Return 10,000 x 35 | 350,000 |  |  |
| Wage 5 x 35,000 |  | 175,000 | 75,000 |
| Variable costs 10,000 x 5 |  | 50,000 |  |
| Depreciation costs |  | 20,000 |  |
| Interest 5% of 1,000,000 |  | 50,000 |  |
| Total | 350,000 | 295,000 | 55,000 |

c. As indicated, this solution involves transaction costs. The workers have to accept their decrease in wages. Negotiations are necessary. However, in the case of closing down the business, they will lose their investments in human capital. Another distribution of the quasi-rent is possible. It is possible that the entrepreneur has a strong bargaining position and is able to reduce the wage for the workers to, for example, $W_2 = 30,000$ Euros. This will increase the quasi-rent for the entrepreneur to € 80,000. The outcome of who is able to capture which part of the quasi-rent depends on available information, bargaining power, and the residual control rights.

d. The mode of organisation here is the single owner. A partnership would involve sharing the total quasi-rent, but it can also include sharing the costs of the investment.

### 2.19 Short- and long-run view of a firm

a.  In a short-term view, what types of costs have to be taken into account when considering the closedown of a firm?
b.  What does it mean if a firm can realise a quasi-rent?
c.  What does the shut-down point mean and what is the shut-down point rule?
d.  What will happen to a firm if it is unable to cover the total average costs in the long run? What will be the role of sunk costs?

### Answer 2.19 short- and long-run view of a firm

a.  In a short-term view, the revenue should at least cover the variable (running) costs incurred by producing. If that is not possible, it is better to close the firm down.
b.  If a firm realises a quasi-rent, the earnings of a production factor used in the firm are higher than the salvage value of production factor (i.e. value of production factor outside the firm).
c.  The shut-down point is the point at which it is better to stop with the production. At this point, **none** of the fixed costs are recovered anymore and below this point the variable costs are no longer being recovered. This is also called the shutdown rule: if for every choice of output level the firm's average revenue is less than its variable cost, then the firm should immediately shut down.
d.  If a firm is not able to cover the total average costs in the long run, the firm will be not able to continue its production activities. In the long run, the total revenue must cover the total cost, including total variable costs and fixed costs. Certain investments of a firm can involve sunk costs (these costs can not be recovered). To keep a firm in production in the long run, the losses caused by sunk costs have to be recovered by other activities.

### 2.20 Flower market

In the flower market, the percentage of the transactions through direct contracts increases over the years at the expense of the percentages of transactions through the auction clock.
a.  Explain this phenomenon based on the transaction cost economics.
b.  Explain this phenomenon based on the structure conduct performance paradigm.

### Answer 2.20 Flower market

a.  Transactions in the flower market are likely to be repeated over time. Flowers are often brought to the auction clock in small lots. One can save a lot on transaction costs by direct contracting; visiting the auction sessions is time-consuming (costly) for buyers. For long-term contracts, one can also save considerably on negotiation- and contract enforcement costs. For large flower growers, selling via the auction is clock is often not more efficient. The transaction costs become too high. The same holds for large flower buyers.

Direct contracting is often facilitated by intermediaries. They work for the ornamental marketing organisation 'FloraHolland'. In 2008 about one-third of the turnover of 4.1 billion Euros of FloraHolland was sold by intermediaries. An important role of the intermediaries is reducing transaction costs.
b.  In the SCP approach, elements of the structure of a market influence its conduct and performance (and *vice versa*). Scale enlargement on the flower growers and purchase side means a change in the market structure. From a situation where both producers and buyers are too numerous to have any control over prices whatsoever (a situation where everyone

is a price taker and no one has market power) to a situation with market power for the involved parties. In other words, the market structure changes from perfect competition to monopolistic competition.

Direct contracts often mean that the market power in the market has been changed or will change: the sellers may increase their market power. Their conduct changes, they are not anonymous price takers anymore, the degree of control over prices increases and they are able to develop a direct contract with a buyer. This has consequences for the performance of the firms. Their costs structure, profits and efficiency may change. Concerning the costs structure, it is possible that e.g. specific investments by the sellers are made to satisfy the requirements of the buyers.

# 3. Embeddedness, institutional environment and governance structures

## 3.1 Pareto efficiency
a. What is Pareto efficiency?
b. Why do economists use this criterion for comparing alternative economic systems?

**Answer 3.1 Pareto efficiency**
a. An allocation of resources is Pareto-efficient if there is no other allocation in which some other individual is better off and no individual is worse off.
b. One reason that economists use this criterion for comparing economic systems is that it is relatively uncontroversial. Stronger criteria are likely to be met with more disagreement.

## 3.2 Analytical framework
a. What four different levels of institutions can be distinguished?
b. Explain how the institution environment can affect the incentives of a society to invest in economic activities.

**Answer 3.2 Analytical framework**
a. At the **first** level we find social embeddedness. Important parts of social embeddedness are social capital and formed norms and values, customs, morals, traditions, and codes of conduct, i.e. the informal rules of the game in the society. The **second** level is referred to as the institutional environment; it includes the formal rules of the game in society. These formal rules include constitutions, laws, rules of law, and property rights. At this level the executive, legislative, and bureaucratic functions of the government, as well as the distribution of power across different levels of government are located. The third level is where the institutions of governance are located. Analysis at the **third** level is about the effectiveness and efficiency of different governance structures; e.g. markets, firms, contracts, clubs, in-house production or vertical integration. The challenge here is: get the governance structure right. At the **fourth** level we have placed the incentive structure. These incentives can be based on rewards (carrot), punishment (stick), building-up reputation, credible commitment and career concerns. The incentives can continuously be changed, and when taken together with other levels, they are very important for the economic outcomes. The challenge here is: get the incentive structure right. The economic outcomes are the results of the four levels.
b. The institutional environment in the western part of the world developed from a situation where monarchs had the monopoly of violence, with which they protected civilians against theft and robbery, to a situation of a constitutional state and parliamentary democracy. In the past, some monarchs used their monopoly of power to rob the people. Slavery, serfdom and toll levy were common. People were hesitant to carry out productive activities, as they were afraid the monarch would seize any returns. Society has a kind of hold-up problem. In other words, lack of property rights or the erosion of these rights creates a negative incentive for people to undertake productive activities or investments.

### 3.3 Institutions and economic or sustainable development
a.  Why is *getting the prices right* often not enough to realise economic or sustainable development?
b.  Why do institutions matter from an economic perspective?
c.  Are good institutions instrumental to economic development? If so, why?

### Answer 3.3 Institutions and economic or sustainable development
a.  In many studies about economic or sustainable development the institutional structure is considered as exogenous and the problem becomes one of 'getting the prices right' so that atomistic agents will behave in a 'correct' (that is, efficient) manner. From this presumption of correct economic behaviour, human actions will help to bring about a proper use of the natural environment, and the realisation of a modern economy. *Getting the prices right* follows logically from the prior problem of *getting the institutions right.* **However, institutions are not always right.**
b.  From an economic perspective, institutions matter because they affect national welfare, primarily through productivity, income growth and employment[1]. Comparison of a broad range of countries provides evidence for the importance of institutions and policies on a country's prosperity. In particular, the experiences of those countries with weak institutions show that the absence of well-developed institutions severely hampered economic growth and caused poverty. Olson[2] concludes: (…) 'the large differences in per capita income across countries cannot be explained by differences in access to the world's stock of productive knowledge or to its capital markets, by differences in the ratio of population to land or natural resources, or by differences in the quality of marketable human capital or personal culture. Albeit at a high level of aggregation, this eliminates each of the factors of production as possible explanations of most of the international differences in per capita income. The only remaining plausible explanation is that the great differences in the wealth of nations are mainly due to differences in the **quality of their institutions** and economic policy.'
c.  On the one hand (good) institutions are instrumental to economic development. On the other hand, it is also clear that some institutions retard rather than accelerate growth. Regulatory agencies prevent entry, courts resolve disputes arbitrarily and sometimes dishonestly, and politicians use government property to benefit their supporters rather than the population at large.

### 3.4 institutions and good government
a.  What is the relationship between institutions and good government?
b.  Which dimensions can be used to describe good government?

---

[1] For instance, a country's educational institutions may promote human capital formation, which raises labour productivity in the long run. Technology policy may enhance research and development. Labour market regulation, taxation, and social insurance influence labour supply and demand decisions and search behaviour of unemployment, and thus affect a country's activity rate, the number of working hours per capita.

[2] Olson, M., 1996. Distinguished lecture on economics in government: big bills left on the side-walk. Why some nations are rich, and others poor. Journal of Economic Perspectives 10: 3-24. Citation on p. 19.

**Answer 3.4 Institutions and good government**

a. Good government is shown to have contributed to the economic development of European countries over the last millennium, and to growth across countries over the last 50 years. This implies that good government is an important condition for good institutions.

b. Dimensions to describe good government are:

1. Good government protects property rights, and keeps regulation and taxes on a reasonable level.

   Perhaps the most standard view is that a good government protects property rights, and keeps regulation and taxes on a reasonable level. The **first dimension** therefore, focuses especially on the quality of regulation and the security of property rights. One area where the interpretation of interventionism is ambiguous is taxation. Some hold that high taxation is a measurement of high intervention, others believe high tax rates are imposed with the consent of the government to finance sought-after public goods. Recent interpretations of higher taxes are consistent with the notion that higher tax rates may go hand in hand with better institutions.

2. Efficiency of the government or quality of bureaucracy.

   A **second important dimension** can be described as the efficiency of government, or the quality of bureaucracy. When a government intervenes, it can do so reasonably efficiently, or with delays, corruption, and other distortions. The government tries to limit time inconsistency. When a government imposes taxes, it can do so with relatively high compliance, or with low compliance, which often leads to corruption and arbitrary variation of effective tax rates across similarly situated taxpayers.

3. The government as provider of public goods.

   A **third dimension** is the government as provider of public goods that are essential for economic development, such as infrastructure, schools, health care, police protection, and a court system. Government performance of a given country should be assessed in part by evaluating the quality of public good provision such as schooling, infant morality, literacy, and infrastructure.

4. Government expenditure and public sector employment.

   A **fourth important indicator** of performance is government expenditure on transfers, its own consumption, and public sector employment. High government expenditure in these areas may reflect the citizen's *willingness to pay* taxes because they like what the government is doing, and this reflects good government. Alternatively, high expenditure on transfers and subsidies or on government consumption may reflect high levels of distortionary taxes and redistribution, and hence represent a failure to protect the public from government intervention.

5. Democratic and politic rights.

   A **final dimension** of good government is democratic and political rights. Political freedom is a crucial element of good government, and because economic freedom generally goes together with political freedom. The relationship between democracy and economic success over a long period indicate that governments that are more limited have presided over more successful development.

**3.5 Models of the government**

a. Which models of the government can be distinguished?

b.  What are the most important characteristics of these models, and what is their focus?

**Answer 3.5 Models of the government**

a.  In their book, The grabbing hand, Shleifer and Vishny[3] distinguished three models of government: the helping hand model, the invisible hand model and the grabbing hand model.

b.  **(1) helping hand model.** According to the **helping hand model**, unbridled free markets lead to monopoly pricing, to externalities such as pollution, to unemployment, to defective credit supply to firms, and to failures of regional development, among other ills. The helping hand model analysis focuses especially on **market failure**. Solutions ranging from corrective taxes, regulations, and aggregate demand management to price controls, government ownership, and planning are then proposed to cure these sources of market failure.

**(2) invisible hand model.** The traditional alternative to the *helping hand model* is the laissez-faire view of the government; it is the **invisible hand model**. This model begins with the idea that markets work very well without any government. The government may perform the basic function needed to support a market economy (such as provision of law, order, and national defence), but other than delivering these few public goods, the less the government does, the better. The adherents of *the invisible hand models* rarely inquire what the reasons are for massive government intervention in real economies or focus on the reforms that would contain the government. The *invisible hand model* of the government was initially conceived as a prescription for an ideal, limited government. Its irrelevance as a descriptive model is quite obvious, since the government intervenes in economic life much more than any version of the *invisible hand model* would allow.

**(3) grabbing hand model.** The third view of government, described by Shleifer and Vishny[4] as the **grabbing hand model**, focuses squarely on politics as the determinant of government behaviour. The *grabbing hand model* shares with the *invisible hand model* a sceptical view of government, but describes more accurately what governments actually do and therefore focuses more on the designs of reforms. The *grabbing hand* and *helping hand models* share their activist interest in reforming government, although since their conceptions of government are so different, their ideas of good reforms rarely coincide. The *grabbing hand model* analysis typically looks for ways of limiting government as opposed to expanding its scope.

At the root of the *grabbing hand* analysis are models of political behaviour that argue that politicians do not maximise social welfare, but instead pursue their own selfish objectives. The *grabbing hand model* is helpful in understanding the existing institutions in different countries, the reasons for the ways in which they have been put together, and the benefits and costs of these institutions for economic development and growth. When writing about institutions in a country, such as ownership patterns, regulatory structures, and legal mechanisms, economists used to focus on the benefits of institutional development

---

[3] Schleifer, A. and R.W. Vishny, 1998. The grabbing hand: government pathologies and their cures. Harvard University Press, Cambridge, MA, USA, pp. 2-13.

[4] Schleifer, A. and R.W. Vishny, 1998. The grabbing hand: government pathologies and their cures. Harvard University Press, Cambridge, MA, USA, pp. 3-4.

### 3.6 Williamson 2000; taking stock and looking ahead[5]

a. Which four levels of institutions does Williamson distinguish and what is located at each level?
b. At which level do we find social capital?
c. In neo-classical economics, the rule is *get the prices right* and everything will function well. What are the rules if we adopt Williamson's levels?
d. An important question concerning the economic organisation of activities is: what is the best governance structure? Please explain why the choice of the governance structure not only depends on the characteristics of the good and the human characteristics, but also on the institutional environment?

### Answer 3.6 Williamson 2000; taking stock and looking ahead

a. The four levels of institutions of Williamson, and their content, are:
   - Social embeddedness; here we find common values and norms, informal rules;
   - Institutional environment; here we find the formal rules;
   - Institutional arrangements; here we find the governance structures like markets, firms and hybrids;
   - Resource allocation and income distribution; here we find prices, incomes, profits, etc.
b. Social capital lies at the social embeddedness level.
c. Getting the formal and informal rules of the game right.
d. The institutional environment consists of the informal and formal rules of the game. They determine how a certain governance structure can function, and influence which governance structure is most preferable.

### 3.7 Social embeddedness and social capital

a. In which field is the analysis of social embeddedness developed and to which idea does the term social embeddedness refer?
b. What can we say about the forms of social capital? What is its dark side?

### Answer 3.7 Social embeddedness and social capital

a. The analysis of social embeddedness is developed in the field of social theory. The term 'social embeddedness' refers to the idea that economic behaviour is embedded within social relationships.
b. Social capital takes many different forms, depending on the type of ties that connect people together. It is identified as involving norms, social beliefs, conventions and sometimes networks that evolve out of processes that are not overtly investment activities. Shared norms are forms of social capital, but specific norms may have different consequences. The norm of reciprocity implies some level of symmetry among those who engage in long-term reciprocal relationships. In this case, the relationship is based on a balance of giving and taking over time. For example, the family structure is considered a form of *bonding social capital*, based on close kinship ties in which people share a common set of values, norms of behaviour and social conditions. There is also a dark side to social capital. Gangs and the Mafia use norms

---

[5] Williamson, O.E., 2000. The new institutional economics: taking stock, looking ahead. Journal of Economic Literature XXXVIII: 595-613.

such as 'an eye for eye' to distinguish between outsiders, and insiders who belong to the 'family'.

### 3.8 Social capital
a.  Do we have to make efforts to create social capital?
b.  Is it useful from an analytical point of view to distinguish between social capital and institutional environment?
c.  What is the relationship between the level of social capital and the Gross Domestic Product?

### Answer 3.8 Social capital
a.  According to Ostrom[6], creation of social capital requires sacrifice: 'investments made in one time period in building trust and reciprocity can produce higher levels of return in future time periods even though the individuals creating trust and reciprocity are not fully conscious of the social capital they construct'.
b.  Institutional environment is also defined as informal and formal rules of the society. However, social capital also includes elements such as informal rules. For that reason, one could say that social capital is a part of the institutional environment, and it is difficult to separate both from each other. However, from an analytical point of view, it is better to distinguish social capital from the institutional environment. Both have some common elements, but also elements that differ, such as the formal rules.
    With regard to common values and norms, they are part of the informal rules, and at the same time, they can serve as a co-ordination principle for groups of people, and they also belong to social capital.
c.  The relationship between the level of social capital and the Gross Domestic Product (GDP) is, that, in general, the higher the level of social capital, the higher the GDP per capita.

### 3.9 Social capital
a.  What is social capital and to which level of institutions does it belong?
b.  Why is social capital so important, for example for economic development?
c.  What are important components of social capital?
d.  Which types of costs can be reduced by a high level of social capital?
e.  Why is social capital also important within firms or organisations?
f.  Suppose you have to investigate the level of social capital in a certain region. Which kind of methods and indicators would you use?

### Answer 3.9 Social capital
a.  Social capital is the shared knowledge, understandings, norms, rules, and expectations about patterns of interactions that groups of individuals bring to a recurrent activity. Some people describe it also as the glue that holds society together. It facilitates cooperation and reduces transactions. Social capital belongs to the social embeddedness level.
b.  There are different reasons why social capital is important for economic development.

---

[6] Ostrom, E., 2000. Social capital: a fad or a fundamental concept? In: P. Dasgupta and I. Serageldin (eds.) Social capital. A multifaceted perspective. The World Bank, Washington, WA, USA, pp. 172-214. Citation on p. 177.

- First, there is more needed for economic success than just the formal rules of the institutional environment and the governance structure. The informal rules and trust in people, society government and in processes are also important.
- Second, it is the glue that holds the society together.
- Third, it facilitates co-operation between people.
- Fourth, it reduces transaction costs.
- Fifth, we see a strong relationship between the level of social capital and the Gross Domestic Product (GDP): the higher the level of social capital, the higher the GDP per capita.

Remark: the second, third and fourth reasons largely result in the fifth one.

c. Important components within social capital are trust in people, society, government, and in processes, common values and norms, reputation, (norms of) reciprocity and connectedness. Trust is perhaps the most important component of social capital; trust is the catalyst that makes an economy function efficiently.

d. A high level of social capital reduces transaction costs.

e. Social capital is also important within firms or large organisations because it helps the firm in reducing transaction costs, agency costs, and influence costs. It facilitates cooperation within the firm and it adds to the firm's goodwill.

f. As well as using literature and data sources, a suitable method would be to survey a sample of the population in the region. The questionnaire should include questions about:
- Trust in society, trust in government, trust in the economy, trust in people with whom they work or who are contract partners, etc.
- Passive and active participation in the society[7].

## 3.10 Social embeddedness and social capital

a. What does an 'under-socialised view of human behaviour' mean and how is this related to the assumption of opportunistic behaviour of Williamson?

b. Why is the role of social embeddedness so important?

c. What is the central thesis of social capital theory?

d. What is a social network, what can it be built upon, and what is basic idea of the social network theory?

e. What is a social network analysis?

f. What is the relationship between social network and network as a governance structure?

## Answer 3.10 Social embeddedness and social capital

a. According to Granovetter[8], the under-socialised view of human behaviour refers to Williamson's assumption that all agents in an economic transaction are motivated to act opportunistically for their own benefit alone. Economic sociologists point out that in reality, opportunistic behaviour is often constrained by social mechanisms such as reputation and reciprocity, which generate the foundation for trustworthy transactions. Furthermore, economic sociologists point out that successful economic transactions are embedded in

---

[7] See page 97 of the textbook.

[8] Granovetter, M., 1985. Economic action and social structure: the problem of embeddedness. The American Journal of Sociology 91: 481-510.

social relationships that are conducted within the informal rules of some cultural context. Therefore, the assumption that economic agents will always display opportunistic behaviour largely ignores the value of trust and how it is created.

b. The social embeddedness is the fundamental level of analysis for understanding the social relationships underlying economic transactions. The embeddedness argument holds that (economic) behaviour and institutions are so constrained by ongoing social relations that to construct them as independent is a grievous misunderstanding. Economists need to acknowledge the role of concrete personal relations and structures (or networks) of such relations in generating social capital (including trust, etc.) and discouraging malfeasance.

c. How behaviour and institutions are affected by social relations is one of the classical questions of the social theory. The central thesis of social capital theory is that social interactions in civic life, the day-to-day and face-to-face encounters in neighbourhoods and communities, are the foundation upon which common values are based and trust is built. In this view, the production of social capital depends on the degree to which social interactions are embedded in a network of social relations. In this sense of the term, social capital is only generated when a network of relations has the capability of creating standards.

d. A social network is a network of relations. It can be built upon social values and the reputation of being trustworthy. It is a social mechanism such that members of embedded economic groups draw initially upon resources of close network ties, but then bridge into more autonomous ties beyond micro-relationship, as their need for larger economic and financial transactions expands.

e. A social network analysis is an analysis of the embeddedness of the social interactions, including economic and financial transactions. For example, does the network consist of strong or weak social ties, are the transactions anonymous or not, etc.? The degree to which economic and financial transactions are an embedded pattern of social relations is fundamental for understanding how transaction are organised and coordinated.

f. Social network refers to the network of relations or the embeddedness of the social interactions. In a network as governance structure, the transaction mechanism is located at the centre.

### 3.11 Social capital in the rural areas

Much empirical research has been done to investigate the concept and level of social capital. For example, in the Netherlands there was quite some research performed on social capital in the rural areas.

a. What do you think about the form of social capital? Does it takes the same form everywhere in the (Dutch) rural areas?

b. What negative aspects of social capital in the rural areas could there be?

### Answer 3.11 Social capital in the rural areas

a. Social capital takes very different forms, depending on the 'type' of society. For example, research in the Netherlands distinguished five different types, from elitist rural areas to closed-community areas. The functions, importance and forms of social capital differ a lot between these different areas[9].

---

[9] For more on this research, see Vermeij, L., and G. Mollenhorst, 2008. Overgebleven dorpsleven, sociaal kapitaal op het platteland. Sociaal en Cultureel Planbureau, Den Haag, pp 11-12.

b. An often-mentioned negative side of social capital (especially in rural areas) is that it may 'close' a community to outsiders. People who come from outside the community, or who used to live there but have quarrels with other members of the community can face enormous difficulties in everyday life. Especially in remote or sparsely populated areas, problems can arise; there are few public facilities and people sometimes depend on social capital for basic needs such as transport and shopping.

### 3.12 The black box of 'institutions'
If we speak about institutions it is not always clear what we mean. The term 'institutions' is often a broad and sometimes a vague concept.
a. How can we open the black box of institutions?
b. What levels of institutions can be distinguished?
c. Suppose we want to analyse **governance structures** as a part of the black box of 'institutions'. What could be important issues?
d. What is meant by rules of the game and play of the game?

### Answer 3.12 The black box of 'institutions'
a. We can open the black box of institutions by:
- distinguishing four levels of institutions – social embeddedness, institutional environment, institutional arrangements and incentives level[10] – and investigating which level we are dealing with;
- making use of suitable and relevant theories, such as transaction cost theory, principal-agent theory, incomplete contract theory, and the old and new property rights theory.
b. Levels of institutions[11]:
- Social embeddedness:
  - Informal rules, culture, norms and values.
- Institutional environment:
  - Formal rules of the society.
  - Rules of the game.
- Institutional arrangements or governance structures:
  - Play of the game.
- Incentives mechanisms:
  - Carrot or stick.
  - Intrinsic of extrinsic motivation.

NB: The four levels of institutions of Williamson[12] are given on page 86 of the textbook. A difference with the theory of Williamson is at the fourth level.
c. Important issues are:
1. What are governance structures?
   - Supporting structures for carrying out transactions;

---

[10] See textbook on page 20.

[11] See textbook on page 20.

[12] Williamson, O.E., 2000. The new institutional economics: taking stock, looking ahead. Journal of Economic Literature XXXVIII: 595-613.

    – They consist of a broad spectrum ranging from the market at one end, to firms/organisations based on 'command and control' at the other end of the spectrum.

2. Why do we need governance structures?
   – They create value;
   – For distributing profits, quasi-rents and residual incomes.
3. What is the origin of governance structures?
   – Transactional motives;
   – Changes in (a) the social embeddedness and (b) the institutional environment.
4. What is the relation between governance structures and coordination mechanisms? Coordination mechanisms are a part of a governance structure, for example, a market is a governance structure and the price is coordination mechanisms. A governance structure can also make use of a mix of coordination mechanisms.

d. The formal rules of the society are *rules of the game*[13] and the *play of game* refers to how activities or transactions are organised. The latter refers to the used mechanisms of governance or government structures, i.e. supporting structures for carrying out transactions.

### 3.13 Institutional environment and institutional arrangement
a. What is the difference between the institutional environment and institutional arrangements? Describe in brief some important differences.
b. What are governance structures?
c. What are the two ends of the spectrum of governance structures?
d. How do we call the in-between governance structures? Please name a few examples.

### Answer 3.13 Institution environment and institutional arrangement
a. The institutional environment consists of the informal and formal rules of the game. It is located for a large part on the second level of framework of Williamson. The institutional arrangements that are often called governance structures are the play of the game.
b. Governance structures are mechanisms or supporting structures for carrying out transactions. It is an institutional arrangement consisting of the rules by which a transaction is carried out. Examples are the market, firms, and hybrids such as clubs and contracts.
c. The two ends of the spectrum of governance structures are markets at one end and hierarchies or organisations based on command and control at the other.
d. The in-between governance structures are called hybrids. Examples are contracts, clubs, associations and cooperatives.

### 3.14 Governance structures
a. What are governance structures?
b. The governance structure 'the firm' is concerned with how firm decisions are made, i.e. the exercise of authority, guidance and control. Could you give some examples of these governance structures?
c. What is the meaning of **decision or control rights** and **income rights?**
d. What is crucial in a governance structure?

---

[13] Rules of game can be considered as the rules in the society; game is used as a metaphor for the society.

e. What is the essence of questions regarding governance structures in the case of incomplete contacts?
f. What is the purpose of a governance structure?

## Answer 3.14 Governance structures

a. It is a mechanism for carrying out transactions. More precisely, a governance structure is often an institutional arrangement consisting of the rules by which an exchange is carried out, and a certain structure for administering the transactions.
b. Examples of topics of the governance structure 'the firm' are the coordination mechanism, the allocation of property rights, the capital structure, the reward system, the board of directors, the pressure of large investors, the competition in the product and labour markets, the organisational structure, the (management) accounting system, and so on.
c. The **decision**[14] **or control rights** concern who may decide on the use of an asset or a firm. The **income rights** determine who receives income from the use of the assets. The rules concerning these rights do not always determine important questions such as: who has the residual control rights and who is able to capture the residual income? On the contrary, this is often unclear or not well defined.
d. Crucial factors in a governance structure are the control rights and income rights. Important questions to assess a governance structure are: 'How are these rights arranged?' and: 'Who has the residual control right and who is able to capture the residual income?'.
e. The essence of governance structure, in the case of incomplete contacts, is: who has the residual control rights and who is able to capture the residual income?
f. The purpose of a governance structure is to:
   - provide the most efficient mechanism for carrying out transactions;
   - maximise the incentives to generate value-enhancing investments, while incentives for developing inefficient activities have to be minimised;
   - define the relative position of parties within a particular governance structure. This position depends on bargaining power and having the residual control rights over the bundle of property rights of the used assets and the ability to capture the residual income;
   - To minimise risk, and to allocate the residual risk to the least risk-averse party.

## 3.15 Governance structures

a. What are the possible origins of governance structures?
b. Why do we need governance structures?
c. What factors determine the outcome of the bargaining process about the quasi-rent or residual income?
d. What theories form the background of the quasi-rent and the residual income?

## Answer 3.15 Governance structures

a. Governance structures emerge in response to various transactional considerations. Transactions refer to *quid pro quo* or an exchange between a performance and a counter performance. However, we see also governance structures come into being as (1) a result of a change in the social embeddedness or (2) a gap in the institutional environment.

---

[14] The decision rights are also often called the control rights.

b.  We need governance structures because they
   - create value, otherwise they would not exist. The value is a surplus or a quasi-rent, however, it can also be non-monetary value;
   - take care of the distribution of the quasi-rent. The distribution of the quasi-rent depends on (1) the bargaining power of the involved parties; (2) specific control rights, i.e. the rights specified by contracts or rules of law; (3) the residual control rights;
   - enable people to deal with a change in the social embeddedness. This can be as a result of a public goods dilemma, i.e. a decreased supply and an increased demand for public goods, such as environmental goods. For example, people in rural areas would like to protect special environmental goods and they establish a club as governance structure;
   - enable people to deal with a change in the institutional environment, for example, a policy change that leaves or creates an institutional gap.
c.  The outcome of the bargaining process about the quasi-rent or residual income is determined by:
   - bargaining power of the involved parties;
   - specific contractual arrangements or rules of law concerning the control rights.
d.  The quasi-rent results from fixed assets (fixed asset theory) and asset specificity (transaction cost theory), and the residual income from the incomplete contract theory.

### 3.16 The choice of a governance structure
a.  What should the choice of a governance structure take into account?
b.  What are important criteria for the characteristics of goods or services and what do these characteristics mean?
c.  What are the consequences of non-rivalry and non-excludability of goods and services?
d.  According to transaction cost theory, which human characteristics are important for the choice of the governance structure, and why?

### Answer 3.16 The choice of a governance structure
a.  The choice for a governance structure should take into account the informal and formal rules of the institutional environment, the characteristics of the goods or services, and the characteristics of human beings.
b.  Important criteria for the characteristics of goods or services are (non-)rivalry and (non-)excludability. The meaning of these characteristics is explained in Chapter 5.4 of the textbook.
c.  In the case of non-rival and non-excludable goods and services, the market will fail and other governance structures like contracts, clubs, or even in-house production of the government could be a better solution.
d.  The choice for a governance structure should take into account the human characteristics of bounded rationality and opportunistic behaviour. Bounded rationality means that we have to be aware that individuals have only limited possibilities and abilities to obtain and process information. People are bounded by their inability to obtain information in order to fully comprehend the complexity of a situation. Opportunistic behaviour is a characteristic which is often described as a condition of self-interest. Both human characteristics can lead to hidden information and hidden actions.

### 3.17 Institutional arrangements or governance structures

a. What are the polar cases of institutional arrangements or governance structures and what is their co-ordination mechanism?
b. Many economists argue that it is too simple to view the market and hierarchies as the only two governance structures for transactions. It is an extremely narrow view of non-market transaction mechanisms or non-market governance structures. Explain their arguments.
c. What kind of co-ordination is used in the third way of co-ordination?
d. Can common values and norms also serve as co-ordination principle?

### Answer 3.17 Institutional arrangements or governance structures

a. The polar cases are *markets* on the one hand and *organisations based on command and control* (also referred to as hierarchies) on the other hand. In markets, co-ordination is based on prices, while in hierarchies it is based on authority or direct order. Hierarchy involves the capacity to supervise and control, including the right to take decisions.
b. Markets and hierarchies should not be viewed as two mutually exclusive governance structures: hybrid forms exist as well. There are areas of overlap, which give rise to hybrid forms. Hybrid forms are characterised by a mix of (1) specific market incentives (= prices); (2) modalities of co-ordination involving some forms of hierarchical relationship (= direct order); (3) rules and directives; (4) mutual adjustment, common norms and values. See also Figure 8.1 in the textbook.
c. The third way of co-ordination consists – according to Figure 8.1 of the textbook – of the 'handshake' and the 'handbook' as coordination mechanisms.
   • In contrast to hierarchical co-ordination – that is mostly vertical – the 'handshake' is a way of co-ordination consisting of forms of horizontal non-market co-ordination, in which more or less equal members have informal communication with each other. Important basic elements of these relationships are motivation, trust and commitment. The co-ordination mechanisms that are used within such organisations are *mutual adjustments* and the *standardisation of values and norms*. Mutual adjustment refers to the co-ordination achieved by informal horizontal communication. Standardisation of norms and values means shared codes of conduct usually for the entire organisation, so that everyone functions according to the same norms of behaviour.
   • The coordination mechanism that is called the 'handbook' consists of rules, directives and safeguards. It is often used for the governance structure 'contracts'. Contracts also often contain a price as a coordination mechanism. In that case the coordination mechanism of contracts consists of a combination of the 'handbook' and the 'price'. More in general, the type of contract determines which coordination mechanism will prevail and what the role of the price will be in the relationship *quid pro quo*. The price could be a compensation (counter performance) or an incentive mechanism (= motivation element).
d. Common values and norms can serve as a co-ordination principle for groups, where groups range from a family to a club, from a church to a volunteer group or team of people (a community) working towards a common goal. Common values and norms diminish the incidence of opportunistic behaviour between the members of the group and thereby reduce transaction costs. Effective co-ordination based on common values and norms coincides with a strong motivation and high commitment of individual members of a group to achieve their common goal.

### 3.18 Important characteristics of clubs
a. What is a club?
b. Which aspects of a club deserve attention?
c. Many environmental cooperatives in the Netherlands have not only farmers and other directly involved people as their members, but also citizens (i.e. non-farmers)[15]. What are the consequences of this from the point of view of club theory?

### Answer 3.18 Important characteristics of clubs
a. A club is a voluntary group of individuals who derive mutual benefits from sharing one or more of the following: (1) production costs of activities and services; (2) the members' characteristics (e.g. members like soccer or golf in the case of a soccer- or golf club, members have land, are farmers, etc.); or (3) a product or service characterised by excludable benefits. These benefits can be internal, which means accessible only for the members. However, it is also possible that the benefits of the club are external. This means that also non-members can enjoy the benefits (e.g. a club that preserves environmental goods).
b. **(1) members choose to belong voluntarily**, because they anticipate a net benefit from membership. The utility or expected income jointly derived from membership and from the use of other goods must exceed the utility associated with non-membership status. Furthermore, the net gain in utility or expected income from membership exceeds or equals membership fees or toll payments.
   **(2) clubs involve sharing**, in the use of an impure public good, the use of the service of the club such as an environmental co-operative, and sharing in the benefits. Crowding and congestion imply that one user's utilisation of the club good decreases the benefit or quality of service still available to the remaining users.
   **(3) A third** distinguishing characteristic of club goods is the **existence of non-members**. For pure public goods, all individuals can be members without crowding taking place, so that non-members do not exist. For club goods, non-members of a given club have two options: they can join another club providing the same good, or they may not join any club offering the club good.
   **(4) A fourth** distinguishing feature of club goods is the presence of an **exclusion mechanism**, whereby non-members and/or non-payers can be barred.
   **(5) A fifth** distinguishing attribute of club goods concerns the **dual decision**, including the membership and the provision decision. The membership decision affects the provision choice, and vice versa, neither can be determined independently.
   **(6) A final** feature concerns **optimality**. Voluntary provision of pure public goods is typically associated with a Nash equilibrium that is sub-optimal; thus government provision may be required. In the case of club goods, members or firms can form clubs that collect tolls through an exclusion mechanism. Under a wide variety of circumstances, these clubs can achieve Pareto-optimal results without resorting to government provision.
c. Because of these citizens, the environmental cooperatives become more heterogeneous. The different 'subgroups' of members may well have different interests. This can hamper the effectiveness and the efficiency of the club. It takes more time and it is much more difficult to come to decisions that all members support. In other words: it will lead to more transaction

---

[15] See textbook on page 114.

costs. On the other hand, if such a club manages to make decisions that are supported by all members, the different goals of the involved subgroups are better balanced. This will increase the impact that this club has in society; its basis in society will be stronger.

### 3.19 Economic theory of clubs
a. For which purpose does the 'club' theory provide a theoretical base?
b. What do Pareto-optimal conditions focus on with regard to clubs?
c. How should the homogeneity condition be interpreted?
d. Which institutional forms of clubs can be distinguished?
e. What are possible objections to government-led clubs?
f. What is the relationship between the optimal size of a club and the number of clubs?
g. What condition needs to be met by a club to offer quasi-public goods in a Pareto-efficient way?

### Answer 3.19 Economic theory of clubs
a. The study of clubs is intended to bridge the gap between private and purely public goods. The 'club' theory gives a theoretical basis for the study of the allocation efficiency of quasi-public goods.
b. Pareto-optimal conditions focus on:
   - the homogeneity of members;
   - the institutional form;
   - the point of view (that of the club members or the total economy);
   - the optimal membership size of the club.
c. Homogeneity of members is not an absolute condition for achieving efficient allocation. The more heterogeneous the members, the more difficult it is to reach an agreement on the nature and significance of the service, membership fee and membership. On the one hand this will lead, among others, to higher transaction costs compared to clubs with homogeneous members. On the other hand, it is possible that different goals are well balanced and the allocation of goods and services of the club becomes Pareto-optimal. Being Pareto-optimal means a situation from which it is impossible to increase the welfare of any party without decreasing that of another party. In other words we have to weigh the costs and benefits of clubs with heterogeneous members against those with homogeneous members.
d. Clubs can range from associations, co-operatives, a group of profit-making private firms, member-owned clubs, to organisations being publicly controlled by the government.
e. Government-led 'clubs' do not have the right incentives compared with those whose members are from overlapping generations, due to their short-term political goals.
f. Limitation of membership size must take place in mutual dependency with the number of clubs, because of, among other things, congestion problems. The presence of crowding requires a restriction of group size, so that membership size and provision are interdependent decisions.
g. Quasi-public goods can be produced in an efficient way by 'clubs' if the following conditions are met:
   - households or people can be excluded, i.e. there is an exclusion mechanism;
   - entrance can be limited;
   - costs resulting from congestion will increase.

– This means that the optimal size of the number of households (= members) of the club in relation to the total population is limited.

### 3.20 Self-organisation
a. What is self-organisation?
b. What factors increase the chance of self-organisation?

### Answer 3.20 Self-organisation
a. Self-organisation arises when people who are in an interdependent situation organise and govern themselves to obtain continuing joint benefits.
b. The likelihood of self-organisation increases if it deals about goods whose use is subject to rivalry, and, by making use of certain rules, people can be excluded from the use of these goods[16].

---

[16] See Ostrom, E., 1998. Governing the commons. The evolution of institutions for collective action. Cambridge University Press, Cambridge, UK, pp. 29-32.

# 4. Information and behavioural economics, and the role of incentives

## 4.1 Why would a person buy insurance?
Insurance companies have to generate enough revenues to cover their costs and make a normal profit – otherwise they will go out of business. This implies that the premiums charged for insurance policies must be greater than the expected payouts to the policyholders. Why would a person ever buy insurance, knowing that the price is greater than the expected payout?

## Answer 4.1 Why would a person buy insurance?
Risk-averse people are willing to pay a premium for insurance. They prefer a certain outcome to a less certain outcome and are willing to give up some expected value in order to reduce risk.

## 4.2 An investment
Suppose that an investment can yield three possible cash flows: € 5,000; € 1000; or € 0. The probability of each outcome is 1/3.
a. What is the expected value and standard deviation of the investment?
b. How much would a risk neutral person be willing to pay for the investment?
c. How much would a risk averse person be willing to pay for the investment?

## Answer 4.2 An investment
a. Expected value = € 2,000; Standard deviation = € 1,825.
b. A risk neutral person would be willing to pay € 2,000 for the investment (ignoring the time-value of the money).
c. Something less than € 2,000 (the exact amount depends on the risk averse level).

## 4.3 Effects of handgun laws
Some states in the United States allow citizens to carry handguns. Citizens can protect themselves in case of robberies by using these guns. Other states do not allow citizens to carry handguns. Criminals, however, tend to have handguns in all states. Use *economic analysis* to predict the effects of handgun laws on the behaviour of the typical criminal. In particular:
a. Do you think criminals will commit more or fewer robberies in the states that have laws that allow the possession of guns?
b. How do you think the laws will affect the *types of robberies* criminals commit? Be sure to explain your *economic reasoning*.

## Answer 4.3 Effects of hand gun laws
Based on economic models, criminals are expected to consider the marginal costs and benefits of their actions in choosing the level and type of crime. Allowing citizens to carry handguns increases the marginal costs of robberies, since the criminals are more likely to get hurt or killed.
a. Thus the economic model predicts that there will be fewer robberies in the states where handguns are allowed.
b. The laws affect the marginal costs of some types of crimes more than others. Crimes involving personal contact are the ones most likely to be affected by the laws. Therefore, economic models suggest that criminals will move away from crimes involving personal contacts in favour of crimes of stealth in states where handguns are allowed.

### 4.4 Teenagers play 'chicken'

Some foolish teenagers play 'chicken' on Friday nights. Two teenagers drive their cars at each other at high speeds. The first to swerve to the side is the 'chicken' and loses. If both swerve out of the way, they are both chickens and both lose. Neither of the drivers wants to get into an accident. It causes a significant loss in utility (possibly death). However, neither wants to be known as a chicken. This causes some loss in utility.
a.  What is the equilibrium of this game?
b.  Do you think the two drivers will necessarily produce an equilibrium outcome?
c.  Do you think the chances are better or worse for achieving an equilibrium outcome if the two players know each other? Explain.
d.  Do you think it matters whether the two players have played the game before? Explain.

### Answer 4.4 Teenagers play 'chicken'

a.  There are two pure strategy equilibria in this game. In each case, one of the drivers will swerve while the other will not.
b.  Unfortunately, there is no guarantee that an equilibrium outcome will be observed. Indeed, sometimes teenagers die in this foolish game (presumably either person would have swerved if he had guessed that the other would not; the equilibrium outcome requires that both players are perfectly rational).
c.  Presumably, teenagers are more likely to reach an equilibrium outcome if they have played the game before and/or if they know the other person (or his reputation in the game).
d.  Having played the game before and/or knowing the reputation of the other person will help each player to make more informed choices of his rival's behaviour and an equilibrium outcome is more likely.

### 4.5 Asymmetric information

a.  What is asymmetric information?
b.  What term is used to describe the inability of people to know all the necessary information?
c.  What type of behaviour includes opportunistic behaviour?
d.  How can asymmetric information restrict contracts from solving incentive conflicts?

### Answer 4.5 Asymmetric information

a.  Asymmetric information means that the involved parties do not share the same information.
b.  Bounded rationality. This is said to arise when the cognitive ability of people is insufficient to deal with the complexity of the world. Hence, people are not in a position to take all circumstances into account when making a decision.
c.  Opportunistic behaviour includes providing selective and distorted information, making promises which are not intended to be kept, and a person pretending to be different from what the person actually is.
d.  With symmetric information, incentive conflicts would be relatively easy to solve. The contracting parties could agree to take certain actions and if they do not take these actions, they can be heavily penalised. **Asymmetric** information, however, can make it difficult to ascertain whether or not a party has honoured the terms of the contract.

## 4.6 Adverse selection or hidden information
a. What is adverse selection?
b. Please, give an example of adverse selection.

## Answer 4.6 Adverse selection or hidden information
a. Adverse selection refers to the tendency of an individual with private information about something that affects a potential partner's benefits to make offers that are detrimental to the trading partner. This phenomenon is also called hidden information.
b. A common example is from the insurance industry. Prospective customers are more likely to know about their health than insurance companies. The customers who are most likely to purchase insurance at a given price are those who are most likely to use it.

## 4.7 Adverse-selection problems and incentive problems
Which of the following examples is an adverse-selection problem and which is an incentive problem? Explain why. In each case, give one method that the restaurant might use to reduce the problem.
a. A restaurant decides to offer an all-you-can-eat buffet that is sold for a fixed price. The restaurant discovers that the customers for this buffet are not its usual clientele. Instead, the customers tend to have big appetites. The restaurant loses money on the buffet.
b. A restaurant owner hires a manager who promises to work long hours. When the owner is out of town, the manager goes home early. This action results in lost profits for the firm.

## Answer 4.7 Adverse-selection problems and incentive problems
a. Adverse selection: a pre-contractual information problem. People seeing the buffet prices know how much they are likely to eat, but the restaurant does not. Consequently, the buffet price tends to attract people who will eat a lot of food. There are many potential ways to address the problem. For instance, the restaurant might raise the prices on the buffet to cover the costs of the largest eaters and then offer deals for other customers such as being able to fill a smaller plate for a lower price.
b. Incentive problem: post-contractual information problem. The manager promises to work hard, but once the owner is not around to monitor her, she shirks. This is a kind of hidden action (see also question 4.11). Potential solutions include:
   - providing incentive compensation (for example, a profit-sharing plan), and
   - increased monitoring.

## 4.8 Practice of tipping
In the USA, in most restaurants, waiters receive a large portion of their compensation through tips from customers. Generally, the customer decides the size of the tip. However, many restaurants require a 15 percent tip for parties of eight or more. Discuss:
a. Why the practice of tipping has emerged as a major method of compensating the waiting staff.
b. Why the customer typically decides on the amount of tip.
c. Why restaurants require tips from large parties.

## Answer 4.8 Practice of tipping

a.  Tipping provides incentives for waiters to do a better job compared to paying them a straight salary. Tipping provides incentives to provide high-quality service and to sell products (since the tip is based on a percentage of the bill).
b.  The customer has the specific knowledge about whether or not the waiter did a good job. She is well able to monitor the waiter.
c.  For tipping to work, the customer must follow through on the implicit promise[1] to tip if the quality of service is good. Individuals in large parties often have incentives to shirk on the tip (free ride). For instance, if each individual agrees to put his share of the bill in a common pool, the amount collected is usually less than the bill plus the normal tip. Hence, large parties are less likely to give reasonable tips unless they are required to do so. Requiring a tip helps to solve this type of agency problems. The waiter has fewer incentives to provide good service. However, the waiter still has incentives to sell products.

## 4.9 Risk and uncertainty

a.  What is the difference between risk and uncertainty?
b.  Is this difference considered useful nowadays?

## Answer 4.9 Risk and uncertainty

a.  Risk refers to situations in which an individual is capable of calculating probabilities on the basis of an objective classification. Uncertainty refers to situations in which no objective classification is possible.
b.  Nowadays this difference is considered less fruitful, because of the expected utility theory, which is the dominant theory of choices under uncertainty.

## 4.10 Hidden information or adverse selection

a.  When does adverse selection arise?
b.  Is adverse selection an *ex-post* or an *ex-ante* problem? Explain.
c.  What could be the consequences of hidden information?

## Answer 4.10 Hidden information or adverse selection

a.  Adverse selection arises when, with a potential transaction in mind, one party is better informed than the other and takes advantage of this information asymmetry.
b.  Adverse selection is an *ex-ante* problem. Adverse selection is a consequence of the hidden information that exists before the transaction takes place.
c.  The consequences of hidden or private information that one party has at its disposal and the other does not, which is relevant for the potential transaction, are that it imposes risks on the other party. These risks could concern price, quantity, quality, etc.

## 4.11 Hidden actions or moral hazard

a.  When does moral hazard arise?
b.  Is moral hazard an *ex post* or an *ex-ante* problem? Explain.
c.  What could be the consequences of moral hazard?

---

[1] Such a promise can be considered as an implicit contract.

d.  What three conditions must be present for moral hazard to arise?
e.  How can we limit the problems of moral hazard?

## Answer 4.11 Hidden actions or moral hazard

a.  Moral hazard arises when one party undertakes actions that the other party cannot observe.
b.  Moral hazard is an *ex-post* problem. The hidden actions occur after the contract has been signed.
c.  The consequences of moral hazard could be that the agreed contracts are not complied with. It could lead to unintentional use.
d.  In order for a *hidden action* problem to arise, three conditions must hold. **First,** there must be some potential divergence of interests between people. **Second**, there must be some basis for gainful exchange or other co-operation between the individuals – some reason to agree and transact – that activate the divergent interests. **Third**, there must be difficulties in determining whether in fact the terms of the agreement have been followed and in enforcing the contract terms.
e.  These three conditions suggest ways to deal with moral hazard problems. The remedies for, or to limit, the hidden action problems can be grouped into: *monitoring, incentive contracts, bonding* and '*doing it oneself*'.

## 4.12 Wages

a.  What is the senior rule concerning age and wage?
b.  Why do wages tend to increase with age?
c.  Wages are not only costs for employers but they also function as a signal. What kind of information do they contain?
d.  To what phenomena is an age-wage pattern a response?
e.  Why is mandatory retirement necessary for increasing pay with age?
f.  Suppose the government wants to stimulate innovation in the national economy. What would be the effect if the government freezes the wages?

## Answer 4.12 Wages

a.  Pay tends to increase with age.
b.  There are different arguments: (1) people have more experience; (2) people stay or would like to stay for a long time; (3) it is a response to adverse selection (hidden information) and moral hazard (hidden actions), e.g. good work attitude, no shirking; (4) firms use it as a form of bonding.
c.  It reveals information about the work behaviour and attitude (good or bad worker), experience and quality of the work.
d.  It is a response to hidden information and hidden actions. It can also be considered as a pay for loyalty.
e.  Otherwise people would want to stay too long. Their marginal costs would become higher than the marginal products.
f.  On the one hand firms can reduce their costs, which can lead to more profits. This creates more possibilities for investments. On the other hand, people become less motivated. This can lead to less innovation. Further, higher wages will lead to more substitution of labour by capital. This can result in more technological developments.

### 4.13 Google

Google Inc., the company behind, amongst others, search engine Google and Gmail, is well-known for its informal company structure. The firm has no fixed team managers, recreational facilities are freely available, and all engineers are free to spend 20% of their working hours on topics of interest of their own choice. On the other hand, selections for job applicants are known to be tough. Applicants always have at least five or six job interviews. Analyse this case from the perspectives of incentives and motivation.

a.  What are the benefits for Google in allowing its employees to spend 20% of their time on topics of personal interest?
b.  Why do you think the 'selection at the gate' is so tough?
c.  What could be an alternative to this solution?
d.  Which solution do you prefer?

### Answers 4.13 Google

a.  The interests for the company are twofold: firstly, it is a sort of 'carrot' to motivate its employees. Their jobs remain challenging and fun, as they are in line with the personal interests of the workers. Secondly, often the interests of the firm and its staff appear to be in line with each other. Some successful recent projects (e.g. GoogleNews) are reported to be the result of the '20% rule' for its personnel[2].
b.  From the perspective of incentives and motivation, it seems wise to look for people who are intrinsically motivated. By selecting (screening) so strictly, they can look for potential employees who seem to fit in this environment with relatively very little monitoring.
c.  An alternative solution is a more classical approach of firm management: a strong hierarchy where managers give strict commands to the team members.
d.  That is a matter of preference, also depending on the specific context (e.g. how costly is it to monitor tasks, costs of screening, type of work that is to be carried out, etc.).

### 4.14 Time inconsistency

a.  When does time inconsistency arise?
b.  What could be the consequences of time inconsistency, for example, on the part of the government?

### Answer 4.14 Time inconsistency

a.  Time inconsistency arises when a policy that initially appeared to be optimal is no longer optimal to the policy makers when it is time to implement the policy or when it becomes no longer optimal after some time.
    The consequences of time inconsistency could be that:
    • The policy loses its credibility.
    • People realise that the government is guilty of time inconsistency; they will anticipate a policy change and behave in such a way that the government will not be able to achieve its initial objectives.
b.  People will demonstrate strategic behaviour.

---

[2] See Washington Post, 21st October 2006.

## 4.15 Expected value

A real estate agent sells objects for Realco. He receives a sales commission from his employer. Suppose the agent has three possible incomes for the year. In a good year, he sells many houses and gets € 200,000, whereas in a bad year he earns nothing. In other years he receives € 100,000. We assume that each outcome is equally likely, and thus has a probability of 1/3 of occurring.
a.  How is the expected value defined?
b.  What is the amount of the expected value?
c.  What is the variability of the payoff?
d.  What is the standard deviation?
e.  Which measures are used as measures of risk?
f.  What is reflected by higher standard deviations?

## Answer 4.15 Expected value
a.  The expected value of an uncertain payoff is defined as the weighted average of all possible outcomes, where the probabilities of the outcomes are used as the weights. The expected value is a measure of tendency – the payoff that will occur *on average*.
b.  Expected value = $(1/3 \times 0) + (1/3 \times 100,000) + (1/3 \times 200,000) = €\ 100,000$.
c.  The variance is a measure of the variability of the payoff.
    The variance = $1/3 \times (0 - 100,000)^2 + 1/3 \times (100,000 - 100,000)^2 + 1/3 \times (200,000 - 100,000)^2$
    = € 6.7 billion.
d.  The standard deviation = $(6.7\ \text{billion})^{1/2} = €\ 81,650$.
e.  Variances and standard deviations are used as measures of risk.
f.  Higher standard deviations reflect more risk.

## 4.16 Expected value and utility

An estate agent – named John Smith – works for ASR Real Estate (formerly Fortis, in de past a large investment company and bank in the Netherlands). He receives a sales commission from his employer. For simplicity, we suppose that Smith has three possible incomes for a year. In a good year, he earns € 400,000, whereas in a bad year he earns € 100,000. In other years, he receives € 200,000. Probability refers to the likelihood that an outcome will occur. In this example, each outcome is equally likely, and thus has a probability of 1/3 of occurring.
a.  What is the amount of the expected value of his earnings?
b.  John Smith marries, buys a house and has children, but remains risk neutral. What is the expected utility (EU) his earnings?
c.  However, as a result of the credit crunch (or credit crisis) in autumn 2008 John Smith becomes risk averse. He values his income Y because of his expected utility as $Y^{0.8}$. What is the **expected utility** of his earnings?

## Answers 4.16 Expected value and utility
a.  EV = $\frac{1}{3}$ x 400,000 + $\frac{1}{3}$ x 200,000 + $\frac{1}{3} \times$ 100,000 = 233,333 Euros.
b.  In the case of being risk neutral, the EU is equal to the EV; EU = 233,333 Euros.
c.  EU = $\frac{1}{3}$ x 400,000$^{0.8}$ + $\frac{1}{3} \times$ 200,000$^{0.8}$ + $\frac{1}{3} \times$ 100,000$^{0.8}$ = 19,241,781 Euros
    •  Note that if we use the sum of EV, the result will be: EU = 233,333$^{0.8}$ = 19,696,154 Euros. However, this way of calculation is not correct, because the chances are raised to the power, although the difference in outcome is small.

### 4.17 Costs concepts
a. Define opportunity costs.
b. What are some characteristics of opportunity costs?
c. A firm paid € 8,325 last year for some raw materials it planned to use in production. When is the € 8,325 a good estimate of the opportunity costs of the material?
d. Define sunk costs and give an example.
e. Why are opportunity costs costly to estimate?

### Answer 4.17 Costs concepts
a. The opportunity costs consist of the returns from the most valuable foregone alternative when making a decision or choice from many options.
b. • Opportunity costs are not necessarily the same as payments;
   • Opportunity costs are forward looking, in terms of what the alternatives are;
   • Opportunity costs can be dated at the moment of final destination.
c. The € 8,325 is an accurate estimate of the opportunity costs if we can resell the material for that amount or we can replace the material, and the future price is expected to be € 8,325. In general, historical costs can be reasonably accurate estimates of opportunity costs if the current market price has not changed and there is a ready market to buy and sell the material.
d. Sunk costs are costs incurred in the past that cannot be recovered and are therefore irrelevant for future decision making. An example of a sunk cost is as follows. A firm purchases 100 Euros worth of a material required in a one-time project. Sixty Euros' worth of the material are used in this project. The remaining 40 Euros have no market value. Using the opportunity costs concept, the historical cost of the remaining 40 Euros is sunk and irrelevant for future uses of this material.
e. Estimating opportunity costs requires the decision-maker to formulate all possible alternative actions and the foregone net receipts from those actions. This is a costly and time-consuming process. Furthermore, the opportunity costs change as the set of alternative actions change.

### 4.18 Past performance and ratchet effects
a. What is a common mechanism for setting performance goals?
b. To what type of incentive can this method lead?

### Answer 4.18 Past performance and ratchet effects
a. A common mechanism for setting performance goals is making use of historical data on past performance.
b. This method often leads to a perverse incentive called the *ratchet effect*. The ratchet effect refers to basing next year's standard of performance on this year's actual performance. But performance targets usually are adjusted in only one direction: upwards. A poor year usually does not cause subsequent years' targets to be reduced at all, or to be reduced only by very little. This 'ratcheting up' of standards discourages employees from exceeding the quota substantially, to avoid raising the standard for future periods by too much[3].

---

[3] Brickley, J.A., Smith, C.W. and J.L. Zimmerman, 2001. Managerial economics and organizational architecture. McGraw-Hill Irwin, New York, NY, USA, p. 401.

## 4.19 Ratchet effect
a. What is a bottom-up budgeting system?
b. What is the ratchet effect in a budgeting system?

## Answer 4.19 Ratchet effect
a. A bottom-up budgeting system means that lower levels in the organisation prepare the initial budgets because they have the specialised knowledge, and as the budget winds its way through the decision ratification process, higher levels in the organisation review the budget and bring additional knowledge to bear.
b. The ratchet effect in a budgeting system refers to basing next year's budget on this year's actual performance if this year's actual performance exceeds this year's budget. If in this year actual performance falls short of budget, next year's budget is not reduced. Budget ratcheting causes employees to reduce output this year to avoid being held to a higher standard in future periods.

## 4.20 Tenure track
Many universities (especially in the USA and Canada, but also in Europe and elsewhere) have a so-called tenure track system. The basic idea is that junior academics (e.g. assistant professors) can obtain a lifetime senior position (e.g. associate professor or personal professor) if they provide a very strong record, indicated by criteria like a minimum amount of articles published in a double-reviewed journal per year, grants obtained, evaluations for educational tasks, bringing in of projects financed by the government or EU, etc.
a. From the point of view of behavioural economics, what are the advantages of such a system?
b. What are the disadvantages?

## Answers 4.20 Tenure track
a. Especially in the USA, job security is seen as an important employee benefit. If this weren't offered, salaries would have to increase significantly to compensate for the risk of losing the job. In addition, the juniors in such a system have strong incentives to perform as well as possible: their career is at stake. Seniors are expected to become more willing to invest in the university where they stay for a long time. It is worth the investment (compare question 4.12). They will also be more willing to invest in talented juniors, as they are no threat to the position of the (lifetime-appointed) seniors.
b. An important disadvantage of this system is that it induces ratcheting effects: juniors can be pushed to the extreme, and requirements may become stricter over time. The criteria are usually quantitative, individual criteria. Hence, juniors will focus on meeting the criteria, and invest less time in other (more qualitative) aspects of their job. They have fewer or no incentives to contribute to their team or group. Another concern is that seniors, once they have a secure job, focus on their personal interests rather than on other common goods of a university. They become more focused on their own career.

## 4.21 Narrow self-interest
One of the main tenets of economic analysis is that people act in their narrow self-interest.
a. Why do people leave tips in restaurants?

b. If a study were to compare the size of tips earned by waiting staff in restaurants on interstate highways with those in restaurants near residential neighbourhoods, what do you expect to find?

### Answer 4.21 Narrow self-interest

a. When a customer comes into a restaurant in the USA they have an implicit contract with the waiter to tip for good service. A customer may honour this contract with the waiter to tip for good service. A customer may honour this contract for two reasons. First, the person might value being fair and not want to shirk on the implicit agreement (economics allows for people to care about fairness). Second, the customer will realise that if he shirks on the tip the next time he comes back to the restaurant the waiter will shirk on service.

b. Tips are likely to be higher at restaurants in residential neighbourhoods because the second effect (the repeat-customer effect) is likely to be large. Restaurants on interstate highways will be frequented by many customers who will not return. These customers have large incentives to shirk on the tip unless they care significantly about fairness to the waiter.

### 4.22 Selling or leasing your house

Two employees are assigned to work overseas for a 2-year period. One person sells his house in the United States, whereas the other leases it for 2 years to another family. Which house do you think will be in better condition after the 2 years? Explain.

### Answer 4.22 Selling or leasing your house

The owned house is likely to be in better condition. Generally, owners take better care of property than renters.

### 4.23 Incentive scheme for teachers

Several school districts have attempted to increase teacher productivity by paying teachers based on the scores their students achieve on standardised tests (administered by external testing agencies). The goal is to produce higher-quality classroom instruction.
Do you think that this type of compensation scheme will produce the desired outcome? Explain.

### Answer 4.23 Incentive scheme for teachers

Compensation plans of this type provide incentives for teachers to emphasise the material covered in the texts. Yet such plans sometimes produce bad side effects.

- Teachers will have strong incentives to focus on test scores. This focus does not necessarily produce better teaching. In part, it depends on how well the tests measure learning.
- Moreover, some teachers are likely to discover ways to 'game the compensation scheme.' For instance, in some school districts, this type of compensation scheme has motivated teachers to teach the material to be tested rather than provide a more general education.
- In extreme cases, teachers get copies of the exam in advance and give the answers to students before the test.

## 4.24 Increased pay of employees

A company recently raised the pay of employees by 20 percent. Employee productivity remained the same. The CEO of the company was quoted as saying, 'it just goes to show that money does not motivate people'. Provide a critical evaluation of this statement.

## Answer 4.24 Increased pay of employees

According to the economic model simply raising a payment by 20 percent is unlikely to increase productivity. The employees may be happier but not more productive. What is important is tying the pay raise to productivity. In this case, employees would be expected to exert more effort to increase the likelihood of the pay raise.

## 4.25 Gains and losses of shirking

Suppose that a worker in a factory is currently being paid € 35,000 per year and that, if fired, his best wage elsewhere is € 30,000. For simplicity we assume that the employment situation is expected to last only one period. Next, we suppose that the worker could earn an expected utility of € 500 by shirking. The probability of getting caught and fired is equal to 5%.
a. What is the amount of the quasi-rent the worker is earning?
b. What are the expected gains from shirking?
c. What are the expected costs of shirking?
d. What wage will discourage shirking in this example?

## Answer 4.25 Gains and losses of shirking

a. Put simply, the worker stands to lose the quasi-rent associated with his employment. The quasi-rent is $(W-W_{alt})$ or 35,000 – 30,000, i.e. the worker is earning a quasi-rent of € 5,000.
b. The expected gains from shirking are € 500.
c. If the employment situation is to carry over X periods, then the cost to the worker of shirking, if detected but ignoring the discounting of future wages, is:
$$X(W-W_{alt}) \tag{1}$$
The probability of getting caught and fired is equal to 5%. Although the worker cannot be certain of getting caught and losing $X(W-W_{alt})$, the worker does know the expected value of being caught and fired. The expected costs of shirking are then:
$$pX(W-W_{alt}) \tag{2}$$
Because we assume that the employment situation only refer to the last one period the expected costs of shirking are $0.05 \times (35,000 - 30,000) = € 250$ (3)
d. The wage chosen by an organisation can cause workers to choose not to shirk. If the benefits of shirking, say R, do not exceed the expected costs of shirking $pX(W-W_{alt})$, shirking will not occur:
$$R \leq pX(W-W_{alt}) \tag{4}$$
If we solve this equation for W, we have found the minimum wage necessary to encourage workers not to shirk. We call this the efficient wage, $W_e$,
$$W_e = W_{alt} + R/(X_p) \tag{5}$$

The wage that will discourage shirking in this example is 30,000 + 500/0.05 = 40,000 Euros. Notice that the efficient wage, $W_e$, exceeds the alternative or opportunity wage $W_{alt}$ by the amount R/(Xp). Thus, the efficient wage offers a quasi-rent[4].

## 4.26 Risk aversion versus risk taking

Lauren Smith decides to bet 2,000 Euros on number 35 on the roulette wheel in a Las Vegas casino. Almost immediately she starts to question her decision. Lauren normally is a risk avoider who hardly ever gambles. But she works at Trilogy Software where the CEO understands that taking risks and suffering the consequences are critical to the firm's success. The CEO wants to develop people who take chances. 'You don't win points … for trying.' Lauren is participating in Trilogy's three-month training program for all new recruits. It educates employees about, among other things, how to evaluate risky projects, not just to immediately accept or reject the project because it is risky. The program also suggests to employees that they will not be rewarded at Trilogy unless they take risks. Thus, although Lauren does not like taking risks, working for Trilogy, she has economic incentives for doing so.

There at least three ways in which the Trilogy training program might be effective:
1. It changes employees' preferences regarding risk bearing;
2. It identifies more effectively individuals with the risk tolerances that Trilogy desires;
3. It communicates better the consequences to Trilogy employees of undertaking risky ventures.
Discuss the likely importance of these three mechanisms.

### Answer 4.26 Risk aversion versus risk taking
It is generally difficult to change a person's preferences toward risk. A brief experience in gambling is unlikely to do so. The training program might identify individuals with the risk tolerances Trilogy desires.
- However, the people have already been hired and this is unlikely to be the major reason for the program.
- Additionally, employees have incentives to behave in a risky manner in the program and it might be hard to distinguish underlying preferences of individuals from their actions.
- The program does a relatively effective job of communicating that risk taking is valued at the company.
- In addition, it gives the employees experience in evaluating risky alternatives.

## 4.27 People give to charity
a. Is giving to charity consistent with the 'economic view of behaviour'? Please explain why.
b. Suppose there is a big drop in charitable giving. At the same time there has been no decline in per capita income or total employment. Using the economic approach, what potential factors might have led to this decline in giving?
c. How might the decline in giving be explained by the institutional environment and social embeddedness framework?

---

[4] Fitz, F.R., Z.J. Acs and D.A. Gerlowski, 1998. Management and economics of organization. Prentice-Hall Europe, London, UK, pp. 314, 324.

### Answer 4.27 People give to charity

a.  There is nothing in the 'economic view of behaviour' that says that people can't gain utility from contributing to good causes. Also they may be doing this to create goodwill in the community. This might result in more business opportunities, less government red tape in completing transactions, etc.

b.  Economic analysis focuses on how changes in constraints (rather than preferences) affect behaviour. One potential variable that might have changed is the tax code. For instance, tax breaks may have been eliminated making it more expensive to give to charity. The economic view would not typically make statements like 'people's preferences changed and thus they no longer felt like giving to charity'.

c.  Based on the 'institutional environment and social embeddedness' framework we can argue that people's behaviour is explained by their upbringing and social background. According to this view, some people who were brought up to care about others will give to charity, while others will not. Perhaps while per capita income has not changed, there has been a shift in income away from the giving group to the non-giving group, making giving less likely. However, there might have been demographic changes due to relocations, deaths, etc. Additionally, it is possible that people's trust in the economy or in society has decreased, for example, as result of the credit crunch (or credit crisis) in autumn 2008. This will affect charitable giving.

### 4.28 High incentive pay

There has been an increased emphasis on compensating employees through incentive pay. High incentive pay, however, is not likely to be productive in all settings.

a.  Discuss the factors that are likely to favour paying high incentive pay to employees.
b.  What is inefficient risk bearing?
c.  What is the trade-off between incentives and inefficient risk bearing?

### Answer 4.28 High incentive pay

a.  The following four factors favour high incentive pay:
    1.  the employee's output is sensitive to her effort;
    2.  the employee is not very risk averse;
    3.  the level of risk that is beyond the employee's control is low;
    4.  the employee's response to increased incentives is high (the employee exerts a lot of more effort).

    These four factors reflect the trade-off between incentives and inefficient risk bearing. When they are met, the benefits of increased incentives are large relative to the risk-bearing costs.

b.  Inefficient risk bearing means that the gains of a high incentive pay (e.g. better performance) are lower than the compensation pay to the employees.

c.  The trade-off refers to the fact that inefficient risk bearing reduces the gains from bargaining in employment relationships. At the same time, incentive compensation is likely to increase the effort of the employee which can increase these gains from trade. In deciding on the optimal amount of incentive pay, the firm must consider this trade-off.

### 4.29 Profit-sharing plans are good

Evaluate the statement: 'Profit-sharing plans are good; they encourage teamwork'.

### Answer 4.29 Profit-sharing plans are good

Economic theory questions the incentive effects of large profit-sharing plans. Participants in these plans seem to have incentives to free ride on the efforts of others. Nevertheless, the widespread existence of these plans suggests that the plans may have positive incentive effects. For example, they may play a role in communicating in a credible way what the firm values. Also, there may be effects that are not well explained by existing economic theory.

### 4.30 Bonus pay

Evaluate the following statement: 'John is paid a straight salary with no bonus pay. Obviously, he has no incentives to do a good job.'

### Answer 4.30 Bonus pay

Incentive pay takes many forms besides bonus pay. John might be paid a straight salary, but still have strong incentives provided by such things as prospects of promotion, and salary increases that are tied to performance. This also means that career concern can function as an incentive.

### 4.31 Tax collection

The Roman Empire taxed many faraway provinces. Rome would auction the rights to tax collection to the highest bidder. The winning bidder was given the right to set the tax rate for the province and the right to collect (and keep) the taxes. In turn, the winner would pay the bid amount to the Roman government. Assume (1) that the Emperor is a young man interested in maximising the present value of all future revenues to Rome from auctioning off the tax rights, and (2) that the auction for the rights to each province is conducted annually.

a. Give two reasons why Rome would auction off the rights to tax collection rather than simply send a Roman soldier to collect the taxes.
b. Discuss two problems this system might generate for the Emperor.

### Answer 4.31 Tax collection

a. The reasons for placing the tax collection out to bid rather than using a soldier are similar to the reasons for franchising rather than owning:
   - The incentives of the winning bidder to collect taxes will be much higher than for a soldier who has incentives to shirk.
   - The winning bidder is more likely to have specific knowledge about who in the community has money to tax than a Roman soldier (there is a reason why the bidder is willing to bid a high price for the rights).
   - The winning bidder is likely to be a person with the skills required for successful tax collection (again, there is a reason why the bidder is making a high bid).
b. The emperor is likely to run into several problems with the system:
   - The potential local bidders might get together and place a low bid for the rights to collect the taxes (rather than compete).
   - The winning bidder has the incentives to collect high taxes in the given year rather than to worry about long-run taxes. Thus, the bidder is likely to overtax the province – reducing investment and future tax revenues.
   - The overtaxing is likely to make people in the province unhappy and increase the likelihood of rebellion.

- If the bidder is risk averse, the bid will be less than the expected value of the tax collections.

## 4.32 Scholarship

The Ministry of Education has developed two systems for scholarships, in cooperation with Rabobank and ING Bank. Both systems are based on the idea that an average student is able to earn 60 ECTS credits per year.

- Under the scholarship of Rabobank, the student receives 400 Euros per month and the money is transferred at the beginning of the month.
- Under the scholarship of ING, the student receives 150 Euros per ECTS and the money is transferred to his account at the end of the academic year.

a. What kind of student is more likely to choose the ING scholarship?
b. Which system would you choose and what information is revealed by your choice?
c. Suppose you are risk averse, which system would you choose, and why?
d. Who bears the risks in the scholarship of ING?
e. What are the costs of the incentive used in the scholarship of the ING?
f. Explain the trade-off between risk bearing and the costs of providing an incentive to an agent.
g. From the efficiency point of view of society, which party should bear the risk? Explain also why.

## Answers 4.32 Scholarship

a. The ING scholarship is more likely to be chosen by students who are risk neutral, hardworking; smart and able to earn 60 or more ECTS per year.
b. It depends on your capacity and your effort level. The revealed information refers, among other, to capacity level, effort level, work attitude, risk attitude.
c. If you are risk averse you will choose the Rabobank scholarship because you will receive a fixed amount of money independent of your effort and results.
d. The student bears the risk in the scholarship of ING.
e. Suppose you earn 60 ECTS. The costs of the incentive are 9000 – 4800 = 4200 Euro. The benefits are that you work hard and will finish your study earlier.
f. The trade-off between risk bearing and the costs of providing an incentive is that the more risk averse an agent is, the higher compensation he will ask for bearing risk. Because of the high costs of giving an incentive, it might be even better for the principal to give a risk averse agent a fixed amount of money. However, in that case there will be no incentive.
g. To avoid inefficient risk bearing, the least risk averse party should bear the risk, because in that case the costs as compensation for bearing risk are lower.

## 4.33 Incentive compensation for police

Communities are frequently concerned about whether police officers are vigilant in carrying out their responsibilities. In some countries, a number of communities have experimented with incentive compensation for police. In particular, some cities have paid members of the police force based on the number of arrests they personally make. Discuss the likely effects of this compensation policy.

## Answer 4.33 Incentive compensation for police

The number of arrests would go up. However, the plan would likely have several undesirable effects.

- First, it encourages the police to make arrests even if the reasons for the arrests are questionable.
- Second, it would encourage police to work on crimes where arrests are easy to make, rather than working on more serious crimes where it is more difficult to make numerous arrests.
- Third, the plan would not encourage co-operation or teamwork (since the bonus is based on *individual* arrests).

## 4.34 Piece rate

Agricultural workers are often paid piece rates. For example, pear pickers are paid a fixed amount for each box of pears they pick. Pear companies, however, pay tree thinners on an hourly basis. These thinners remove excess fruit from trees so that the remaining fruit can grow larger (each piece of fruit must be at least six inches apart on the tree).

Why do you think these companies pay thinners by hour? Presumably, they would work harder if they were paid by the tree.

## Answer 4.34 Piece rate

Good tree thinning involves both quantity and quality.

- Quality means that no fruit is wasted and there is at least 6 inches between each piece of fruit.
- Paying by the tree emphasises quantity and not quality. Workers would be expected to underinvest in quality to increase output.
- For instance, thinners might break branches to remove the fruit at the top of trees, rather than take the time to set a ladder to appropriately thin the fruit.
- It is difficult for an outside monitor to tell whether the worker is doing a quality job by simply observing the tree after the fact. The worker could claim that the tree already had broken branches from previous storms.

## 4.35 Risk attitude

a. How, and in which mathematical functions, are preferences and aversion to risk manifested?
b. What is the expected utility function in a risk neutral situation?
c. What is the expected utility function in a risk averse situation?
d. What does a concave utility function mean?
e. Which risk attitudes are the most common?

## Answer 4.35 Risk attitude

a. Preference and aversion to risk manifest themselves in the slope and shape of the indifference curve, but also in the characteristics of the utility function from which these indifference curves are differentiated.
b. In a risk neutral situation, the expected utility function is linear.
c. In a risk averse situation, the expected utility function is concave.
d. A concave utility function implies that a fixed amount of money is valued higher than an uncertain amount of which the weighted average would yield the same amount of money.

e. Risk-neutral and risk averse behaviour are the most frequent risk attitudes. In a P/A situation risk-loving behaviour is often left out of consideration. One assumes for the greater part that the principal is risk neutral and the agent is either risk neutral or risk averse.

### 4.36 Neumann-Morgenstern utility function (N-M utility function)
a. What are the labels for the horizontal and vertical axes for the expected utility function?
b. To which category does the N-M utility function belong?
c. What quality does an expected utility function satisfy?
d. What does a positive affine transformation mean?
e. What is the result a positive affine transformation?
f. What does the expected utility framework imply for the measurability?
g. What is an important property of the N-M utility function?

### Answer 4.36 Neumann-Morgenstern utility function (N-M utility function)
a. The horizontal axis of the expected utility function is labelled income, and the vertical axis is labelled utility.
b. The N-M utility function belongs to the category of expected utility functions.
c. An expected utility function is unique to a positive affine transformation.
d. A positive affine transformation simply means multiplying by a positive number and adding a constant. We say that a positive affine transformation can be written in the form of: $v(u) = au + b$ where $a > 0$.
e. It turns out that if you subject an expected function to a positive affine transformation, it not only represents the same preferences (this is obvious since an affine transformation is just a special kind of monotonic transformation) but it also still has the expected utility property. Economists say that an expected utility function is 'unique up to an affine transformation'. This just means that you can apply an affine transformation to it and get another expected utility function that represents the same preferences. But any other kind of transformation will destroy the expected utility property.
f. The expected utility implies that sub-utility indices of the expected income from every action, that can be weighted and added to the total expected utility, are cardinally measurable.
g. An important property of the N-M expected utility function is that sub-utility indices that are weighted and added to measure expected utility are cardinally measurable. It means that it is not only the amount of the outcome of the expected utility function that represents a ranking, but that the differences in utility indices also have a meaning of ordering.

### 4.37 Loss aversion
a. What is an important difference between the prospect theory and the expected utility theory?
b. What is a central concept in the prospect theory?
c. In valuation studies we often find a substantial difference between the willingness to pay (WTP) and the willingness to accept (WTA). What is an explanation of this valuation disparity?
d. What is the consequence if we have to compensate people for the loss of their property as a result of a taking by the government or a disaster (e.g. a flooding)?

### Answer 4.37 Loss aversion

a.  An important difference between the prospect theory and the expected utility theory is the risk attitude concerning profits and losses.
b.  Loss aversion is a central concept in the prospect theory. People feel the pain of a loss stronger than the joy of a gain. Losses and gains are not valued the same.
c.  One of the explanations of this valuation disparity between WTP and WTA is the loss aversion, for example, for environmental goods.
d.  The consequence will be that a compensation based on the market price does not meet the loss experience of the people involved.

### 4.38 Lotteries and insurances

a.  If people are generally risk averse, why do so many people around the world take part in national lotteries?
b.  What is the idea of an insurance for policyholders and of an insurance company? Which types of people are prepared to pay premiums in order to obtain insurance; risk averse, risk neutral or risk-loving people?
c.  Why are insurance companies unwilling to provide insurance against losses arising from war or 'civil insurrection'?

### Answer 4.38 Lotteries and insurances

a.  An explanation can be found in the loss aversion approach. According to the prospect theory, in a loss situation decision makers prefer to have an uncertain loss. It means that for losses, this theory predicts that people have a risk-seeking preference. In a loss situation, they prefer an uncertain loss (e.g. 50% chance of a loss of € 2,000 and 50% of a loss of € 0) above a certain loss of € 1000. In a lottery the chance of a loss is uncertain. There is a chance of a loss (the purchase price of lottery ticket, e.g. € 25), say 90%, and a chance of say 10% on a loss of € 0 in the case of a prize of € 25 (or the prospect of a profit with a higher payment). The loss still remains uncertain. Another argument of the prospect theory is that people overestimate small chances.
b.  Insurance is a way of eliminating risks for policyholders. Being risk averse, people are prepared to pay premiums in order to obtain insurance. Insurance companies, on the other hand, are prepared to take on these risks because they can spread them over a large number of policies. According to the law of large numbers, what is unpredictable for a single policyholder becomes highly predictable for a large number of them, provided that their risks are independent of each other.
c.  The claims would be enormous. These types of risks are not independent of each other.

### 4.39 Valuation of an uncertain income

a.  How is the certainty equivalent of the uncertain income y defined?
b.  What does the risk premium consist of?
c.  When is an individual unwilling to pay a risk premium?
d.  Is there a relationship between the distribution of risks between the principal and agent and the reward structure?

## Answer 4.39 Valuation of an uncertain income

a. The certainty equivalent of an uncertain income y can be calculated as follows:

$$y = E(y) - 0.5 \ r \ Var(y) - C(a)$$

where
$y$ = valuation of the uncertain income;
$E(y)$ = expectation of the uncertain income;
$r$ = risk characteristic of the individual;
$Var(y)$ = income variation;
$C(a)$ = costs involved with the activity.

b. The risk premium consists in the first place of the 'nature' of the individual (careful or more adventurous), reflected by r (r = 0 when risk neutral or r > 0 when risk averse). In the second place, the risk premium consists of the variation of the uncertain income (Var(y)).

c. An individual is unwilling to pay a risk premium if the income is not accompanied by any uncertainty (Var(y) = 0) or if he is risk neutral (r = 0).

d. Distribution of risks between the principal and agent can be differentiated from the reward structure. An agent would be prepared to take more risks if he is compensated by a higher expected compensation.

## 4.40 Prisoners' dilemma

A famous, non-economic example of game theory is the so-called prisoners' dilemma. Imagine the following situation: Andrew and Barack (the players of the game) were caught while stealing bikes. This is a reason to put them in jail for five years. However, they are also *suspected* of bank robberies, a crime serious enough to be imprisoned for 15 years. The police need confessions for the convictions. Both are therefore interviewed separately, and informed about their possibilities:

- If both deny the crime, they will both be imprisoned for five years.
- If one confesses he robbed the bank and the other does not, he will have an incredibly low punishment of two years imprisonment only; the other is found guilty of robbery and lying, and will get the full fifteen years.
- If both confess their crime, both will have a reduced sentence of ten years.

a. Draw a scheme of this situation.
b. If Andrew and Barack act in their own interest only (selfishly), what will they choose?
c. Would this be different if they had agreed beforehand to help each other out?
d. If they are caught later on again, and are offered comparable possibilities, would they make the same choice?

## Answer 4.40 Prisoners' dilemma

a.

| | | Barack's choices | |
|---|---|---|---|
| | | Confess | Deny |
| Andrew's choices | Confess | A 10 years<br>B 10 years | A 2 years<br>B 15 years |
| | Deny | A 15 years<br>B 2 years | A 5 years<br>B 5 years |

b. Both will confess. To see why; think of Andrew's strategy. He (being selfish) is prepared to see Barack suffer for 15 years, if he can get away with only two years. The same goes of course for Barack.

c. Provided that they stick to their agreement, that would indeed change the situation. Both would deny, and end up with five years in prison.

d. Such situations are called 'repeated games' in game theory. People are then supposed to adapt their behaviour on the basis of earlier experiences. The brothers in crime could have learned from this experience, and make an agreement for next time. Even so, it remains open whether they would stick to that agreement.

### 4.41 Nash equilibrium
a. What is a Nash equilibrium?
b. Explain why a joint confession is the Nash equilibrium in the prisoner's dilemma.

### Answer 4.41 Nash equilibrium
a. A Nash equilibrium is a set of actions (or strategies) such that each player is doing the best it can, given the actions of its opponents.
b. A joint confession is the Nash equilibrium in the prisoner's dilemma. Given one person confesses, it is in the interests of the other party to confess as well (indeed, confession is a dominant strategy – it is in a player's interest to confess no matter what the other player does).

### 4.42 Dominant strategy and a Nash equilibrium
a. What are strategies?
b. What is characteristic of strategies?
c. What is the relation between a dominant strategy and a Nash equilibrium?

### Answer 4.42 Dominant strategy and a Nash equilibrium
a. Strategies are actions, or a series of actions, that a player can undertake to strengthen his own position.
b. Typical of strategies is that they influence the actions of others.
c. All dominant strategies are Nash equilibria. However, not all Nash equilibria are dominant strategies. Dominant strategies are optimal no matter what the other party does. Nash equilibrium strategies are strategies that are individually optimal given the strategy of the other party[5].

### 4.43 Game theory
a. What is generally discussed in the game theory?
b. Why, in a conflict situation, are there interactive situations?
c. What distinction can be made in the game theory and what type is most frequently used in economics?
d. What solution is used in a non-co-operative game?
e. How is a Nash equilibrium defined?
f. What does the co-operative game theory refer to?

---

[5] See also Chapter 6 of the textbook.

g. When does a co-operative game change into a non-co-operative game?
h. Can the game theory also be applied to contracts or management agreements between the government and farmers for preserving wildlife and landscape?

**Answer 4.43 Game theory**
a. The game theory generally discusses situations in which there are conflicting interests.
b. Conflict situations concern interactive situations because individuals realise that when they consider their possible actions, they influence each other from both sides.
c. Game theory distinguishes co-operative and non-co-operative games. In the theory of economics, the non-co-operative game theory is most frequently used.
d. The non-co-operative game theory uses the Nash equilibrium as a solution.
e. A combination of strategies is called a Nash equilibrium when none of the players has the incentive to change his chosen strategy.
f. The co-operative game theory refers to situations in which, before the game is played, players can negotiate about what to do during the game.
g. If in a co-operative game the non-negotiable outcomes are not stated, the co-operative game changes into a non-co-operative game.
h. Game theory can also be applied to management agreements. The principal (government) offers the agent (farmer) a contract that the agent can either accept or reject. If the agent accepts the contract, he chooses an action to carry it out.

**4.44 Game theory and two students**
Sometimes a problem in game theory yields more than one equilibrium. Consider the following situation. You and a fellow student have to hand in a paper, due in one day's time. It turns out that both of you use a different text processor, and that the systems are not compatible with each other. You (player A) prefer text processor OO, player B has a preference for text processor MW. Of course, both of you prefer using the program you are used to. However, both of you also prefer using the program of the other over failing to coordinate at all. For the sake of the argument, assume that you have no possibility to discuss with your colleague and agree upon the use of a specific choice; each of you has to decide separately.

The pay-offs of the possible combinations can be summarised as follows:

| | | Choice of your colleague (player B) | |
|---|---|---|---|
| | | OO | MW |
| Your choice (player A) | OO | A 2 B 1 | A 0 B 0 |
| | MW | A 0 B 0 | A 1 B 2 |

a. What are the Nash equilibria in this case?
b. In game theory there is also the concept of 'mixed strategy Nash equilibria'. In a mixed strategy, one calculates the probility that a player will choose a certain strategy. So in this case we look for a Nash equilibrium where player A and player B choose WP and MW with

a certain probability. Calculate these probabilities. (Hint: for such equilibria, a player must be exactly indifferent to the outcomes both of his pure options, and all options must have a positive probability).

## Answer 4.44 Game theory and two students

a. The 'normal' Nash equilibria are: (OO, OO) and (MW, MW). In other words, the situations where both players choose the same processor are equilibria.
b. Denote the probabilities for player 1 with q, and for player 2 with p. Remember that the probabilities for a player must total to one. Begin with player one. There are two options, choose OO or MW, and player 1 should be indifferent to the outcomes of these options. Multiplying (unknown) probabilities, we get:
$$q(2) + (1-q)(0) = q(0) + (1-q)(1) \tag{1}$$
Solving gives: q = 1/3. A similar equation can be set for player 2:
$$(1-p)(1) + p(0) = (1-p)(0) + p(2) \tag{2}$$
Now solving yields p = 1/3. Hence, there is a Nash equilibrium where a player chooses the system of his colleague with probability 1/3 and his own system with probability $2/3$[6].

## 4.45 Striking as threat

A labour leader has announced that her union will go on strike unless you grant the workers a significant pay raise. You realise that a strike will cost you more money than the pay raise. Should you concede to the wage increase? Explain.

## Answer 4.45 Striking as threat

Not necessarily. It is important to ask if the threat by the labour leader is credible. Is it really in the interests of labour to strike if you do not concede to the wage increase? The labour union leader may simply be making an 'idle threat' in an attempt to get you to make a wage concession.

## 4.46 Consumer surplus

The consumer surplus is an important measure of the welfare of people. An increase in consumer surplus means an increase in welfare of consumers and a decrease in consumer surplus means a decrease in welfare. Suppose that all consumers have an identical demand for a product. Each person's demand curve is:
P = 30 - 2Q
The marginal cost of production is € 2.
a. Determine the quantity sold if the price is € 2.
b. Devise for this firm a two-part tariff that will exhaust the consumer surplus.

## Answer 4.46 Consumer surplus

a. At a price of € 2, the quantity sold is 14.
b. The firm could charge marginal costs of € 2 and an up-front fee equal to the consumer surplus. As said, at a price of € 2 the quantity sold is 14. Consumer surplus is equal to the area of the

---

[6] For a more extended discussion of this type of problem, see Jehle, G. and P. Reny, 2000. Advanced Microeconomic Theory. 2nd edition. Pearson Education, Addison Wesley, p 277.

triangle below the demand curve, but above price line of € 2 (tip: draw figure). The resulting up-front charge is € 196.

### 4.47 Consumer and producer surplus

Suppose the demand and supply of a certain product can be described as follows:

$Q_d = 10 - p$
$Q_s = p - 2$
$Q_d = Q_s$

Where  $Q_d$  = demanded quantity;
       $Q_s$  = supplied quantity;
       p   = price per unit.

a.  Make a clear diagram of this situation.
b.  Determine the price, and the demanded and supplied quantities for this situation.
c.  Determine the willingness to pay (WTP) and willingness to sell (WTS) in this situation.
d.  Determine the consumer surplus (CS) and producer surplus (PS). What do these concepts present?

**Answer 4.47 Consumer and producer surplus**

a.

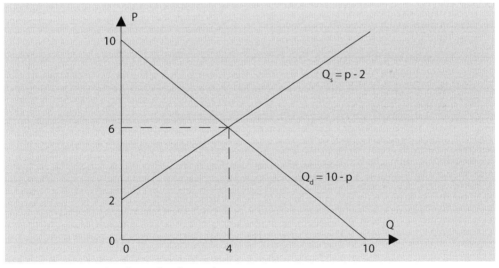

Figure 4.1. Demand and supply of a product.

b.  $Q_d = Q_s$                                                  (1)
     $10 - p = p - 2$                                  (2)
     $p = 6$                                              (3)
     $Q_d = Q_s = 4$                                    (4)

c.  WTP $= 4 \times 6 + \frac{1}{2}(4 \times 4) = 24 + 8 = 32$                                         (5)

   WTS $= \frac{1}{2}(8 \times 4) = 16$                                                                (6)

d.  CS $= \frac{1}{2}(4 \times 4) = 8$                                                                 (7)

   PS $= \frac{1}{2}(4 \times 4) = 8$                                                                   (8)

The CS is the difference between what a consumer is willing to pay for a product (indicated by the area under the demand curve) and what he/she has to pay. It is a surplus because the consumer gains an excess of benefits from the purchase of the good over the amount paid.

The PS is the area above the supply curve and below the price line $P_e$ representing the difference between the minimum amount the seller will accept for any unit sold (given by the WTS line) and its actual price. It is a surplus because the WTS line is higher than the actual $P_e$ over the considered area in the Figure.

### 4.48 Bargaining over a sale

Consider two people; a buyer and a seller. The seller produces a product in which the buyer is interested. The buyer believes that the seller values the product at either 20 or 15 Euros. The seller believes that the buyer values the product at either 30 Euros or 10 Euros.

a.  The buyer assigns a probability of 0.2 to the seller's valuing the good at 15 Euros and correspondingly, a probability of 0.8 that it is worth 20 Euros to her. Please calculate the expected value.

b.  The seller assesses a probability of 0.2 that the buyer's valuation is 10 Euros and a probability of 0.8 that it is 30 Euros. Please calculate the expected value.

c.  How can we show or represent this situation in a figure or graph? Please indicate the bargaining area, and the expected values in this figure.

d.  Suppose there are a number of the same goods, and one buyer and one seller. At a price of 30 Euros, the buyer would like to buy 5 units of the product and at a price of 10 Euros he would like to buy 30 units of the product. At a price of 15 Euros, the seller is prepared to sell 10 units and at a price of 20 Euros, he is prepared to sell 25 units of the product.

e.  Please show the bargaining area in a graph.

### Answer 4.48 Bargaining over a sale

See text book

# 5. Attributes of transactions and transaction cost economics

## 5.1 Reasons for non-market transactions
a. Why are not all transactions conducted through markets?
b. What factors create a comparative advantage for non-market transactions over the costs of market exchange?
c. What is in general the relationship between these factors and the complexity of a transaction?
d. What is often the most important attribute of a transaction for determining the best suited governance structure? And what does this attribute mean?

## Answer 5.1 Reasons for non-market transactions
a. Ronald Coase[1] provided the answer to this question by arguing that market transactions involve costs; there is a cost of using the price mechanism. For instance, they involve the cost of searching for trading partners and negotiating the relevant price. In other words, we have to deal with transaction costs.
b. Factors that can make the costs of market exchanges higher than the costs of non-market transactions are (1) asset specificity and the associated hold-up and lock-in effects; (2) uncertainty; (3) frequency and duration; (4) difficulty of performance measurement; (5) connectedness and (6) non-rivalry and non-non-excludability. For examples of such factors, see the textbook.
c. In general, if these attributes occur, the complexity of the transaction will increase. In practice, this will lead to higher transaction costs if a transaction occurs. The complexity can be so large, and because of that the transaction costs would become so high if we carry out the transaction via the market, that other governance structures would be preferable.
d. The most important attribute of a transaction for determining the best suited governance structure is often the asset-specificity attribute, connected with hold-up and lock-in effects. Assets are specific to certain uses if the goods and service they provide are highly valuable only in that use. The degree of specificity of an asset can be defined as the fraction of its value that would be lost if it were excluded from its major use.

## 5.2 The firm as organisational unit
a. Why do we have firms?
b. Can a firm be considered as a contractual structure? What did Alchian and Demsetz[2] assume about the type of contracts, and what is a weak point?
c. What is the view of Jensen and Meckling[3]? To what does it refer?
d. What is the background of the **make or buy** decision?

---

[1] Coase, H.R., 1937. The nature of the firm. Economica 4:386-405.

[2] Alchian, A.A. and H. Demsetz, 1972. Production, information costs and economic organization. American Economic Review 73: 777-795.

[3] Jensen, M. and W. Meckling, 1976. Theory of the firm: managerial behaviour, agency cost and capital structure. Journal of Financial Economics 3: 305-360.

## Answer 5.2 The firm as organisational unit

a. As Coase said: there are costs linked to carrying out transactions via the market. The size of these transaction costs depends on the nature of the good, the nature of the transaction and the way in which it is organised. It may be more efficient and effective to enter into an organisational relation, instead of hiring labour every day via a market. In other words, a firm as an organisational unit can exist if it can carry out its coordination function at lower costs than by undertaking market transactions each time.

b. Alchian and Demsetz considered a firm as a contractual structure. The acquisition of the resources, the production and the delivery of the end-product are organised via contractual relations. They assumed **complete contracts.** However, it is almost impossible to conclude complete contracts.

c. Jensen and Meckling viewed firms as broadly defined contractual structures and stated that organisations such as firms, non-profit organisations and government agencies consist of a *nexus of contracts*. These contracts can be internal or external. With an internal contract, the firm decides to provide the requirements from within the organisation, and with an external contract, the provisions are delivered by a third party. This refers to the classic **make versus buy** decision, which is an important subject of research.

d. The background of the **make or buy** decision is the firm's choice of whether it should make an intermediate good in-house or secure it in some market or via contracts. The **make or buy** decision also refers to the fundamental question regarding the reason for existence of organisations and how they function.

## 5.3 Basic elements of transaction cost economics (TCE)

a. What does TCE try to explain?
b. What is the unit of analysis?
c. What are the exogenous and endogenous variables?
d. What drives the choice of the governance structure?
e. What factors determine, according to Williamson[4], which particular governance structure is most efficient?

## Answer 5.3. Basic elements of transaction cost economics (TCE)

a. The TCE tries to explain which governance structure has a comparative advantage in carrying out transactions.
b. The unit of analysis is the transaction, while governance structures are chosen depending on:
   1. the characteristic of the environment (asset specificity, uncertainty and frequency);
   2. the human characteristics of the decision-makers (bounded rationality and opportunistic behaviour).
c. The exogenous variables are (1) and (2) and the endogenous variable is the governance structure.
d. The choice of the governance structure is driven by minimising the transaction costs.
e. According to Williamson, the dimensions of the transaction consisting of the level of asset specificity, degree of uncertainty and frequency, complemented with the human characteristics, together determine which particular governance structure is most efficient.

---

[4] Williamson, O.E., 1998. Transaction cost economics: how it works, where it headed. The Economist 146: 23-58.

## 5.4 Transaction costs approach
a.  What is the empirical object of transaction cost economics?
b.  What is a firm in the transaction costs approach?
c.  What are markets, firms and hybrids in this approach?
d.  What type of transaction costs does Williamson distinguish?

## Answer 5.4 Transaction costs approach
a.  The empirical object of TCE is formed by governance structures in which transactions are carried out and administrated: markets, organisations and other institutional arrangements which lie in between these two outer cases. However, the results of these transactions are strongly influenced by the institutional environment, but also by the social embeddedness.
b.  In the transaction costs approach, a firm can be seen as an institutional solution to avoid costs linked with the market mechanism and to realise specific contracts which do not easily arise in market relations.
c.  Markets, organisations, and hybrid forms such as contracts are mechanisms *for carrying out* transactions.
d.  He distinguishes transaction costs of **ex-ante** and **ex-post** types. Ex-ante costs arise before the transaction occurs. They consist of the cost of *drafting, negotiating, and safeguarding an agreement*. The ex-post costs of contracting take several forms; (1) maladaption costs incurred when transactions drift out of alignment, including the opportunity costs of maintaining the contract under changed circumstances; (2) the haggling cost incurred if bilateral efforts are made to correct ex-post misalignments, including the adaptation costs in case of changes in the contract; (3) the set-up and running cost associated with the governance structure to which disputes are referred; and (4) the bonding cost of effective secure commitments.

## 5.5 Comparative advantages of transaction mechanisms
a.  What types of characteristics of the transaction determine, according to Williamson, the comparative advantages of a governance structure?
b.  What are the human characteristics according to Williamson?
c.  What are the environmental characteristics according to Williamson?

## Answer 5.5 Comparative advantages of transaction mechanisms
a.  The *characteristics of human decision makers* and *environmental characteristics* of the transaction determine the comparative advantages of a governance structure.
b.  The human characteristics are *bounded rationality* and *opportunistic* (strategic) *behaviour*. The human characteristic *bounded rationality* has a practical significance in a complex and uncertain environment. It may be too costly or impossible to consider all the consequences of a decision and to use the market for carrying out the transaction. The transaction costs of an internal organisational relation (i.e. **make** by in-house production/vertical integration) can be lower than of a market relationship (i.e. **buy**).
    *Opportunistic behaviour* is also a human characteristic consisting of the provision of selective and distorted information, making promises which are not intended to be kept, and a person pretending to be different from what the person actually is. The phenomena of *hidden information* and *hidden action* are included in Williamson's approach. In his view, it

is sufficient if some of the agents behave differently from the way they are and it is difficult or expensive to determine who they are and how they behave in reality.

c.  The environmental characteristics which influence the size and nature of transaction costs are: (1) asset specificity; (2) the uncertainty; and (3) the frequency.

## 5.6 Transaction cost economics
a.  What is, according to the transaction costs economics, the fundamental unit of analysis?
b.  What is the relationship between 'transaction' and the concept of 'exchange'?
c.  Why is the transaction mechanism or the governance structure important?

## Answer 5.6 Transaction cost economics
a.  According to transaction cost economics, the fundamental unit of analysis is the transaction.
b.  Transaction is synonymous with the economic concept of exchange. It is a two-sided mechanism: the transfer of goods or services from one individual to another including the trade-off between performance and counter performance, *quid pro quo,* and the transfer of property rights. The *quid pro quo* could refer to concluding an agreement (by sale and purchase) or a contract. A special assignment must be carried out.
c.  Transactions can be carried out in various ways. Each transaction of a good or service involves costs. The choice of the governance structure influences these (transaction) costs and the one with the lowest transaction costs (including the costs for distribution of quasi-rent) should be used (other things being equal). The choice of the governance structure is driven by minimising transaction costs.

## 5.7 Fundamental transformation
a.  What is the background of the fundamental transformation of Williamson?
b.  What concept is strongly related to the idea of the fundamental transformation of Williamson? What theory is the background of this concept and what does this concept mean?
c.  What is meant by the fundamental transformation of Williamson?

## Answer 5.7 Fundamental transformation
a.  The background of the fundamental transformation of Williamson is the type of investment within a certain relationship. The investment is characterised by a high level of asset specificity and it creates a lock-in situation.
b.  The 'concept of being trapped' is strongly related to the idea of the fundamental transformation of Williamson. It is based on the fixed asset theory. The 'concept of being trapped' means that your alternatives are strongly reduced, for example, because of the low salvage value of your investments or the high level of sunk costs of your investments.
c.  The fundamental transformation of Williamson means that an original situation with a large number of potential transaction partners is transformed into a situation of monopoly; i.e. an original situation of large numbers of transaction partners is transformed into a situation of some numbers transaction partners. The final situation can be a bilateral monopoly.

## 5.8 Transaction cost theory and quasi-rent
a.  Why is the quasi-rent an important topic in the transaction cost theory?
b.  What role can the type of governance structure play?

## Answer 5.8 Transaction costs and quasi-rent

a. Firstly, quasi-rents arise as results of investments or the use of assets with a high level of asset specificity. Secondly, the distribution of the quasi-rent is important. Ex-ante and ex-post haggling over the distribution of the quasi-rent can involve high transaction costs. Especially the human characteristic of 'opportunistic behaviour' – as assumed to exist by Williamson – contributes to the level of transaction costs.

b. The type of governance structure can reduce the transaction costs about the distribution of the quasi-rent. For example, a small family firm will have no distribution problem with the quasi-rent if it realises a quasi-rent within the firm, because there is no third party involved to share with. Vertical integration or in-house production can also reduce these transaction costs (see also question 3.14).

## 5.9 Predictions of transaction cost economics

a. Which transactions will be carried by the governance structure the market?

b. What is the most suited governance structure for transaction with a high level of asset specificity and a high level of uncertainty?

c. According to Williamson, the market is an appropriate governance structure in cases of high level of uncertainty. What do you think about his view?

d. Could you give an example of a transaction between two parties that is specific and occur infrequently or not very often. What does it mean for the governance structure?

## Answer 5.9 Predictions of transaction cost economics

a. Transactions with a low level of asset specificity will be carried out by the governance structure the market.

b. The most suited governance structure for transactions with a high level of asset specificity and high level of uncertainty is the hierarchy; i.e. vertical integration or in-house production.

c. Other governance structures making use of common values and norms, reputation mechanisms and the build-up of trust are also possible, e.g. short- or medium-term contacts. However, because of the assumption of opportunistic behaviour, Williamson predicts the market as governance structure. This view is disputed because of this assumption.

d. An example is buying a house. Such a transaction is not often carried out (mostly once or maybe twice in a lifetime). Most people will make use of an external intermediator, a real estate agent. Williamson calls this a trilateral governance structure.

## 5.10 Transactions with relation-specific investments

a. Which party finds itself in a disadvantageous position and why?

b. What are the reasons that the investing party has a disadvantageous position?

c. What types of problems are created?

d. How is the surplus of this type of investment called?

e. What questions are emphasised in this type of transaction?

## Answer 5.10 Transactions with relation-specific investments

a. The party which has made the relation-specific investments finds itself in a disadvantageous position. The non-investing party may try to appropriate a high share of value created by the investment.

b. The reasons are:
- the asset specificity or the sunk character of the investments, ex-post there are hardly alternatives available;
- the human characteristics of opportunistic behaviour and bounded rationality; and
- contracts are incomplete, as a result of bounded rationality, people are not omniscient, and transaction costs; writing complete contracts would involve huge transaction costs.
c. The factors mentioned in (b) create hold-up and lock-in effects.
d. The surplus of this type of investment is called the quasi-rent.
e. The emphasis is on the (1) value creation of the investment expressed in (quasi-)rents and the (2) distribution of the (quasi-)rents. The distribution of the (quasi-)rents can also be considered as the appropriation of the quasi-rents.

### 5.11 Framework of attributes of transactions
a. What attributes are decisive for the choice of governance structures and how does this differ with the view of Williamson?
b. What is in general the relationship between these attributes and the transaction costs?
c. What factors determine the preferable governance structure?

### Answer 5.11 Framework of attributes of transactions
a. All together, these attributes consist of:
   1. level of asset specificity;
   2. degree of uncertainty;
   3. level of frequency and duration;
   4. difficulty of measuring the performance of the transaction;
   5. level of connectedness of assets and co-specialised assets;
   6. non-excludability and non-rivalry of the goods.

   This is an extension and deepening of the approach of Williamson. For more on his ideas, see the text book.
b. In general, a higher level of these attributes will lead to higher transaction costs if a transaction occurs.
c. Transaction costs, the level of the quasi-rent, and the distribution of the quasi-rent determine which governance structure is preferable.

### 5.12 Hold-up and lock-in
a. What is the root of the hold-up problem and with what type of investment is it related?
b. What is the effect of hold-up problems? Are they real costs and do they recur often?
c. What does lock-in mean and how does it occur?
d. What is the difference between lock-in and hold-up?
e. Suppose we have two co-specialised assets. When do we have two really co-specialised assets and what could happen if we would like to maximise the benefits?

### Answer 5.12 Hold-up and lock-in
a. The root of the hold-up problem is that certain assets are specific to certain uses; asset specificity. The degree of specificity of an asset depends on the fraction of its value that

would be lost if it were excluded from its major use. It is related to the phenomenon of 'sunk investment'.

b.  The fear of being *held-up* can prevent people from investing in specific assets. It will affect a society's total welfare. These are the real social costs of a hold-up problem. Hold-up problems are very common and recur frequently.

c.  Lock-in means that your alternatives are strongly reduced. This can be because of functional, technical, or institutional reasons. Lock-in effects can be the result of being *held-up*.

d.  Lock-in effect is an ex-post phenomenon, while hold-up is more of an ex-ante problem.

e.  Co-specialised assets are in some respects unique and are also complementary. It is a condition of two assets in which each is more productive when used with the other. Both parties are often locked-in. In that case, any breakdowns in the transaction will lead to large costs on both sides. Maximising the benefits requires using both assets together.

## 5.13 Natural monopoly

a.  What is characteristic for natural monopoly?

b.  For what type of provisions are they very common?

c.  What kinds of governance structures are possible?

## Answer 5.13 Natural Monopoly

a.  Natural monopolies are characterised by a large part of fixed costs and a relatively small part of variable costs. The total average costs will decrease if the production capacity increases. The investments are often asset-specific.

b.  Natural monopolies are a common phenomenon for the provision of electricity, gas, water and other 'network' services, such as railways.

c.  Possible governance structures are:
   *  The national government is owner and a public utility company takes care of all the activities involved. This is the in-house production solution.
   *  The national government is the legal owner of the network and the network is leased to private operators. This a variety of a franchising contract solution.
   *  The local government is the legal owner of the network and gas, water and electricity is delivered by a private company.

## 5.14 Hold-up and lock-in effects in railway

As explained in question 1.6, the organisation of the Dutch railway system is rather complicated. Based on a contract, the government makes the policy, sets quality criteria and gives orders (as of 2008, the involved parties themselves can decide how to meet these quality criteria, and are judged ex post by the ministry). A separate organisation, ProRail, is the 'rail infrastructure manager' and as such responsible for the building and maintenance of the rail. It also regulates the capacity. The government owns all the shares of ProRail. Several other organisations, NS being by far the largest and most well-known, take care of the actual transport. Given its large share, NS can also be considered as a monopolist. The government owns also all the shares of NS.

a.  What kind of problems can arise?

b.  What are possible solutions to these problems?

## Answer 5.14 Hold-up and lock-in effects in railway

a. The problems that arise are related to the concepts of hold-up and lock-in. Large (specific) investments have to be made in building and maintaining the physical infrastructure (e.g. network of railways). These tasks have to be done by ProRail, but this company will be reluctant to make such huge investments if it is not able to increase the tariffs for the use of the railway. This creates a hold-up problem. As soon as the important investments have been carried out, a lock-in effect arises. ProRail is dependent on NS for earning back his investment.

The benefits of those investments largely accrue to the parties that actually use the railway. The user of the railway is NS (and may also be the government as the owner of all the shares of NS). Further, the users of the railway have no incentive for avoiding abuse or overuse of the infrastructure, as the costs go to the infrastructure manager (ProRail). The problems are worsened by the form of the market, where large monopolists have enormous market power. Because both ProRail and NS can be considered as a monopolist, we have a situation of bilateral monopoly. Exclusive contracts between both can create negative welfare effects because of hold-up and lock-in effects.

b. The problems can be mitigated by designing long-term contracts that build in incentives to make the user pay for the real costs connected with the actual use, and the benefits of investments also go to the party that has to make the actual investments. A conflict-resolving mechanism such as an NMa can be useful, if the transaction costs are not too high. Increasing competition may also help. However, it is questionable if infrastructural projects of this scale and with such specific investments indeed become more efficient from increased competition[5].

## 5.15 Uncertainty

a. What is, according to the transaction cost theory of Williamson, the reason for uncertainty?
b. Could you give some other reasons for uncertainty?
c. Which theories are very helpful for analysing the effects of uncertainty?

## Answer 5.15 Uncertainty

a. According to the transaction cost theory of Williamson, the degree of uncertainty is a result of the incompleteness of contracts and the possibilities of ex-post renegotiation.
b. In practice, due to a number of reasons, uncertainty and complexity exist.
   - **Firstly,** contracts can be very complicated, e.g. a contract for the construction of a railway line from Rotterdam to Germany or for a long tunnel. Such contracts will give rise to uncertainty and complexity. Specific unforeseen events may not have been taken into account.
   - **Second**, even if all events could be predicted, it is difficult for the parties to negotiate over so many possibilities. There would be far too many events to take into account in the contract.
   - **Third**, even if the parties could take all possibilities in the future into account and negotiate them, it would still be extremely difficult to lay it all down in an agreement that, in the case of a conflict of opinion, could be examined by an outsider, e.g. a court of law, with regard to the content and meaning of the agreement, and be enforced.

---

[5] Based on information from the Dutch Ministry of Traffic and Water management; http://www.verkeerenwaterstaat.nl/onderwerpen/openbaar_vervoer/trein/organisatie_spoor/.

c. The expected utility theory and prospect theory (loss aversion) can be very helpful for this type of analysis.

## 5.16 Frequency and duration
a. What mechanism can be used for transactions of a 'once in lifetime' nature, or transactions which occur infrequently?
b. What can be expected in the case of parties that interact frequently?

## Answer 5.16 Frequency and duration
a. One of the mechanisms for transactions which occur infrequently is making use of external intermediators. Most people only buy a house once or twice during their lifetime. Intermediators, like a real estate agent, may reduce transaction costs, such as search costs, surveys, inspection costs and dispute resolving. An important incentive for them to do their job well is the reputation mechanism.
b. In the case of parties that interact frequently, one may expect a mechanism that is specially designed for the particular aspects of their relationship. A special-purpose governance structure is often worthwhile.

## 5.17 Difficulty of measuring performance or counter performance in the transaction
a. What is an important factor for the choice between in-house production and contracting out?
b. What is an important condition for applying performance-based pay or financial incentives?
c. Please name at least three circumstances that give a reason for avoiding formal financial performance incentives.

## Answer 5.17 Difficulty of measuring performance or counter performance in the transaction
a. For the choice between in-house provision and contracting out, it is necessary that (1) you know what you want; (2) the quality of the goods or services that you want are contractable.
b. An important condition for applying performance-based pay or financial incentives is that it is relatively cheap to measure performance accurately. If this is possible, performance-based pay can be a good solution.
c. Three circumstances are: (1) when performance is difficult to measure; (2) situations in which **care** is very important but difficult or costly to measure; (3) when the problem of motivating the person to honour his or her responsibilities is great, e.g. because of the crowding-out effects. In such cases the best system may be to avoid offering any formal financial performance incentives.

## 5.18 Connectedness and co-specialised skills
a. What is important about the 'connectedness' attribute and what is the effect when assets are connected?
b. Is the 'connectedness' attribute also important for the asset of human capital?
c. What is the solution?

## Answer 5.18 Connectedness and co-specialised skills
a. Transactions differ in how they are connected to other transactions, especially those involving investments which are highly asset-specific. It is even possible that the assets or services they

yield are strongly complementary. A high level of one may significantly increase the value of the other.

b. The connectedness of transactions can also be a result of the people involved. Human capital is one of the most important kinds of assets. The skills and knowledge of a person are often tied to the person in question. The transferability of human capital is problematic if those skills are specific to an organisation or asset.

c. Maximising the benefits requires using connected assets together in one organisational mode. With regard to human capital, teams are very common in hospitals, research institutions, government bureaus, and in firms. Mostly they are charged with specific tasks demanding specific knowledge and expertise. The team is an organisational mode. Co-specialised skills and knowledge are often characteristic for working in a team.

### 5.19 Non-excludability and non-rivalry

a. What characteristics of goods are crucial for a well-functioning market?
b. To what does 'non-excludability' refer concerning property rights, and what does it mean?
c. What is the effect of non-excludability on (1) the choice of the market as a governance structure and (2) the level of transaction costs?
d. What is the cause of non-rivalry in production and consumption?
e. What is the relationship between non-rivalry, asset-specific investment, sunk costs and natural monopoly?

### Answer 5.19 Non-excludability and non-rivalry

a. The goods should be excludable and rivalrous.
b. Non-excludability refers to a lack of property rights. In the case of complete non-excludability, it is impossible to exclude people from the consumption of the good and nobody is prepared to pay for it.
c. The choice of the market as a governance structure involves high transaction costs, because of the difficulties of the allocation of transferable property rights. In the case of a high degree of non-excludability, the level of transaction costs are often prohibitive.
d. Non-rivalry in production is caused by the imperfect divisibility (or lumpiness) in the production sphere. Non-rivalry in consumption is caused by the imperfect divisibility (or lumpiness) in the consumption sphere.
e. Non-rivalry in production is caused by the imperfect divisibility (or lumpiness), caused by the fact that in order to provide a good, a certain scale is needed. A certain minimum size is necessary, otherwise offering the good is not efficient. For many provisions such as networks and infrastructure, we have to deal with indivisibility and investments that are asset-specific. Just as with natural monopolies, they are often characterised by a large part of fixed costs and a relatively small part of variable costs. These large fixed costs and indivisibility lead to non-rivalry in consumption and the marginal costs of use are often zero.

### 5.20 Public and private transaction costs

a. What are public and private transaction costs?
b. How can we measure transaction costs?

## Answer 5.20 Public and private transaction costs

a. Public transaction costs are the transaction costs for the government and private transaction costs for private persons, firms and organisations.

b. There are different ways of measuring transaction costs:
- One way is to estimate transaction costs by making use of demand and supply curves of goods and services. This is applied in Figure 5.5 of the book. The difficulties here are the availability of the data and the estimations of the curves.
- A second method is by using surveys or interviews. However, these methods involve high costs and are time-consuming. Respondents in a survey and interview are asked to estimate future costs or recall costs of the past, which could lead to less reliable results
- Finally, a possibility is to carry out simulation, in which researchers themselves go through all the steps of a transaction.

## 5.21 Transaction cost economics and transition costs

a. What is the empirical object of transaction cost economics and transition costs?

b. What is the difference between transaction and transition costs?

## Answer 5.21 Transaction cost economics and transition costs

a. The empirical object of transaction cost economics formed by governance structures in which transactions are carried out and administrated: markets, organisations and other institutional arrangements, such as contracts, clubs, etc. The empirical object of the transition costs is the institutional structure in a country.

b. Transaction costs should be distinguished from transition costs. Transition costs are the costs of creating, building up or changing a system or institutional structure. They are the costs of an institutional provision that will change the institutional environment. Extrapolating the transaction cost theory to provisions involving transition costs is not in line with the transaction cost theory as comparative static analysis, and it will therefore lack a sound theoretical basis.

## 5.22 Internet

Imagine a company that markets computer products over the Internet (for example, through a web search). In what ways does the company create value? Is it likely to capture much of this value? Explain.

## Answer 5.22 Internet

The answer to this question depends on the example you developed. Internet companies often create value by reducing transaction costs. In discussing the potential to capture value, you should focus on the effects of competition and whether or not these effects are likely to reduce the ability of the firm to capture profits.

## 5.23 Enlarging team size

A leading business school currently uses study teams in the MBA program. Each team has five members. Some of the work in the first year is assigned to study teams and graded on a group basis. Discuss the trade-offs involved with enlarging student study groups in the MBA program from five people to six people.

## Answer 5.23 Enlarging team size

Increasing the team size from five to six will increase the amount of knowledge on the team. Thus, the teams will have more skills to complete projects. However, it is harder to control free-rider problems in larger groups. It can be more difficult for six people to reach consensus and coordinate their actions than for five.

## 5.24 Transaction cost economics, asset specificity and connectedness of assets

Russia wants to build an oil pipeline from its main production site in central Russia to the east. It has to choose between a pipeline to the Chinese oil city of Daqing (in inland China) and its own Siberian port city of Nachodka. Daqing is now only an oil exploitation area, but oil reserves here are becoming exhausted. China may build a refinery plant here. From Nachodka the oil can be transported by ship to Japan, but this option is twice as expensive as the pipeline to China. China prefers the Daqing option; Japan prefers the Siberian option.
a.   What are the advantages and disadvantages of both options from a transaction cost economics perspective?
b.   How can China and Japan persuade Russia to choose their favoured option? In other words, how can they resolve the disadvantages of that option?

## Answer 5.24 Transaction cost economics, asset specificity and connectedness of assets

a.   The disadvantage of the pipeline is that it is not only an asset-specific investment (only suitable for oil), but the oil pipeline to China is also specific to one customer. An oil pipeline to China also creates a high level of connectedness with the refinery plant in Daqing. It makes Russia dependent on one customer. This will weaken the bargaining power of Russia. The advantage of the pipeline to the Siberian port city of Nachodka is that it is not specific to one customer. From a port with oil-loading facilities, oil can also be transported to other customers. This pipeline becomes a less specific asset compared to the oil pipeline to China.
b.   One option would be that China takes part in the investment of the pipeline. The investment of the pipeline can be a result of a joint venture of China and Russia. Another option would be that the refinery plant to be built in Daqing has a much larger capacity then needed for its own oil production. In this view the refinery plant can be considered as a dedicated asset for the transaction with Russia.
    Japan can invest in the pipeline to Nachodka or in the port facilities in this city. This can be done, for example, in the form of a joint venture. One the one hand this reduces the costs for Russia and on the other hand it ties Japan to this oil transaction. It creates a kind of lock-in effect, guaranteeing that Japan continues to be a client for the Russian oil. Of course, it is possible that Japan considers it all as sunk costs and ends the relationship.

## 5.25 Transaction cost economics and prepacking

More and more vegetables sold in the supermarket are prepacked. The companies that sort, clean and pack the vegetables are all owned by the vegetable growers themselves (either individually or jointly with other growers).
Can you explain, using transaction cost economics, why no independent vegetable packing companies exist?

**Answer 5.25 Transaction cost economics and prepacking**

Chapter 5.4. of the book provides a list of decisive attributes for the choice of governance structures. For the question why no independent vegetable packing companies exist we have to look at the following transaction attributes:

1. level of asset specificity;
2. degree of uncertainty;
3. level of frequency and duration;
4. difficulty of measuring performance of the transaction.

No independent vegetable packing companies means that prepacking of vegetable takes place in-house. In the first place, for prepacking of vegetables specific machines are necessary. These are mostly machines with a narrowly defined use (i.e. physical asset specificity). The machine can also be made at the request of a particular transaction partner (i.e. dedicated asset specificity). A high level of asset specificity is, according to transaction cost economics, a reason for in-house production (i.e. a form of vertical integration).

In the second place, the degree of uncertainty concerning the right supply (in terms of quality and quantity) can be a reason for in-house production. The third attribute refers to frequency. For an independent vegetable packing company, a continuous supply is necessary. Taking care of that can involve high transaction costs.

The fourth attribute refers to difficulty of measuring performance of the transaction. Measuring performance is an important factor for the choice between in-house provision and contracting out of prepacking of vegetables. The option of contracts requires (1) that a firm knows exactly what it wants to contract out; and (2) that the quality of the vegetables are contractable. In the case that a firm does not know exactly (or cannot specify exactly) what it desires, the contract will be very incomplete and the costs associated with renegotiations will be considerable, so that the transaction costs become very high. If you are not able to measure the performance, it is possible that the contract taker has a strong tendency to reduce the costs, and this is accompanied by a reduction in (non-contractible) quality. The adverse effect of cost reduction on quality could be significant. In this situation, in-house production is likely to be a better solution.

# 6. Principal-agent theory

## 6.1 Agency theory

a. What two streams within the agency theory can be distinguished?
b. What is the basic unit of the positive agency theory (PAT)?
c. How is the firm viewed within the PAT?
d. What are important research questions within the PAT?
e. Of what type of costs do agency costs consist?
f. What two parties are involved in an agency relationship?

### Answer 6.1 Agent theory

a. Within the agency theory, two streams of literature can be distinguished: the positive agency theory (PAT) and the principal-agent (P/A) theory.
b. In the PAT, the basic unit is the agency relationship. This can concern asymmetric relationships (shareholders with managers, for example). However, in the most complex version, the analysis is related to the whole nexus of contracts and to the organisational structure. The representation of this agency relationship is contingent on the organisational phenomenon studied, which can be, depending on the case, the board of directors, the entire quality management or the financial structure (regarded as a particular organisational mechanism). For example, for the board of directors, the unit of analysis may be the agency relationship between shareholders and managers, but this can be expanded to a nexus of relationships between shareholders, managers, employees, financial creditors and other stakeholders: the board of directors is therefore assessed on its capacity to minimise the agency costs on the whole nexus of relationships (contracts).
c. Within the PAT, the firm is viewed as a nexus of contracts. The firm is an entity that consists of *various parties with different interests.*
d. Important research questions are: how do contracts affect the behaviour of participants, and why do we observe certain organisational forms in the real world? In general it is assumed in the PAT that existing organisational forms are efficient. If they were not, they would not continue to exist. The theory is not (yet) expressed in the forms of mathematical models.
e. The agency costs consist of monitoring costs, bonding costs and residual losses (bonding costs are the costs that are associated with the mechanisms allowing the agent to reassure the principal on the credibility of his commitments, for example, the costs associated with a voluntary audit).
f. Principal and agent.

## 6.2 Principal-agent (P/A) theory

a. What is the standard representation of the principal-agent theory?
b. What sort of problems can be analysed with the principal-agent theory?
c. What does the P/A model assume about the information available and the objectives?
d. What is the essence of the P/A problem?

### Answer 6.2 Principal-agent (P/A) theory

a. The most simple principal-agent relationship consists of two people. One person (the principal) hires the other (the agent) to perform a certain task. The relationship is often governed by a contract, which is chosen and designed by the principal. Subsequently, it is the agent who decides whether or not he will accept the contract. Finally, the agent chooses a level of effort or an investment decision. Effort refers to many things, like the number of hours worked, the intensity of activities, etc.

b.  The principal-agent theory offers a framework for a coherent analysis of situations involving: (1) conflict of interests between principal and agent (for example, between a landlord and tenant about the lease price; politician and civil servants; employer and worker); (2) asymmetric information and uncertainty; (3) making an agreement or setting up a contract; (4) issues such as how contracts influence the behaviour of the participants. An interesting basis for the principal-agent problem arises when the principal is willing to pay more for the execution of a task than it will cost the agent, i.e. a surplus can be generated. The question is: who will get/capture this surplus?

c.  The P/A model assumes that the principal has less access to information than the agent. The P/A model also assumes that principal and agent have different objectives.

d.  The essence of the principal-agent problem is the development by the principal of a payment incentive that motivates the agent to carry out those activities that are in the best interests of the principal.

### 6.3 Examples of incentive conflicts
Give examples of incentive conflicts for the relationship between:
a.  shareholders and managers;
b.  co-workers in teams.

### Answer 6.3 Examples of incentive conflicts
a.  Managers might want to invest in prestigious projects, rather than projects that increase shareholder value. They might also prefer to spend company resources for personal consumption rather than on productive investment projects. Many other examples are possible.
b.  One prominent example is the classic free-rider problem. Individually, team members can have incentives to shirk and hope that everyone else in the team works hard.

### 6.4 Potential problems in agency relationships
What potential problems exist in agency relationships?

### Answer 6.4 Potential problems in agency relationships
An agent agrees to act in the interests of the principal. However, the agent may subsequently act in his own self-interest at the expense of the principal. For example, a real estate agent has a legal obligation to represent the seller of a house. Nevertheless, the agent might provide confidential information to a prospective buyer (for example, the lowest price which the seller is willing to take) to speed up the sale of the house and the receipt of the agent's commissions.

### 6.5 Monitoring as a solution for eliminating incentive problems
Is it worthwhile for shareholders to seek to eliminate incentive problems with managers and directors completely through means such as monitoring? Why or why not?

**Answer 6.5 Monitoring as a solution for eliminating incentive problems**
Generally speaking this is not worthwhile. It is optimal to incur out-of-pocket expenses to reduce agency problems only up to the point where the marginal reduction in the residual loss is equal to the marginal increase in out-of-pocket expenses. A firm might want to stop employees from taking company pencils home for personal use. However, the costs of completely eliminating this behaviour are likely to be too high to justify.

**6.6 Capital investment and agency problems**
You are the owner and CEO of a large divisionalised firm, with operations in a number of diverse industries. A number of division managers report to you. Division managers have considerable decision-making responsibilities with respect to the day-to-day operations of their divisions, but you must approve of any capital investments above $ 100,000 before they are made.
a.  As owner, what type of capital investments would you like your division managers to be proposing to you?
b.  Is there a potential agency problem between you, as owner, and your division managers with respect to capital investments? What is the nature of that problem? Why is it a problem?
c.  How might you attempt to solve that agency problem?
d.  Do you think you can solve the problem entirely? Why or why not?

**Answer 6.6 Capital investment and agency problems**
a.  All positive net present value (NPV) projects, no negative NPV projects. In other words, you only want investments that will yield a net positive result in the future.
b.  Division managers may propose negative NPV projects because these increase their (the division managers') utilities even though they do not increase the owner's utility. Also, division managers may not propose some positive NPV projects because they derive no benefit from them.
c.  It is a problem because managers want to maximise their own utilities, not the owners' utility. You could think of the following solutions:
    •   link pay to investment performance;
    •   pay via stock-based compensation (but a free-rider problem may arise if you do so);
    •   pay a deferred compensation based on long-term performance;
    •   acquire knowledge so you can better evaluate the projects that managers propose and identify when they are not proposing the projects that they should be propose.
d.  Probably not. Anything you do to reduce the likelihood that a manager proposes a negative NPV project increases the likelihood that he or she will not propose all positive NPV projects, and *vice versa*.

**6.7 First-best and second-best solutions**
a.  Under which condition is a first-best solution possible?
b.  What is a forcing contract?
c.  What can be solved with a forcing contract and under what conditions?
d.  What is mostly the reality: first-best or second-best solutions?

**Answer 6.7 First-best and second-best solutions**
a.  A first-best solution is possible under perfect information.

b.  In a forcing contract, the effort of the agent is equal to the optimal effort level of the agent, seen from the perspective of the principal.
c.  A forcing contract solves the moral hazard or hidden actions problem. The conditions are observation possibilities and no problems caused by adverse selection or hidden information.
d.  We do not live in a perfect world. First-best solutions are hardly ever possible. Mostly we have to deal with a lack of information. This means that only second-best solutions are possible.

### 6.8 Position of principal in a situation with adequate information available
a.  What type of utility function of the principal is used as a base?
b.  What does compensation of the agent by the principal depend upon?
c.  If the principal is able to observe $a$ (or $\theta$) and knows the relationship $x(a,\theta)$, he can also observe $\theta$ (or $a$). To what extent does the principal need to know the variable $z$ and what does this mean for the payment schedule?
d.  In a situation such as the above, are we dealing with moral hazard?

### Answer 6.8 Position of principal in a situation with adequate information available
a.  The P/A theory assumes that the principal has a utility function of the form $u(x-y)$, in which the risk aspects, just as the expected outcomes, influence the valuation. Here $x$ = outcome or result for the principal and $y$ = compensation for the agent (by the principal).
b.  The compensation by the principal for the agent is a function of:
    $y = y(x,\theta,a,z)$
    where:  $y$ = compensation for the agent;
            $x$ = outcome or result for the principal;
            $\theta$ = environmental factors;
            $a$ = the activity carried out by the agent;
            $z$ = incomplete information about $a$ or q which is available without charge.
c.  The principal does not need the variable $z$. Further (imperfect) information is unnecessary. The compensation schedule will then only have to depend on $\theta$. The principal chooses a compensation schedule and a value for $a$, such that it will lead to maximisation of his utility; this is limited in such a way that the agent will receive a reward at least as high as his next best alternative.
d.  In such a situation there is no moral hazard.

### 6.9 Crucial elements in a principal-agent relationship
a.  What are crucial elements in principal-agent relationship?
b.  What will be the effect of hidden information?
c.  What are the possibilities for the principal to solve the hidden information problem in a P/A relationship?
d.  How can we control the effect of hidden actions?
e.  What is important to know if the principal wishes to apply an incentive pay?
f.  How can an optimal contract be realised?

### Answer 6.9 Crucial elements in a principal-agent relationship

a. Crucial elements are (1) limiting hidden information or adverse selection; (2) limiting hidden actions or moral hazard (including time inconsistency); (3) realising an optimal contract by making use of self-selection conditions and truth-telling as dominant strategy.

b. The possibility of hidden information can lead to adverse selection.

c. The principal has to develop a mechanism for revealing the private information (= hidden information) of the agent. This private information can refer to characteristics of the agent such as efficiency (inefficient or efficient agents are possible), productivity, capability, diligence or laziness, etc. The mechanism should stimulate the agent to let the principal know something about his characteristics. Such a mechanism is called a revelation mechanism.

We can also make use of self-selection conditions. These conditions are a particular form of the compatibility conditions incentive. They are composed of both the participation conditions and those incentive conditions that lead to contracts, so that the agents choose the contracts which are meant for them. We have a direct revelation mechanism if the participation and incentive conditions are formulated in such a way that *truth-telling* or *being honest* is the optimal strategy for the agents. A direct revelation mechanism means that the agents voluntarily choose to be honest.

d. To control the problem of hidden actions, the principal can offer the agent a performance incentive (for example, the principal can offer the agents a contract where their reward depends directly on the amount of effort they exert. This requires performances that can be measured and monitored, but how feasible is this, and how enforceable are such contracts?).

e. We have to know something about the risk attitude of the agent. If the agent is risk averse, the principal has to give a higher compensation compared to a risk neutral agent.

f. An optimal contract for the principal means:
   - No hidden information or adverse selection.
     - making use of self-selection conditions; agents should reveal their real characteristics;
     - if necessary, making use of a participation bonus to simulate all potential agents to participate in the bidding process.
   - No hidden actions or moral hazard.
     - making use of performance incentive conditions; this means agents do their job well and have no reason for shirking.
   - Lowest possible expected costs for the principal and a good performance by the agent.

### 6.10 Optimal strategy

a. How can an optimal strategy be achieved?

b. What is this principle called?

c. What does a self-selection condition imply?

d. How can a Nash equilibrium be formalised?

e. How can we ensure that as many contractors as possible are willing to participate?

### Answer 6.10 Optimal strategy

a. To achieve an optimal strategy, we need to build in a mechanism which ensures that the participation conditions are met, and an incentive so that truth-telling about the reservation price is the optimal strategy for participants.

b. This mechanism is known as the revelation principle.

c.  Self-selection conditions imply the truth-telling strategy.
d.  In Section 6.5 we formalise a Nash equilibrium as a linear programming problem. The truth-telling or the self-selection condition can be written as a constraint function and the minimisation of the expected costs (of the principal, e.g. the government) as an objective function.
e.  By giving a participation bonus we can ensure that as many contractors as possible are going to participate in the bidding process.

## 6.11 Optimal bidding process

Imagine that a new education building has to be designed and constructed. Ten constructing companies have shown interest in the order. It will be given to the lowest bidder.

a.  How can you make sure that all the potential companies participate in the bidding process and make a well-defined tender?
b.  One of the current major problems in the contracting out process of big building and infrastructural projects is that construction companies collude. Give some reasons based on transaction cost economics as to why constructing companies try to collude.
c.  What can we do about this?
d.  From the point of view of informational economics, who should make the technical drawings? The construction company or the customer? Why?

## Answer 6.11 Optimal bidding process

a.  To ensure that all the potential construction companies participate in the bidding process and make a well-defined tender, we can give them a participation bonus. This bonus is meant as a compensation for the costs of making the tender and as an incentive to reveal their real costs for constructing the new education building[1].
b.  Making a good tender is costly. The investment has often a high level of asset specificity. If they fail, it will be all sunk costs. The uncertainty is often high. They have to make an estimation as to whether they will be awarded the project. The frequency of making tenders can be irregular. In that case, setting up a special division for making tenders becomes difficult. Another reason can be the connectedness of transactions as a result of the people involved. Designing buildings requires specialist skills and knowledge which are often tied to certain persons. The transferability of such human capital is problematic if those skills are specific to an organisation or asset. Co-specialised skills and knowledge are often characteristic for working in a team. This requires a certain scale and regularity in transactions.
c.  A well-defined participation bonus can reduce the collusion problem. In this case it is necessary that the bonus contains an incentive to reveal their real costs of construction companies for the construction of new buildings.
d.  We can distinguish different views. One is based on the reputation building or reputational capital. The technical drawings should be made by the construction company. If things go wrong, the company will loss its reputation and that can be very costly. On the other hand we also assume opportunistic behaviour. Then, it is better that the customer makes the technical drawings. In that case, monitoring is necessary and may be complemented with high sanctions.

---

[1] The principle is worked out in the textbook on page 231.

## 6.12 Position of the principal in a situation of incomplete information

a. Under what conditions does a real moral hazard problem arise?
b. What does this imply for the principal?
c. What solution does the principal have at hand to correct this?
d. What are the consequences for the principal of adding the incentive condition?
e. What does this mean for achieving the optimal risk-sharing solution?

## Answer 6.12 Position of the principal in a situation of incomplete information

a. There is a real moral hazard problem if the principal can observe neither $a$ (i.e. the activity carried out by the agent) nor $\theta$ (the environmental factors).
b. For the principal, this means that he must recognise that given the payment schedule, the agent will choose the nature and level of the effort of the activity to maximise his own utility. In general, this means that the value of the activity of the agent differs from the value that would make the payment schedule optimal.
c. The principal can try to correct this by adding an extra condition in the form of an 'incentive condition'.
d. The principal must then take into account that his choice for the compensation schedule, the nature and level of the effort of the activity to be carried out by the agent through the agent's maximising procedure, will determine the agent's behaviour. This can lead to strategic behaviour.
e. The result will be that one will move away from the point of the optimal risk-sharing solution. There will be a trade-off between the benefits of risk sharing and the need to control how the agent carries out the activities.

## 6.13 Compensation schedule

a. What is the central problem of the P/A theory?
b. What is important for the sharing of risks?
c. What does optimal risk sharing mean in the case of a risk neutral principal and a strongly risk averse agent?
d. What, in this case, is the problem for the principal?
e. What limitations must the principal take into account?

## Answer 6.13 Compensation schedule

a. The central problem of the P/A theory is finding a compensation schedule resulting in an optimal trade-off between the benefits of risk sharing and the costs of giving an incentive to the agent.
b. A very important element for sharing risk is the risk attitude. The more risk averse the agent is, the higher the compensation he will ask for bearing the risk. This means that the costs of providing an incentive to a risk averse agent can become very high. It is usually most efficient to allocate the risk to the least risk averse party. In that case, the compensation for bearing the risk will be lower and, with that, the social costs will also be lower.
c. Optimal risk sharing, in the case of a risk neutral principal and a strongly risk averse agent, means that the agent will receive a fixed payment. The principal will bear all the risks. However, this outcome is determined by the risk-attitude level of the agent. For an explanation see Table 6.1 of the textbook.

d. The problem for the principal is to develop a compensation schedule in such a way that, from the principal's point of view, the agent performs the best actions.
e. The principal must take the following into account:
- The agent can have a better alternative to revert to; this limitation is known as the participation condition.
- The principal is not able to influence the agent directly. Given the compensation schedule of the principal, the agent chooses the best action for himself. The principal can only influence the action of the agent by the choice of his compensation schedule. This limitation is known as the incentive compatibility or incentive payment schedule.

## 6.14 Costs to the principal
a. What types of costs arise for a principal if he makes use of an agent?
b. When do high consequence costs arise?
c. What are the total costs for the principal?

## Answer 6.14 Costs to the principal
a. The costs to the principal can include participation, stimulation, inspection and consequence costs.
- Participation costs are those that the principal has to bear to persuade the agent to participate. These costs form the agent's reservation price.
- Stimulation costs are the costs that the principal has to bear to formulate regulations and compensation in order to influence or restrict the degrees of freedom. Participation costs can also be part of this.
- Inspection costs are the costs that the principal has to bear to monitor whether the agreed conditions are being complied with.
- Consequence costs are the benefits that accrue to the agent and that the principal will to try to avoid by formulating certain conditions.
b. If the output does not meet certain criteria, then this may lead to high consequence costs for the principal.
c. The total costs can also be specified as the compensation for the activities of the agent (e.g. the contractor) and transaction costs are the cost for carrying out the transaction.

## 6.15 Principal-agent and risk attitude
a. What are important issues in the Principal-Agent approach concerning risk?

Suppose a principal would wishes to conclude a contract with two agents for carrying out activities. The estimated time for carrying out these activities is about one year. One agent is risk neutral (named A) and the other is risk averse (named B). The expected utility function for the risk neutral agent (A) is given in Equation (1):

$$U(y,a) = y - a \qquad (1)$$

and, the expected utility function for the risk averse agent (B) is given in Equation (2):

$$U(y,a) = \sqrt{(y - a)} \qquad (2)$$

where: *U* = expected utility;
  *y* = expected income for the agent;
  *a* = own costs for the agent.

The principal states that agents can earn € 250,000 if they conclude the contract. This means *y* = € 250,000. For both agents the efforts (or costs) that they have to make are € 50,000 (thus *a* = € 50,000).

b. Calculate what both agents will do, participate or not, and explain your answer.
c. What should be the **minimum** value of y to make sure that the risk averse agent B participates? What does it show for the level of risk averseness?
d. Explain the trade-off between risk bearing and the cost of providing an incentive in the case of the risk averse agent.
e. Why is it efficient to allocate the risk to the least risk averse party?
f. In the case of a risk averse agent, would a fixed salary of 60,000 Euros per year be a good alternative? Who bears all the risk in this case?
g. Suppose the exponent of the risk averse agent is not $y^{0.5}$ in Equation (2) but $y^{0.9}$. Would this agent participate or not?

### Answer 6.15 Principal-agent and risk attitude

a. Important issues in the principal-agent approach concerning risk are:
   - the risk attitude of the agents;
   - the level of risk aversion of the agents;
   - the trade-off between the cost of risk bearing and the costs of giving an incentive;
   - the developing of a payment schedule.
b  **Agent A (risk neutral):**
   250,000 - 50,000 = 200,000 → he is willing to participate.
   **Agent B (risk averse):**
   $\sqrt{250,000}$ - 50,000 = - 49,500 → he will not participate.
c. The value of y should at least $50,000^2$ Euros. This extremely large amount of money shows that the agent is very strong risk averse. In that case it would be better to look for another solution, for example, such as fixed compensation.
d. The more risk averse an agent is, the higher the costs for compensating the agent for the bearing of risk. This also means that the costs of providing an incentive to the risk averse agent are higher.
e. In that case, the compensation for bearing risk will be lower. Or more in general, the social costs for carrying out (risky) activities will be lower.
f. A fixed salary per year will be a good alternative for both parties. In that case, the principal bears all the risk, but the agent will be less motivated to carry out his task properly.
g. This means the expected utility function will be:
   $U(y,a) = y^{0.9}$ or $U(y,a) = 250,000^{0.9}$ - 50,000 = 72,135 - 50,000 = 22,135
   Given this expected utility function, he will participate. This relatively small change in the value of the exponent (from 0.5 to 0.9) indicates the importance of the risk attitude level.

## 6.16 Franchising contract in a principal-agent setting

A franchisor (principal) rents a retail formula to a franchisee (agent). The agent expects that he has an 80% chance of realising a net return of € 200,000, and a 20% chance of a net return of € 50,000.

a.  What is the expected value (EV) of this net return?
b.  Would it make a difference for the expected utility (EU) of this net return if the agent is risk neutral or risk averse?
c.  For the risk neutral agent, the expected utility of the net return is equal to the expected value. However, the risk averse agent values the net return (= Y) because of his expected utility of this return as $(Y)^{0.8}$. Please calculate the expected utility of the net return for the risk averse agent.
d.  The franchisee pays a fixed amount of 20,000 Euros yearly as rent to the franchisor. Who bears all the risk in this case?
e.  The agent = franchisee would like to build a specialised store. You have to give him advice. What can happen and what are possible solutions?

## Answer 6.16 Franchising contract in a principal-agent setting

a.  $EV = 0.8 \times 200,000 + 0.2 \times 50,000 = 170,000$
b.  Yes, a risk averse agent will value the net return lower than a risk neutral agent.
c.  $EU = 0.8 \times 200,000^{0.8} + 0.2 \times 50,000^{0.8} = 15,077.51$
d.  The franchisee (= agent) bears all the risk.
e.  Building a specialised store means an asset-specific investment. This involves ex-ante a hold-up effect, and ex-post a lock-in effect. The solutions are a long-term contract and sharing the costs of the investment across both parties.

## 6.17 The government as principal and farmers as agents for nature preservation

a.  What problems could arise with the development of an incentive schedule by the government as a principal, who focuses, for example, on preserving nature and landscape by farmers as agents?
b.  What kinds of imperfect information are we dealing with?
c.  What is the central problem of moral hazard and is there a way out?
d.  The same situation as above, but this time in a situation of adverse selection.

## Answer 6.17 The government as principal and farmers as agents

a.  The incentive schedule can lead to the following problems:
   -  The relation between input and output is not always known.
   -  The incentive schedule can be inadequately tuned to the relationship between input and output, through lack of (good) information.
   -  Environmental factors are probably not fully determined.
   -  The behaviour of the farmers – and therefore their activities – cannot be observed perfectly.
b.  There could be:
   -  Adverse selection or hidden information: The government cannot observe the objective function of the agent. The government does not know with what type of farmer it is dealing. This type of incentive problem is identified as adverse selection or hidden information.

- Moral hazard or hidden actions: The government cannot observe the activities of the farmers perfectly. This would provoke unintentional behaviour or hidden actions.

c.  When the principal is unable to observe the agent properly, the incentive condition is of major importance. The incentive condition must give incentives such that the agent will be prepared to carry out the wishes of the principal. The question is whether such an incentive can be developed and whether it can be properly applied.

d.  If the principal does not know what type of agent he is dealing with, the participation constraint is of major importance. The participation constraint must be such that the principal contracts the agents who can carry out the task in the most efficient way.

**6.18 Principal and agent; both are risk neutral**
Assume a farmer has realised, as the next best alternative to nature preservation, a net added value of € 1,500 per ha through regular agricultural activities. The government wants to stimulate the farmers to produce in an environmentally-friendly way. It therefore imposes a levy of € 250 per ha on farmers who do not produce in such a way. Concluding a management agreement, farmers can receive compensation for nature preservation at two levels: (1) a minor effort towards nature preservation is rewarded by compensation of € 500 per ha and (2) a considerable effort towards nature preservation is rewarded by a compensation of € 1,250. However, with a nature management agreement, the net added value of regular agriculture production will go down from 1,500 to 1000 Euros per ha.

The following assumptions should be considered:
1.  Both the government and the farmers are risk neutral.
2.  The expected utility function is given in formula (6.2) in Section 6.2 of the book.
3.  We suppose for the sake of simplicity that the net added value of regular agricultural production is expressed in expected utility.
4.  The reward for nature production can be made dependent on the level of nature production, in this case the intensity of the management package.
5.  The following distribution of probability exists:
    - If the farmer works hard (with a cost or monetary value of effort equal to $a = € 250$) at nature production this will result in a probability of:
        - 0.6 in nature production worth € 1,250;
        - 0.3 in nature production worth € 500;
        - 0.1 in no nature production.
    - If the farmer does not exert himself much ($a = 0$) this will result in a probability of:
        - 0.1 in nature production worth € 1,250;
        - 0.3 in nature production worth € 500;
        - 0.6 in no nature production.
6.  The government is able to observe the level of nature production.

Assume the government wants to offer a contract based on the assumptions mentioned above. What actions will the farmers choose?

**Answer 6.18 Principal and agent; both are risk neutral**
The farmer can choose from the following alternatives:

1. Reject the contract and continue with the next best alternative of € 1,500 per ha and pay a charge of € 250, which yields € 1,250 net.
2. Accept the contract and respond with a low effort level ($a = 0$). This will lead to a net expected utility of $(y\text{-}a)$, which is:
   $0.1(1,250) + 0.3(500) + 0.6(0) = 275$ Euros.
   Together with the net added value of the marketable products, this will yield: $1000 + 275 = 1,275$ Euros.
3. Accept the contract and respond with a high level of effort ($a = 250$). This will lead to an expected utility of $(y\text{-}a)$, which is:
   $0.6(1,250) + 0.3(500) + 0.1(0) - 250 = 650$ Euros.
   Together with the net added value of the marketable products, this will yield: $1000 + 650 = 1,650$ Euros.

In this case the farmer, given the three options, will choose option (3). The government will also consider this a good result. The farmer will strive for nature production for his own interest.

### 6.19 Principal and agent; principal is risk neutral and agent is risk averse

Assume a farmer has, as the next best alternative to nature production, a net added value of € 1,500 per ha. The government wants to stimulate the farmers to produce in an environmentally-friendly way. Concluding a management agreement, farmers can receive compensation for nature production at two levels: (1) a minor effort towards nature production is rewarded by compensation of € 750 per ha and (2) a considerable effort towards nature production is rewarded by a compensation of € 1,250. However, with a management agreement, the net added value of regular agriculture production will go down from 1,500 to 750 Euros per ha.

The following assumptions should be considered:
1. The government is risk neutral and the farmers are risk averse.
2. The expected utility function is given in formula (6.3) in Section 6.2 of the book.
3. We suppose for the sake of simplicity that the net added value of regular agricultural production is expressed in the expected utility.
4. The reward for nature production can be made dependent on the level of nature production, in this case the intensity of the management package.
5. The following distribution of probability exists:
   - If the farmer works hard (with a cost or monetary value of effort equal to $a = €$ 250) at nature production this will result in a probability of:
     - 0.6 in nature production worth € 1,250;
     - 0.3 in nature production worth € 750;
     - 0.1 in no nature production.
   - If the farmer does not exert himself much ($a = 0$), this will result in a probability of:
     - 0.1 in nature production worth € 1,250;
     - 0.3 in nature production worth € 750;
     - 0.6 in no nature production.
6. The government is able to observe the extent of nature production.

a. Assume the government wants to offer a contract based on the assumptions mentioned above. What actions will the farmers choose?

b.  What can be observed when this is compared to question 6.12?

### Answer 6.19 Principal and agent; principal is risk neutral and agent is risk averse

a.  The farmer can choose from the following alternatives:
    1.  Reject the contract and continue with the next best alternative of € 1,500 per ha.
    2.  Accept the contract and respond with a low effort level (a = 0). This will lead to a net expected utility of $U(y,a) = \sqrt{y}$-a, which is:
    $0.1\sqrt{(1,250)} + 0.3\sqrt{(750)} + 0.6\sqrt{(0)} = 11.75$ Euros
    Together with the net added value of the marketable products, this will yield: 750 + 11.75 = € 761.75
    3.  Accept the contract and respond with a high level of effort (*a* = 250). This will lead to an expected utility of $U(y,a) = \sqrt{y}$-a, which is:
    $0.6\sqrt{(1,250)} + 0.3\sqrt{(750)} + 0.1\sqrt{(0)}$ - 250= -220.57 Euros
    Together with the net added value of the marketable products, this will yield: 750 - 220.57 = € 529.43
    In this case the farmer, given the three options, will choose for option (1). There will be no management agreements.

b.  In the case of a risk neutral agent (farmer), it was possible to reach an agreement where the interests of the principal and the agent were parallel. The agent received the highest expected utility. This coincided with the interests of the principal. To convince a risk averse farmer to sign a contract, given the probabilities, a much higher compensation is needed (this result is strongly determined by the chosen (square root) utility function, which gives enormous values for the Arrow-Pratt measures. However, this is beyond the scope of the course).

### 6.20 Optimal risk sharing

a.  What does optimal risk sharing mean if the government (principal) wants to see more nature and landscape values 'produced' by famers, when the government is risk averse and the farmers (agents) are risk neutral?
b.  The same as above, but then for a risk neutral government and risk averse farmers.
c.  The same as above, but then for a risk neutral government and a risk neutral farmer.

### Answer 6.20 Optimal risk sharing

a.  In that case, the government will impose a fixed levy on all agricultural land used by farmers. The levy will be reduced in the case of demonstrable nature and landscape values 'produced' by farmers.
b.  In that case, the government will reward the farmers in the form of a fixed amount for the 'production' of nature and the landscape values.
c.  In that case, the government will give the farmers a reward that corresponds directly to the level of effort the farmer exerts to 'produce' nature and landscape values.

### 6.21 Stimulating 'production' of nature and landscape values by risk averse farmers

a.  How can risk averse farmers be stimulated to 'produce' more nature and landscape values?
b.  How can this be accomplished as efficiently as possible?
c.  What, intuitively, is the optimum?

*Chapter 6.*

### Answer 6.21 Stimulating 'production' of nature and landscape values by risk averse farmers

a. Risk-averse farmers can be stimulated to produce more nature and landscape values by, first of all, placing all the risk with the government.

b. This can be accomplished as efficiently as possible by minimising the expected compensation reward under the following conditions:
   - The farmer signs the contract; i.e. he will participate (participation condition).
   - The farmer chooses to make a greater effort (incentive condition).

c. Intuitively, the optimum is as follows. The government does not want to pay the agent more than is absolutely necessary to get him to engage in nature production. The government also does not want to burden the agent with a greater risk than is necessary to get his full effort, because it is an expensive proposition for the principal to saddle the agent with risks. In that case, the government would have to work with much higher compensations. This is why the government will choose to pay a fixed compensation.

### 6.22 Allocation of risks to risk averse farmers

a. What possibilities are there for persuading risk averse farmers to sign management agreements?

b. Which possibility has the government's preference? Explain.

c. How will the best possible contract appear to the principal?

### Answer 6.22 Allocation of risks to risk averse farmers

a. There are two possibilities for persuading risk averse farmers to sign management agreements, namely (1) paying a fixed compensation or (2) paying a high compensation depending on the effort. In case (2) the level of compensation depends on the risk-attitude level of the farmer.

b. Assuming the expected utility function $u (y,a) = \sqrt{y}-a$ it will be extremely costly for the government to allocate the risks to the strongly risk averse farmers. In that case, they will ask a ridiculously high expected compensation. To the government it is less expensive to pay a fixed compensation.

c. The best possible contract to the principal must satisfy the following conditions:
   - Minimising the payments by the principal (goal function).
   - The preconditions are that the agent (farmer) will accept the contract (participation condition) and will exert a high level of effort (effort condition).

### 6.23 Risk-aversion and utility function

a. What does risk-aversion imply for the shape of the mathematical function?

b. What mathematic conditions will a risk averse utility function need to meet?

### Answer 6.23 Risk-aversion and utility function

a. Risk-aversion implies that there will be a concave utility function.

b. A risk averse utility function meets the following conditions:
   The first derivative is greater than zero (first order condition) $\frac{\delta U}{\delta y} > 0$.
   The second derivative is less than or equal to zero (second order condition) $\frac{\delta^2 U}{\delta^2 y} \leq 0$.
   If the utility function meets these conditions then we have a concave utility function.

### 6.24 Risks of management agreements
a. What can the risks of management agreements be related to?
b. In a situation of nature and landscape preservation where the reward is dependent on results, can we speak of greater uncertainty? What factors contribute to this?

### Answer 6.24 Risks of management agreements
a. The risks of management agreements can be related to:
- The amount of management compensation. The norms on which this amount is based can change.
- The level of land price. The landowners or land users may fear that the value of land subject to a management agreement will fall.
- Time inconsistency of the government, i.e. policy change. At the moment the government is striving for heavy nature management packages. They feel that land brought under light limitations concerning nature preservation is less important. This will change the rules of game.
b. In such a situation the uncertainty is greater. The compensation is based on the results. However, farmers cannot control all factors, such as environmental factors.

### 6.25 The principal-agent approach and the bureaucracy
a. Who are the principals and who are the agents in this application?
b. In a bureaucratic situation, how does the principal-agent problem arise?
c. What are the objectives of the civil servants in Niskanen's hypothesis and what does this imply?
d. Which sources of uncertainty arise when carrying out a task or an activity?

### Answer 6.25 The principal-agent approach and the bureaucracy
a. Ministers and other politicians – and in the last resort the voter – are the principals. The agents are the civil servants who carry out the work.
b. The principal-agent problem arises because:
- Civil servants carrying out the work (the agents) can strive for objectives that differ from those of the politicians (the principals).
- Principals receive incomplete information about the methods and objectives of the civil servants (asymmetric information) and do not have enough instruments to collect this information.
c. In most cases, civil servants aim for budget maximisation. This is usually not in accordance with the objectives of politicians, and it will break down the effectiveness and efficiency of the policy.
d. There are various sources of uncertainty:
- The tangible execution of a task depends on the circumstances. A distinction can be made between environmental factors ($\theta$) and remaining factors ($z$) of formula 6.1 in Section 6.2 of the book.
- The objectives of the agents in practice.
- The effort exerted by the agent.

### 6.26 The principal-agent approach and policy
a. What is x-inefficiency?
b. When does x-inefficiency arise and what does it cause?
c. Why do agents in the principal-agent model dislike providing all the information to their principals?
d. What are the types of indicators usually used in the public sector to determine the productivity of the agents and where will this lead?
e. How is this expressed in environmental policy?

### Answer 6.26 The principal-agent approach and policy
a. X-inefficiency means that actual costs are higher than minimal necessary costs in a household.
b. X-inefficiency arises when agents make no, or very little, effort to work effectively and efficiently. In that case the actual costs are higher than the minimum one. It is caused by lack of information and the behaviour of agents in a bureaucracy.
c. Asymmetric information is to the advantage of the agent. In the public sector, the phenomenon of information asymmetry between principal and agent is stronger than in the market sector. In the public sector, the exact relationship between input and output is often unknown, and so is the relationship between the agent and output.
d. Usually, the principals will manage the agents by using indicators that are more focused on input than on actual output. This will lead to budget maximisation and inefficiencies.
e. Environmental policy is based on conserving species diversity, i.e. biodiversity, which can be seen as the final objective. Since it is difficult to make such an objective operational, the government has translated its policy into input measures. A good example is the Ecological Main Structure. It is based on input maximisation. The government wants to convert agricultural land into conservation areas. The budget of the government is often the only limitation. However, this does not guarantee more biodiversity.

### 6.27 Government intervention and credit crunch crisis
One of the constructions to 'rescue' banks during the credit crunch crisis, was the acquisition of so-called toxic assets. The Dutch government did so for ING. The bank had a portfolio with American mortgages from the Alt-A category (middle range of risk) with a value of 39 billion dollars. Although there were no problems with the repayment of the mortgages, the portfolio could not be sold anymore, and was hence considered toxic. The Dutch government took over 80% of the economic risk. ING is still the formal owner of the portfolio, but its (accounting) balance looks a lot better after this construction. According to the Ministry of Finance, not only ING, but also the State (and therefore the taxpayers) were better off. Two scenarios were calculated: a base scenario (75% chance of materialising) and a bad scenario (25% chance). In the first scenario, the state would make a profit of two billion Euros, and in the second one, it would lose 600 million Euros[2].

a. Evaluate whether the government, purely judging its own outcomes, should make this intervention.
b. What does calculation assume about the risk attitude? What do you think about that?

---

[2] Source: Volkskrant, 31 January 2009.

c. Is the Dutch taxpayer indeed better off?

**Answer 6.27 Government intervention and credit crunch crisis**
a. The expected value of the pay-off is positive, so the government could make this intervention. Note that there are only real costs for the Dutch government (apart from arrangement costs) if the repayment of the mortgages actually fails.
b. The calculation assumes that the government is risk neutral. However, the next question is whether the tax payers are risk neutral. Most of them will be risk averse or have loss aversion.
c. That is questionable. Based on these (standard) risk calculations (i.e. expected value), the taxpayer is better off. However, we do not know the underlying assumptions of the calculations. The near economic future was very difficult to predict at the time when the decision had to be taken; there were many uncertainties. As most taxpayers will be risk averse or have loss aversion, it is well possible that safer investments would have contributed more to their wellbeing.

### 6.28 Intertemporal aspect of principal-agent relationships
In practice, most principal-agent relationships develop over time, during which the agent takes actions several times and the principal observes output several times. What possibilities therefore arise for incentive schemes?

**Answer 6.28 Intertemporal aspect of principal-agent relationships**
**(a) Smoothing over time.** In a repeated relationship, the principal can arrange a stream of payments to the agent that smoothes the agent's consumption. Conversely, it makes the principal's profit more volatile, but a risk neutral principal does not care about this. A risk averse agent benefits from smoothing; in fact if the discount rate is very low, the smoothing effectively brings the agent close to risk neutrality and the outcome close to the first best solution.

**(b) Aggregation over time.** Here we consider a situation lasting over several periods. The agent takes an action each period, resulting in an outcome with a random component. The principal cares only about the outcome aggregated over all the periods. If the incentive scheme rewards the agent differently for outcomes in different periods, either directly or indirectly, this gives the agent an opportunity to play the system to the disadvantage of the principal. For example, with a step-function scheme for the aggregated outcome, an agent who has good luck in the early periods may relax in the later periods, and one who has very bad luck in the early periods (making it unlikely that he will meet the quota for the aggregated period) may give up. If the outcome is multidimensional and the threshold in the incentive schemes covers only one easily verifiable dimension, this opens up further opportunities for playing the system. We find such effects in the operation of job training and partnerships.

**(c) Rewards, punishments and reputation.** If an action is observable with a delay, then repeated relationships allow for incentive schemes with appropriately designed time-varying payments. If the agent can be punished for past actions, the threat of such punishments may be enough. But if the agent can quit, then it may be necessary to devise a cost of slackening in the form of the loss of a reward. A particularly interesting example is the *efficiency wage* scheme (Remark: Question 4.23 gives an application).

Consider an agent who provides a good or service whose quality is observed with a lag. Producing higher quality is more costly for the agent, so he can make more profit in the short run by degrading the quality. A solution is to give some rent each period, pay him more than the extra cost of the high quality, as long as he is not discovered to be cheating. To eliminate his temptation to cheat, the rent should just equal the interest on the one-time profit he can make by cheating.

Repetition also helps mitigate the moral hazard (= hidden action) on the principal's side – the temptation to renege on a promised payment to the agent. To counter this, it is not necessary that the particular relationship be repeated; it may suffice if the principal is in business for a long time or in many activities, and reputation for misbehaviour on one occasion can affect his ability to attract agents to work for him later or elsewhere. For this reason this moral hazard problem may not matter for most public sector agencies. In adverse selection (= hidden information) problems, repetition creates scope for building a reputation about one's types. This can be especially important in matters like the ability of a worker or the quality of a product or service.

**(d) Career concern.** In repeated relationships, it may be unnecessary to provide explicit incentives to induce effort in the early stages; the prospect of indirect incentives in the form of a better prospect of future rewards can suffice. The general conclusion of a lot of research is that workers at early stages of their careers will exert effort without explicit contractual incentives (or with weak ones) to influence perceptions of their abilities. Such efforts will gradually decline as the information is revealed, so senior workers late in their careers will cash in on their reputations, and sharper explicit incentive at that stage will be needed to keep them exerting effort.

**Implicit incentives** are very important in all organisations; they are likely to be especially important in the public sector where explicit incentives are often weak or constrained. If 'career' is interpreted to mean not just tenure in a particular agency relationship but an individual's lifetime, then a manager may be motivated by the possibility of rewards in the form of future employment by someone else.

**(e) Ratchet effects.** Suppose we have an adverse selection-situation (= hidden information) of two periods. In a two-period situation, if the principal cannot bind himself to a contract for two periods, the agent will be more reluctant to reveal his information in the first period, as he fears that the principal will exploit this to his own advantage in the second-period contract. The principal can offer a sufficiently high rent in the first period to induce revelation, but the cost of this may be so high that he finds it better not to try to separate the types of agents in the first period, offering instead a common or pooling contract to several types.

If an addition element of moral hazard (= hidden action) is present, then the ratchet effect can run counter to the career concern effect for young workers, because greater effort when young can lead the principal to infer greater ability and therefore offer less rent in the future. Conversely, career concerns can reverse a presumption of the moral hazard approach that greater uncertainty means weaker incentives: greater uncertainty about the type of the agents leads to a greater uncertainty about the outcome for the principal, but this can cause him to offer the agents sharper incentives because it elicits larger effort from the young in an attempt to prove their ability[3].

### 6.29 Agency Theory

a. Mr. Bean is manager of a company of which he owns all the shares. Mr. Bean investigates whether it is profitable for him to sell a fraction of his shares to outsiders. Explain why Jensen and Meckling[4] do not think that this is profitable for Mr. Bean.

b. Mention two reasons why Mr. Bean will sell part of his shares to outsiders in spite of the conclusion of Jensen and Meckling.

c. Consider a situation with a landowner and a farmer-tenant who is working on a plot of land of the landowner. Who is the principal and who is the agent?

d. Why would the landowner be risk neutral and the agent be risk averse?

e. What are important issues that the landowner must consider when designing the reward contract for the farmer that is optimal from the landowner's point of view?

---

[3] See Dixit, A., 2002. Incentives and organizations in the public sector: an interpretative review. The Journal of Human Resources 37: 696-727.

[4] Jensen, M. and W. Meckling, 1976. Theory of the firm: managerial behaviour, agency cost and capital structure. Journal of Financial Economics 3: 305-360.

# 7. Contract theory[1]

## 7.1 Complete and incomplete contracts
a. What are complete contracts?
b. Why are contracts often incomplete?
c. What is the role of the transition costs?
d. What is emphasised in the transaction cost view and what in the incomplete contract theory view?
e. What are the consequences of the incompleteness of contracts?

### Answer 7.1 Complete and incomplete contracts
a. A complete contract specifies what each party is to do in every possible situation, and arranges the distribution of realised costs and benefits in each contingency so that each party individually finds it optimal to abide by the contract's terms. Every contingency is anticipated and all relevant information is available. Such a contract is considered to be complete because, when signed, it can be immediately implemented. All the ordinances in the contract are verifiable, so that one of the parties can call upon a third party, for example a judge, to enforce the contract. Complete contracts can easily solve the problems of coordination and motivation problems. There are no problems about property rights
b. Most contracts are incomplete. There are several reasons which lead to incomplete contracts. **First,** in a complex and highly unpredictable world, it is difficult to forecast and take into account all possible events. Specific and unforeseen events may not be factored into the contract agreement. With perfect foresight, we could develop a better contract.
**Second**, even if all events could be predicted, it is difficult for the parties to negotiate over so many possibilities. There would be far too many events to take into account in the contract, and a common language (for which prior experience does not exist) would also be needed in order to describe all the diverse states of the world
**Third,** even if the parties could take all future contingencies into account and negotiate over them, it would still be extremely difficult to write it all down in an agreement in such a way that the content and the meaning could be examined and enforced by an outsider, e.g. a court of law, should a conflict arise. As a result of these factors, the concerned parties generally formulate a contract which is incomplete. Not only is the feasibility of a complete contract in question, but also the high transaction costs mean that it is simply too difficult to achieve a complete contract.
c. Not only is the feasibility of a complete contract questionable, because of lack of information and bounded rationality, but also because of the high transaction costs for obtaining the required information, concluding the contract, for monitoring and enforcing the agreements.
d. The transaction costs view emphasises that it is too costly to design a complete contract, while the incomplete contract theory focuses on all the contingencies that can arise that were not foreseen or not specified in the contract.
e. This incompleteness has important consequences. In a complete contract, income can be distributed in such a way that there is no return such as a residual income. If contracts are

---

[1] A good example about contracting issues is given by www.fao.org/ag/ags/contract-farming/index_cf/en/.

incomplete, at least two questions arise: (1) who has the residual control rights and (2) who has the residual income rights? This depends on who has the 'residual power'.

### 7.2 Transaction costs, incomplete contracts, principal-agent approach and quasi-rents
a. What is the transaction cost view about the quasi-rents and its distribution?
b. What are predictions of transaction costs theory concerning the distribution of the quasi-rents compared to those of the incomplete contract theory?
c. What is the view of the incomplete contract theory about the quasi-rent?
d. What is the view of the standard principal-agent approach about the quasi-rent?

### Answer 7.2 Transaction costs, incomplete contracts, principal-agent approach and quasi-rents
a. According to transaction costs theory, asset specificity generates a flow of quasi-rents that are associated with ex-post haggling and opportunism. This means that all forms of asset specificity associated with quasi-rents can lead to a dispute as each party to a contractual arrangement attempts to appropriate those rents. The bargaining power and opportunistic behaviour (including moral hazard) play an important role here.
b. The predictions of transaction costs theory concerning the distribution of the quasi-rents are less robust[2] than those of the incomplete contract theory.
c. Incomplete contract theory states that contracts are incomplete; there will be residual control rights and a residual income. This will lead to a dispute about who has the residual control right in a contract and who is able to capture the residual income. Instead of the term quasi-rent, the incomplete contract theory uses the term residual income.
d. The standard principal-agent approach is usually based on the assumption of a complete contract. Consequently, the standard principal-agent approach assumes no quasi-rents, no residual control rights and no residual income. The crux of the principal-agent approach is that the actors have diverse objectives and interests, and the principal has insufficient information over the actions of the agent. Because of asymmetric information, an incentive problem arises.

### 7.3 Residual control rights and residual income
a. What is the relationship between the residual power and residual control rights on the one hand, and residual control rights and residual income on the other hand?
b. What can happen if residual control rights and residual income are separated?
c. Suppose John Smith and Bill Bush have a profit-sharing contract. The total profit is TP and it is agreed ex-ante that John Smith receives:

$$0.6(TP) \tag{1}$$

and Bill Bush receives:

$$TP - 0.6(TP) \tag{2}$$

and TP = € 250,000
Who is the residual income claimant?
d. Are the residual control rights divisible in the same way as the residual income?

---

[2] Concerning issues such as residual control rights and residual income, the incomplete contract theory is better defined than the transaction cost theory. See also the textbook.

e. Which arguments are used to allocate – as much as possible – residual control rights and residual income to one person or into one organisation?

**Answer 7.3 Residual control rights and residual income**
a. The one with the '*residual powers*' often has also the '*residual rights of control*'. Further, in many cases one might expect the holder of the residual control rights to have significant residual income rights, i.e. residual control rights and residual income should often go together.
b. If residual control rights and residual income are separated, a hold-up problem will often arise.
c. If all the costs and yields are completely verifiable – with low transaction costs – such a profit-sharing contract will not be that difficult. Both Smith and Bush are the residual income claimants.
   • John Smith receives 0.6(250,000) = € 150,000
   • Bill Bush receives 250,000 - 0.6(250,000) = € 100,000
d. The *residual control rights* are not divisible in the same way as *residual income rights*. Suppose there are two parties and one *asset*, then it is reasonable that one party or the other has *residual control rights*. It would be difficult or impossible to allocate 60% of the rights to one party and 40% to the other.
e. **First** as already said, if *residual income* and *residual control rights* are separated, then a *hold-up problem* arises. Certainly, if *control rights* and *income rights* are to a great degree complementary, then it is efficient to allocate both to one and the same person. **Second,** in some situations it is not possible to measure or determine all aspects of the stream of returns from an asset. A return can consist of two components (1) a short-term income generated by current activities and (2) a long-term component resulting from the value-appreciation of the asset. The long-term income accrues to the person who has *control rights*, because he can decide whether or not to sell the asset. The short-term income accrues to the person who *uses the asset*. This person will attempt to maximise this income, without regarding the long-term value of the asset (this person actually has no control rights). This may lead to a very inefficient outcome. It is better to bundle the short-term *income rights* with the *control rights*. **Third,** goods exist for which it is not feasible to separate *residual income* from *residual control rights*.

**7.4 Contracting costs**
a. What are contracting costs?
b. Give a few examples of contracting costs.
c. What effect does the existence of contracting costs have on market economies?

**Answer 7.4 Contracting costs**
a. Contracting costs include search and information costs, bargaining and decision costs, and policing and enforcement costs.
b. Examples include the search and negotiation of prices in the contract, legal disputes about contracts, monitoring employees, and so on.
c. Contracting costs imply that markets are not always the best way to organise economic activities. Sometimes the creation of firms can lower contracting costs. Therefore, in most market economies, you see market transactions, contractual transactions as well as

transactions that occur within firms. Sometimes contracting costs are reduced by organising transactions within firms.

### 7.5 Standard principal-agent theory and complete contracts
a. What does the standard principal-agent theory assume about complete contracts?
b. Is this assumption realistic in practice?

### Answer 7.5 Standard principal-agent theory and complete contracts
a. In the standard principal-agent (P/A) theory, it is assumed that both parties are perfectly informed about each other with exception of 'blindness' presupposed in models with asymmetric information. The inability of individuals to make direct observations is compensated for in these models through the use of economic incentives. Hence, one can speak of incentive contracts. In the principal-agent model with moral hazard, the incentive is embodied in the incentive schedule offered by the principal to the agent. In this model, the principal knows from the beginning the agent's reaction function as well as his reservation utility.
   In the adverse selection P/A model, incentives are reflected in the self-selection constraints, which also constitute an incentive schedule for the principal. In this adverse selection model, the principal knows the utility functions and the abilities of the agents but can not tell which individual agent is which type. According to this terminology, the P/A models are complete contracts, in the sense that a complete contract is one that specifies each party's obligations in every conceivable eventuality.
b. The standard principal-agent theory assumes that it is possible to draw up complete contracts. However, in reality there are a number of factors, ignored in the standard principal-agent theory, that may result in incomplete contracts. One important factor missing from the principal-agent view is the recognition that writing a (good) contract itself is costly. This is a theme that lies at the heart of the large body of transaction cost literature.
   According to the transaction cost literature, contracts are not comprehensive and are revised and renegotiated all the time. This has led to the development of the incomplete contract theory, see section 7.2 of the book.

### 7.6 Key elements for classifying contracts
a. What types of contracts can be distinguished?
b. What five key elements can be used for classifying contracts?
c. Please give a description of classical, neoclassical and relational contracts based on these five key elements.
d. Why are contracts a second-best solution?
e. What is the role of the price in neoclassical contracts?

### Answer 7.6 Key elements for classifying contacts
a. Three types of contracts can be distinguished: classical, neoclassical and relational.
b. Based on: (1) identity of the parties; (2) duration; (3) how to deal with unexpected events (degree of completeness); (4) role of written documentation; and (5) the role of enforcement procedures in case of conflicts – we can distinguish classical, neoclassical and relational contracts.

c.  A **classical contract** is of short duration, the identity of the parties and personal characteristics are of no importance. The duration of the relationship in a classical contract is specified. Its duration can be extremely short, such as within the spot market. Transactions which take place in a way similar to that in a spot market can be considered as classical contracts. In the classical contract, the price is the most important coordination mechanism. Asset specificity is small. Safeguards and written procedures are of limited meaning. The economic advantage for both parties is the driving power of the transaction.

The duration of **neoclassical contracts** is in between the classical and relational contract. It can be a yearly repeated contract or a contract for a longer period. The identity and personal characteristics of the parties matter and are important. Price as a coordination mechanism is less important here as compared to the classical contract. Where contracting parties make relation-specific investments which can not be redeployed at low cost, neoclassical contracts are more suitable, effective and efficient. Some provisions in the contract are necessary, like a longer duration and safeguards. Otherwise, certain investments will not take place and a *hold-up problem* arises[3]. A longer period of a contract can limit the threat of opportunism by the other party since this would mean foregoing the chance to realise relation-specific investments.

As investments in specific assets increase, there will be a greater need for safeguards in the form of written documentation and legal rules as protection against lock-in[4] effects. Further, there can be a need for an arbitration procedure or a conflict-solving mechanism in the case of disputes. If special characteristics increase (e.g. level of asset specificity or the relation-specific investment), the importance of 'safeguards clauses' increases, while that of the price as coordination mechanism declines.

On the other side of the spectrum is the **relational contract**. The duration of a relational contract is left unspecified, but the identity and the personal characteristics are obviously of importance here. These contracts are intended for long-term relationships. The price as coordination mechanism plays a subordinate role in the partnership. In classical contracts, written documents overrule any verbal agreement, in the neoclassical verbal agreements provide a basis for further negotiations, while in the relational contract it is used as an official document of agreement. However, an important difference is that in the relational contract, the relationship is often more important than the content of the contract (for example, in a marriage). Contracts at the *relational* side of the spectrum include strong personal involvement, have a long duration, and anticipate the possibility of events as a normal part of the continuing association between the parties. Marriages and long-term labour relations are well-known examples of relational contracts.

---

[3] The possibility of hold-up arises in every contractual relationship which is incomplete. The reasons may be diverse. As soon as a person has selected a specific technology or relationship, the discontinuation or termination of the relationship can be extremely expensive. Further, as a result of unforeseen circumstances, the position of one of the parties in the contractual relationship can result in a deterioration or change in the negotiation position of the parties over time. Termination of the relationship can be costly.

[4] Lock-in effects mean that your alternatives are strongly reduced. It can be the result of being held-up. It is an ex-post phenomenon, while hold-up is more an ex-ante problem.

d. Contracts are – because of their incompleteness – a second-best solution. Such contracts involve hidden information and hidden actions. The reason for this is that we do not live in a first best world; see also section 6.2 of the textbook.
e. One characteristic of neoclassical contracts is the restricted role of prices as a factor of adjustment. This is caused by the presence of specific assets, while complete self-enforcing safeguards are difficult to implement. Taken together, these factors have consequences for the role of the price as coordination and motivation mechanism.

## 7.7 Incomplete contracts
a. Suppose you have to conclude contracts with other researchers for carrying out a large research project for the EU. The duration of the project is 5 years. What would be an important selection mechanism?
b. How can we make sure that people who conclude incomplete contracts keep to the rules and show enough credible commitment?
c. Suppose you have to deal with activities/transactions with a high level of asset specificity, a high degree of uncertainty, a high frequency and a long duration, difficulties in measuring performance. What organisational mode would be a good alternative for incomplete contracts?

## Answer 7.7 Incomplete contracts
a. The reputation of the researchers would be important; i.e. making use of the reputation mechanism.
b. By making use of monitoring, graduated sanctions and conflict-resolving mechanisms.
c. A good alternative would be in-house production, vertical integration or unified ownership.

## 7.8 Properties of contracts
a. What are properties of contracts?
b. What is an important difference between a contract and a regulation from the government?

## Answer 7.8 Properties of contracts
a. Contracts can be verbal or written, and most of them possess the following properties: (1) they concern voluntary exchange; they contain (2) a coordination mechanism and (3) a motivation mechanism; (4) they are explicit or implicit; (5) they can be global or detailed.
b. A contract is a voluntary exchange, and a regulation of the government is not.

## 7.9 Coordination
a. What four (groups of) coordination mechanisms can be distinguished and how does coordination take place?
b. Which coordination mechanism is less important for contracts, and why?
c. What is the coordination mechanism for classical, neoclassical and relational contracts?

## Answer 7.9 Coordination
a. The four (groups of) coordination mechanisms are: the invisible hand, the handbook, the visible hand and the handshake. The coordination can take place by one of the four groups or a certain mix of them.

b. The group of coordination mechanisms that is called the 'visible hand' is not relevant for contracts in general. Mostly, contract parties are not vertically integrated with the other party. Contract giver and contract taker mostly retain their separate external identity.

c. The coordination mechanism for the classical contract is a mix of the 'invisible hand' and 'handbook', but the emphasis is on the price as coordination mechanism. For the neoclassical contract, the price as a coordination mechanism is less important, compared to classical contracts. In that case, the coordination mechanism of contracts consists of a combination of 'handbook' and 'invisible hand', but there is a shift in the mix towards the direction of the 'handbook' as a coordination mechanism, compared to classical contracts. Dependent on the identity of the parties, the mix can also include parts of the 'handshake'. The price as coordination mechanism often plays a subordinate role in relational contracts. In such contracts, the relationship itself could be even more important than the content of the contract (think of a marriage). Such contracts indicate a certain continuity in the relationship between the parties. It means that the identity of the parties matters. The 'handshake' is often used as a coordination mechanism for such types of contracts. However, the actual coordination is complemented with the price. Hence, the coordination mechanism is a mix of the 'handshake', 'invisible hand', and to a lesser degree the 'handbook'.

## 7.10 Motivation
a. Why do motivational problems exist?
b. What kind of motivations can be distinguished? What does the trade-off between the two types of motivation mean?
c. What can be the effect if the motivation is based more on the stick than on the carrot?

## Answer 7.10 Motivation
a. Motivation questions arise because individuals have their own private interests, which seldom correspond perfectly to the interests of other parties, the group to which the individuals belong, or the society as a whole. Such problems arise because specific plans cannot be described in a completely enforceable contract.

b. Two kinds of motivations are distinguished: intrinsic and extrinsic motivations. It is argued that there may be a trade-off between the two, such that too much emphasis on extrinsic motivation can drive out intrinsic motivation. Thus, motivations activated by external factors, such as monetary incentives and direct order (as in hierarchical governance structure), can crowd out motivations that are internal to the individual, such as more **altruistic concerns.**

c. Motivation more based on the stick than on the carrot can have a negative effect on motivational elements, like wishing to do your work well, trustworthiness and having or building up a good reputation.

## 7.11 Explicit and implicit contracts
a. What is the difference between an explicit and implicit contract?
b. How can we enforce implicit contracts?
c. When is a party able or prepared to build up the desired reputation?
d. For what types of contracts is reputation-building important?

### Answer 7.11 Explicit and implicit contracts

a.  An explicit contract is one in which there is a written document about the agreement. An implicit contract is one which has no formal record of the terms and conditions agreed upon by the parties.
b.  Such contracts are enforceable by the *reputation mechanism.*
c.  A party with a long-term horizon is more willing to invest in a reputation than a party with a short-term horizon. Next, investing in a reputation at the beginning of a game is more attractive than at the end.
d.  Reputation is more important for neoclassical and relation contracts. However, in order to build a reputation, the game has to be played several times.

### 7.12 Global and detailed contracts

a.  What is the difference between a global and a detailed contract?
b.  Can global contracts work effectively? What is important in that case?
c.  What can we say about the relationship?

### Answer 7.12 Global and detailed contracts

a.  A detailed contract is a contract that describes in detail what each party has to do and which rules should be followed. The parties agree on detailed plans and actions. Flexibility is hardly present. However, in a global contract an agreement is set up which frames the relationship. The parties agree on:
    • goals and objectives;
    • general provisions that are broadly applicable;
    • the criteria to be used in deciding what to do if unforeseen contingencies arise;
    • who has what power to act and the bounds limiting the range of actions that can be taken; and
    • dispute resolution mechanisms to be used if disagreements do occur.
b.  Such contracts can in fact work quite effectively; at least when the potential conflicts are not too great and the parties are not inclined to be opportunistic in their dealings with one another. Motivational elements, such as - wishing to do your work well, trustworthiness and having or building up a good reputation, are important. Such contracts could be relational contracts only.
c.  The relationship in a global contract is often more important than the content of the contract.

### 7.13 Credible commitment

a.  In which type of contract can credible commitment be a serious problem?
b.  What can be the consequence of a lack of credible commitment?
c.  What are the pros and cons if we open the possibilities of renegotiating the contract *ex-post?*
d.  What is a good remedy against reneging?

### Answer 7.13 Credible commitment

a.  Credible commitment can be a serious problem, especially in **incomplete contracts** because what has to be done in diverse circumstances is not always written down explicitly and so remains open to interpretation.

b.  Reneging can be a consequence of a lack of credible commitment. If reneging occurs in the form of not carrying out the agreed transactions, it clearly affects efficiency. However, often the problem with reneging is not that it impedes efficiency directly, but rather that it affects performance indirectly. The threat of getting cheated may prevent an efficient transaction from ever occurring in the first place.

c.  In specific circumstances, it is advantageous for both parties to *renegotiate* the contract *ex-post*. At least one of the parties would like the contract to continue, but with some changes in the provisions. New information may have become available, or some conditions may have changed. Re-opening or renegotiating the contract *ex-post* can appear attractive to both parties. At first, this does not seem to be a problem. If both parties really want to renegotiate, it is possible that the original contract included the wrong incentives. In that case it is not possible to generate the desired behaviour with that contract. However, opening the possibility of renegotiating can also be – at same time – an incentive for opportunistic behaviour.

d.  A good remedy against reneging can rely on the reputation of those involved in the contract. Reputations are formed on the basis of behaviour displayed, and particularly on the perception of others regarding that behaviour. Reputation can be seen as an institutional device that may be considered as a part of human capital, or the capital stock of an organisation. Choosing contracting partners on the basis of their *reputation* is one defence against being exploited by a reneging contracting partner.

## 7.14 Contract theory and a gas company

Suppose you have a contract with the NUON gas company that it will supply the gas and provide the gas transport services (gas-line infrastructure and maintenance) to meet your home energy requirements. However, you receive a telephone call from another gas provider suggesting that you will save significant costs in your annual gas bill if you switch to them as your new gas supplier, while maintaining NUON as your gas transport service provider. Let's assume that the new company can use the existing gas-line infrastructure to supply gas to your home without compensating NUON for using its gas-lines.

a.  Why can this new company offer such low gas prices?

b.  What problem is the new company creating for NUON and why does this problem occur?

c.  What can NUON do to secure your business and reduce the threat of outside offers?

d.  If you choose to switch to the other gas provider, what would you expect NUON to do as your gas transport service provider?

## Answer 7.14 Contract theory and a gas company

a.  The new company is proposing to supply you with gas, but has not invested in supplying the service infrastructure such as the underground gas lines that are highly specific investments. Thus, their operating costs are significantly less than those of NUON.

b.  The new company is using the specific assets of NUON and thus creating a situation in which NUON is in a weaker bargaining position to negotiate lower contract prices given their previous investment in the gas-line infrastructure. This is the hold-up problem. This problem occurs because the investment in putting in gas-lines to each home is highly specific with no alternative use. The new company creates a sunk cost problem for NUON.

c.  NUON can use long-term contracts (neoclassical contracts) rather than the classical spot market contract to protect themselves from opportunistic switching. They can build a good

reputation with their clients as a reliable service provider such that the risk of switching to an unknown company is perceived to be a higher cost than the cost savings incentive.
d.  One could expect NUON to increase their service provider rates or to provide a lower level of customer service.

### 7.15 The value of reputation
a.  What is reputation?
b.  What is reputational capital?
c.  What determines the value of reputation?
d.  What are the driving factors behind the incentives to build and maintain a larger *reputation*? For which contracting partner do the arguments hold?
e.  Which party has the most to lose from a damaged reputation?
f.  Which party should have the discretion to direct activities in unforeseen events?

### Answer 7.15 The value of reputation
a.  Reputation is the view formed of an individual or organisation by another based on past experience, and used especially as a basis for forecasting future behaviour. In some cases, it is possible that a contract taker is able to make favourable information known about himself (e.g. information that he is a desirable contract partner). This impression is made credible by actions in an early period of a long-term relationship. That is, through the time a contract taker was able to develop his reputation.
b.  Individuals with a good reputation are able to realise rent from keeping their reputation intact; this is called reputational capital. The notion of reputational capital is similar to human capital – it is rent that a party receives for being trustworthy.
c.  The value of a reputation – and thus the costs incurred in building and maintaining a good one – depends on how often it proves to be useful. This in turn is related to the frequency of similar transactions, the time horizon over which similar transactions are expected to occur, and the profitability of the transactions.
d.  The incentives to build and maintain a *reputation* are greater when the transactions are more frequent, the time horizon is longer, and the transactions are more profitable. It is clear that these arguments hold not only for the contract taker, but also for the contract giver.
e.  This is likely to be the one with the longer time horizon, the higher visibility, the greater size, the greater frequency of transaction. This outcome also indicates which party in contracting should have the discretion to direct activities in unforeseen events.
f.  It should be the one with the most to lose from a damaged reputation. In the case of contracts between private parties and the government, this is mostly the government.

### 7.16 Reputation and contracts
How do reputational concerns work in the enforcement of contracts?

### Answer 7.16 Reputation and contracts
Individuals can find it in their best interests to honour contracts and not engage in 'short-run' opportunistic actions because they fear the loss of future business and profits from developing a bad reputation.

### 7.17 Efficient and most suitable contract
a. What is the most suitable contract?
b. What is an efficient contract?
c. What are the criteria for (most) suitable contracts?

### Answer 7.17 Efficient and most suitable contract
a. The most suitable contract strongly depends on the attributes of the transaction. For a simple transaction a simple contract is sufficient. Indicators for simplicity are: how are the five key elements (see Section 7.3 of the book) taken into account.
b. An efficient contract contributes to optimising coordination and motivation in the cheapest way possible. In other words, it minimises the costs of planning, monitoring, and motivating, and therefore minimises transaction costs.
c. Criteria for most suitable contracts should include:
   * coordination and motivation elements;
   * public and private transaction costs;
   * reducing hold-up and lock-in effects;
   * distribution of residual income;
   * minimising cost of risk;
   * allocation of risk to the least risk averse party.
   This implies that not only efficiency but also income distributional arguments (= equity) are important.

### 7.18 Guidelines for contract design
a. Which two important purposes must every contract serve?
b. Do these purposes conflict? What could be the result? What is often a source of conflict?
c. Why are coordination, motivation and transaction costs so important as design issues?
d. Do these objectives conflict?
e. What could be the role of social capital/trust and reputation?

### Answer 7.18 Guidelines for contract design
a. Contracts must *coordinate* activities, for example to make sure that the right producers are producing the right quantity and quality of the right products/services at the right time and place. Next, contracts must motivate the parties, giving them private interest in making the coordinated decisions that maximise the integrated profit, or satisfying their intrinsic motives.
b. Coordination and motivation aspects will often conflict. A solution achieving the best possible coordination while respecting the potential motivation is usually called a second-best solution. A common conflict between coordination and motivation is derived from the dual role of prices. In many economic mechanisms, prices send coordination signals and affect the allocation of gains (or residual incomes) from contracting.
c. Coordination, motivation and transaction costs are important as design issues:
   * coordination: to ensure that the right products are produced at the right time and place;
   * motivation: to ensure that the parties have individual incentives to make coordinated decisions;
   * transaction costs: to ensure that coordination and motivation are provided at the lowest cost.

d.  The various objectives in contract design may conflict, and different means may have both desirable and non-desirable effects. Objectives can have trade-offs, and must therefore be balanced.
e.  Social capital (including trust) and reputation improve coordination and motivation, and they can therefore reduce transaction costs.

### 7.19 Hidden information

Compensation for nature and landscape management agreements is based on the assumptions about the 'quality' of the average farmer. Quality in this context means a certain level of efficiency. Assume the government wants to conclude management agreements in a certain area:
a.  What type of farmers will be attracted to sign such an agreement?
b.  How will efficient farmers react to undifferentiated compensation?
c.  What sort of solution is there to this problem?
d.  What does the optimal solution look like?
e.  What is meant by 'self selection conditions'?

### Answer 7.19 Hidden information

a.  It could be that the nature and landscape management agreements are more attractive to inefficient farmers than to efficient ones.
b.  For efficient farmers it is appealing to pose as an inefficient farmer. By doing this, the efficient farmer receives a reward that is sufficient to cover his costs (to meet his reservation price), leaving him room for a surplus. His cost function is at a lower level than that of an inefficient farmer. Because the efficient farmer poses as an inefficient farmer his output in nature production will be considerably smaller than what is possible according to his marginal cost function (is also the supply curve).
c.  A solution to this problem could be to change the compensation. The government could decide to raise the reward for the efficient farmer to a point where it covers all costs and leaves room for a surplus. This solution is however not efficient for the government. It pays more than necessary.
d.  The optimal solution implies that the reward for the inefficient farmer is reduced. This will lead to lower production by the inefficient farmer. Two advantages will arise; the government will have to pay less to the inefficient farmer and the amount produced decreases. By paying the inefficient farmer less, it is no longer attractive to the efficient farmer to be inefficient and produce less. If the efficient farmer still chooses to produce the output level of the inefficient farmer, the government will have to pay less to the efficient farmer.
e.  Self-selection conditions consist of participation conditions and those that lead to contracts so that the agents choose the contracts which are appropriate to them.

### 7.20 Long-term contracts

a.  Why should we stimulate long-term contracts?
b.  What types of problems can be reduced by long-term contracts?
c.  How can we reduce hold-up and lock-in problems?

### Answer 7.20 Long-term contracts

a. Contracts should induce parties to take the long-term effects of their actions into consideration. It is important that contracts encourage the right investments. A party that has invested in specific assets is vulnerable to the contracts being terminated. This leaves the party with specific assets in a weak bargaining position in negotiations once the investment has been made. This is ex-ante the **hold-up problem** and **ex-post the lock-in problem**.

b. Long-term contracts can reduce hold-up problems because the terms are settled before one of the parties makes specific investments. Because of their duration, they can also limit lock-in effects. Long-term contracts can also alleviate **ratchet effects**, i.e. the tendency to under-perform in early contracts to avoid tough contracts later on, and facilitate the development of know-how through planned experiments.

c. Hold-up- and lock-in problems can be reduced in different ways. **First**, long-term contracts can reduce the hold-up problem and, due to their duration, also limit lock-in effects. **Second**, if both parties make specific investments, the balance in the bargaining position can remain unchanged. **Third**, the reputation mechanism may also prevent the parties from holding up or locking the other party. A party with a good reputation may be reluctant to devalue its reputation by holding up a contract partner, because this may ruin its chance of making contracts with other agents.

### 7.21 Balance pros and cons of renegotiations

a. What are the advantages of renegotiations?
b. What are the disadvantages of renegotiations?

### Answer 7.21 Balance pros and cons of renegotiations

a. Renegotiations facilitate flexible contracts and enable the parties to adjust the contract to changes in the environment. Hence, the parties can remove ex-post inefficiencies through renegotiations.

b. Renegotiations reduce commitment and may lead to strategic behaviour. Hence, renegotiations can lead to ex-ante inefficiencies.

### 7.22 Minimising the cost of risk and sharing risk

a. Please give some examples of risk and some possible solutions for reducing the costs of risk.
b. Why is risk sharing an important topic in contract design?
c. Why is the risk attitude or level of risk-aversion so important?
d. What is the implication of minimising the cost of bearing risk for a risk averse agent?
e. From the efficiency point of view of society, who should bear the risk? Why?

### Answer 7.22 Minimising the cost of risk and sharing risk

a. Activities are subject to different types of risk. For example, agricultural production and marketing deal with biological, climate and weather, price and institutional risks. In addition, there is behavioural risk, because one party does not know what actions the other parties are taking. Normally, an uncertain payment is considered less valuable than a certain payment with the same expected value. The parties can reduce this cost of risk and uncertainty in two ways. They can minimise the risk or they can share the risk between them. One way of minimising risk and uncertainty is choosing a robust contract that leads to reasonable outcomes even if the initial assumptions do not hold true. Information collection is another way of minimising risk.

b. Risk sharing is an important topic in contract design because it affects both the cost of risk bearing (risk premium) and the motivation to behave in certain ways (incentives). An optimal arrangement (or contract) therefore involves a *trade-off* between the efficient (cost-minimising) *risk sharing* and the *provision of incentives.*

c. The more risk averse the agent is:
- the higher compensation he will ask for bearing risk. It means the cost for compensating risk will be higher for the principal;
- the higher the cost of providing an incentive to the risk averse agent for the principal;
- the more likely that it is better that the principal bears all the risk, and gives the agent a fixed amount of money.

d. Minimising the cost of bearing risk also means reducing the possibility of providing incentives (e.g. performance incentives) to the agent.

e. From the efficiency point of view of society, the least averse party should bear the risk:
- The compensation for bearing risk would be lower;
- The social cost would be lower, because the compensation for bearing risks is a cost for society.

### 7.23 Rules of thumb for contracting
a. What three aspects can be used to categorise the ten rules of thumb?
b. Please give an overview of the ten rules of thumb and discuss them.

### Answer 7.23 Rules of thumb for contracting
a. The ten rules of thumb can be grouped into three categories corresponding to the objectives of coordination, motivation and minimisation of transaction costs.
b. For an overview of these ten rules, see Table 7.1 of the textbook. A discussion is given in section 7.6 of the textbook.

### 7.24 Direct government production
a. What are the motives for government intervention?
b. Does government intervention necessarily mean that the government has to deal with all the aspects that can be distinguished in the production of goods and services?
c. In what situation is direct government production likely to be superior?

### Answer 7.24 Direct government production
a. Market failure, failing to reach sector or macro-economic goals, or own goals of the government can be motives for the government to take control of property, management, financing and production of certain services. This is the most comprehensive form of government intervention. Decision making, financing, implementation and exploitation are in the hands of the government. It makes use of scarce means of production with alternative opportunities (land, labour and capital) for producing goods and services.
b. No, the government can choose for: (1) public provision, i.e. in-house production by the government; (2) private provision by contracting out (3) private provision with strong

government regulation (e.g. through regulatory takings, see Chapter 11), aimed at ensuring that, for example, farmers use their land or produce food in the desired way.

c.  Unified ownership or do-it-yourself (for example, by government) can be an alternative to private provision by contracting out. There are two situations in which direct government production is likely to be superior. **First**, the government may not know what it wants. In that case, a contract will be very incomplete and the costs associated with renegotiations will be considerable, so that contracting becomes very expensive. **Second,** if the contract party has a strong tendency to reduce costs, but this is accompanied by a reduction in (non-contractible) quality. The adverse effect of cost reduction on quality is significant. In both situations, government production is likely to be a better solution.

### 7.25 Cable television companies and contracting

a.  Cable television companies lay cables to individual households in the communities they serve to carry the television signal. How specific is this investment?
b.  What kind of arrangements would you expect the cable companies to make with local communities about the pricing and taxation of cable services? Explain.

### Answer 7.25 Cable television companies and contracting

a.  This investment is highly specific; in its next best use, the value of the cable is greatly diminished – if not useless (no other product can be transmitted over the cable; phone lines already exist). The difference between the cable's current value and its next best use value is its quasi-rents. Thus the quasi-rents are extremely high and you would expect strict **contractual arrangements** between the cable company and local community subscribers to prevent ex-post contractual opportunistic behaviour by both parties.
b.  The cable company might increase subscription costs to capture these rents as subscribers have no other cable TV alternative (they would be forced to watch only channels 1-3, for example). Cable companies will also charge additional flat fees for special channels and pay-per-view options for viewers addicted to cable.

Conversely, local communities have the power to raise taxes on local industry. Once the cable has been installed, taxes could be raised to capture the quasi-rents. The cable company will be forced to pay as their cable is useless for anything else. They wouldn't dig up or take down the cable and go to another town.

Thus, you would expect strict regulation of the cable industry – prices can't be altered much and taxes can't be changed. If either party breaks the regulation they would rely on the courts to settle the dispute or implicit market behaviour (example: If the cable company increases rates, the next town they go to will require them to pay more in taxes).

### 7.26 Leasing a pub

Suppose you are working for a landlord who has real estates, such as pubs, hotels, offices and land. Your task is leasing out the real estate objects.

a.  To evaluate the options, you are studying two of types of contracts for leasing out pubs:
   *   (1) contracts with a fixed lease price, for example, on a yearly basis; and
   *   (2) contracts whereby you share the return with the leaseholder (= tenant), e.g. on a 50% basis.

- We suppose for the sake of simplicity that the fixed lease price on a daily basis for a pub is € 1000.
What is the effect of such lease contracts on the use of assets and the income of the tenants?
b. How would you lease out the pubs to the tenants: (1) based on fixed lease rent or (2) a fixed rent plus a share of the return? What would the tenants prefer?
c. What role could the risk behaviour of the tenants play?
d. Is it possible to create a lease contract that serves both the interests of the real estate owner (landlord) and the tenant? How should such an agreement be drawn up and what would be included?
e. What are the disadvantages of very detailed contracts?
f. Why is sharecropping such an important type of land use in developing countries?

## Answer 7.26 Leasing a pub

a. For working out this question we have data from a pub similar to the one the real estate owner has. This tenant keeps his pub open for 10 hours a day. His variable costs are € 200 per hour. The building, design and equipment belong to the owner. Table 7.1 presents the variable costs and the return for the tenant.

Table 7.1. The variable costs and the return for the tenant.

| Hours open | 0 | 1 | 2 | 3 | 4 | 5 | 6 | 7 | 8 | 9 | 10 |
|---|---|---|---|---|---|---|---|---|---|---|---|
| Variable costs in € | 0 | 200 | 400 | 600 | 800 | 1,000 | 1,200 | 1,400 | 1,600 | 1,800 | 2,000 |
| Return in € | 0 | 500 | 1,400 | 2,100 | 2,600 | 3,000 | 3,300 | 3,500 | 3,600 | 3,600 | 3,500 |

To analyse both forms of lease contracts, we assume that both tenants set their marginal return equal to the marginal costs (MR = MC). This means that the profit is also maximal.

Table 7.2 shows the marginal costs and the marginal benefits of both types of lease contracts. In the case of a fixed lease price contract, the lease price belongs to the fixed costs of the tenant. As Table 7.2 shows, the MR are equal to the MC when the pub is open for 7 hours a day. This is the optimum from the viewpoint of the tenant. However, this is not the case for the tenant with a lease price of 50% of the return. His marginal return is only half of the marginal return with a fixed lease price. This affects the optimum for the tenant; this reaches an optimum when the pub is open for 5 hours.

Table 7.2 The marginal costs and benefits for a fixed lease price and share lease price contract.

| Hours open | 0 | 1 | 2 | 3 | 4 | 5 | 6 | 7 | 8 | 9 | 10 |
|---|---|---|---|---|---|---|---|---|---|---|---|
| Marginal costs | | 200 | 200 | 200 | 200 | **200** | 200 | **200** | 200 | 200 | 200 |
| Marginal return for **fixed** lease price | | 500 | 900 | 700 | 500 | 400 | 300 | **200** | 100 | 0 | -100 |
| Marginal return for lease price based on **sharing** | | 250 | 450 | 350 | 250 | **200** | 150 | 100 | 50 | 0 | -50 |

From this example we learn that a lease price based on a share of the return can lead to less intensive use of assets.

- In the optimal case for the tenant, the return of the pub with a **fixed lease price** is a return of € 3,500 and his surplus is € 3,500 - € 1,400 = € 2,100 per day. Subtracting the fixed lease price of € 1000, the surplus of the tenant is then € 1,100 per day;
- With a lease price of 50% of the return, the optimum for the tenant is a return of € 3,000, but his surplus is € 1,500 - € 1000 = € 500 per day.

This means that contracts based on a high share of the return have a negative effect on the use of an asset such as pubs and land, but also on the income of the tenant. This example shows that the tenant's response to sharing is important. Of course, it is possible that the tenant chooses for the share contract and tries to shirk on keeping the accounts of the sales (hidden actions).

Suppose that in the case of a fixed lease price contract, the lease price is € 1,500 per day. The net surplus for the tenant will be € 2,100 - € 1,500 = € 600, while the landlord has the same revenue as in the case of the share contract, but without any monitoring problems. This example also shows that a sharing contract is **not** the best alternative for both parties.

b. A fixed lease price contract is better for the tenant. It gives him an incentive to work harder and longer, compared to lease price based on a high share of the return. An alternative could be:
- a fixed rent plus a relatively small share of the return (however, the effect of sharing the marginal return will exist);
- a sharing contract that shares the input costs and the return.

Such contracts create better possibilities to combine the interests of landlord and the tenant and to provide both the right incentives. However, they involve higher transaction costs.

c. For analysing risk behaviour, we can use the expected utility theory and the prospect theory. Based on expected utility theory, we may expect that risk neutral tenants would prefer a fixed lease price. For a risk averse tenant, the risk-attitude level is important. It is possible that they have an aversion against paying a high yearly fixed rent and therefore prefer a lease price based on a share of the return. A sharing contract often also means a sharing of risk; it assigns some risk to the other contract partner. A basic argument is that a fixed lease price contract causes the tenant to bear all the production risk, in the absence of insurances or other means for diversifying risk.

According to the prospect theory, the subjective classification of an outcome plays a role. In terms of profits, most people are risk averse, just as in the expected utility theory. Conversely, the prospect theory predicts that decision makers prefer an uncertain loss (e.g. 50% chance of a loss of € 2,000 and 50% chance of € 0) above a certain loss with the same average value (in this case € 1000). This outcome can partly explain why tenants prefer a lease price based on share of the return.

d. It is possible to create a lease contract that serves both the interests of the real estate owner (landlord) and the tenant. This can be a long-term lease contract in which the tenant is protected from hold-up- and lock-in effects. An alternative could be a lease contract in which tenant and landlord or real estate owner share not only the benefits, but also the costs. Input cost-sharing is a common arrangement in share contracts. It is a convenient way of ensuring that inputs are used at an efficient level by the tenants. Although the tenant receives only a part of the product, he only pays a part of the costs. A lease contract with a fixed rent plus a certain share of the return offers the possibilities to combine the interests of landlord and the tenant to provide both the right incentives. That is also the basis of formulae such as those used by McDonald's and franchising applications.

e. Detailed input costs and benefits sharing contracts can lead to high transaction costs.

f. A common answer is that sharecropping is a response to uncertainty, asymmetric information, and lack of power of tenants. Furthermore, for poor farmers, a poor harvest with a small return can mean that they only have to pay a low land rent. One may also view it as a response to different types of market failures, in capital, in insurances, credit, land, and other inputs. However, this does not mean that institutions such as sharecropping will lead to efficient outcomes. Finally, it might also be the case that it is determined culturally. For example, in the USA – which is not a poor country – almost 25% of the land lease is share lease. It is mostly routine for farmers and landowners to share input costs and the return, usually on a 50-50% basis[5,6].

### 7.27 Interlinked or costs sharing contracts

In developing countries, it is quite common to find so-called interlinkage contracts between farmers and traders. In an interlinkage contract, the output and input are linked. This means that the trader not only has agreed to buy the products from the farmer, but that he has also agreed to provide inputs to the farmers (e.g., seeds, fertilisers, credit). Repayment (by the farmer) of the inputs will be settled together with the payment (by the trader) of the outputs.

a. To what type of contracts do these contracts refer?

b. What are the advantages of this type of contract?

c. What are the disadvantages of this type of contract?

d. What does this contract mean for the willingness of the farmer to make specific investments (asset specificity), for example, investments in a special crop variety?

### Answer 7.27 Interlinked or costs sharing contracts

a. These contracts have the characteristics of sharecropping contracts.

b. The advantages are:
- risk sharing for both parties;
- both parties will have common interests;
- making use of interlinkage contracts also involves a kind of screening (hence the identity of the party matters);
- by providing specific inputs, the trader has some control over the quality of the output of the farmer. This means lower transaction costs;
- the farmers obtain access to input (such as seeds, fertilisers, credit) that otherwise would be difficult or costly to obtain;
- lower risk of opportunistic behaviour of the traders;
- if sale of the products has been guaranteed, the farmers have fewer transaction costs.

c. The disadvantages are:

---

[5] Allen, W.D. and D.L. Lueck, 2002. The nature of the farm: contracts, risks and organization. MIT Press, Cambridge, MA, USA, p. 22.

[6] An excellent article about the theory of sharecropping has been written by Singh, N., 2000. Theories of sharecropping. In: P.Bardhan and Ch. Undry (eds.) Readings in development Microeconomics, Volume 1: micro-theory. MIT Press, Cambridge, MA, USA, pp. 19-71.

- it places farmers in a lock-in position. Farmers are mostly obliged to deliver their product to the traders even if they pay a low price;
- the distribution of the bargaining power; who has the residual control rights and who is able to capture the residual income? This will be mostly the trader;
- farmers can become dependent to a large extent;
- the transaction costs for making such contracts can be relatively high;
- weakness of enforcement mechanisms.

d. In general, farmers are only prepared to invest in special crops variety if they have a guarantee that someone is willing to purchase these products. By providing the seeds, fertilisers and credit, the trader commits himself to purchasing the special crops.

# 8. Coordination mechanisms and organisational modes

## 8.1 Central issues in economic organisation theory
a. Why is coordination a central issue economic organisation theory?
b. What does motivation include?
c. What is the relationship between a governance structure and motivation?
d. What type of motivation mechanism can be used for inducing persons (or organisations) to do what they are required to do?

## 8.1 Central issues in economic organisation theory
a. Coordination includes
   - what needs to be coordinated, for example, the right producers should produce the right quantity and quality at the right place and right time;
   - how coordination is achieved in spot markets, in organisations and in hybrid forms (such as contracts);
   - which alternatives there are for achieving coordination between organisational units and how each part of a system fits together.
b. This includes what and who needs to be motivated, which incentives are needed, what alternative kinds of incentive mechanisms there are, and what needs to be done to make incentive mechanisms effective and efficient.
c. Each governance structure contains a *motivation element*. For example, many contracts have a steering mechanism which defines performance criteria and the means to measure the performance. Motivation is also often included in the specification of a reward structure which marks the level of payment if a minimum level of performance is attained.
d. Two types of motivation mechanisms can be distinguished: intrinsic and extrinsic motives. Intrinsic motives refer to the desire to do your work well, trustworthiness, having or building a good reputation and altruism. Motivation can also be driven by extrinsic motives, such as monetary incentives and direct order (as in hierarchical governance structure).

## 8.2 Governance structures and coordination mechanisms
a. What are important differences between coordination mechanisms and governance structures?
b. What does the governance structure consist of?
c. What is the mutual relationship between coordination mechanisms and governance structures?
d. Why is the distinction between coordination mechanisms and governance structures important?

## Answer 8.2 Governance structures and coordination mechanisms
a. Coordination mechanisms are part of governance structures. Another important difference between coordination mechanisms and governance structures is that coordination is – as a central issue in economic organisation – more oriented towards the nature of the coordination mechanism such as the price, mutual adjustments, the contract rules or safeguards, and direct supervision.

b. The governance structure or organisational mode often consists of more than just a coordination mechanism and a motivation mechanism. In the case of a firm, it also includes the legal formal rules concerning legal ownership, corporate status, and tax regimes

c. A mutual relationship exists between coordination mechanisms and governance structures: the nature of the coordination mechanism determines for a large part the type of governance structure. For example, in a contractual relationship, the nature of the coordination mechanism determines for a large part the type of the contract.

d. The distinction between governance structures and coordination mechanisms is key to understanding the different governance structures and the potential possibilities of combining coordination mechanisms into governance structures.

### 8.3 How to organise matters
a. What is revealed in the applied governance structure or organisational mode?
b. What does 'boundary of the firm is subject of analysis' mean?
c. What characterises the type of the governance structure?

### Answer 8.3 How to organise matters
a. The way in which transactions are organised and carried out is revealed in the applied organisational mode or governance structure.
b. Governance structures are a response to various transactional considerations. It means that the type of governance structure can be adapted, it is a dependent variable (see also Section 5.3 of textbook). It should be noted that we can see the firm as a metaphor for any institutional arrangement or governance structure.
c. **First** of all, the nature of the coordination mechanism characterises for a large part the type of the governance structure. In the **second** place, according to the transaction costs theory, the governance structures are a response to various transactional considerations. Transaction cost economics (TCE) tries to explain which institutional arrangement has a comparative advantage in carrying out transactions. In the **third** place, governance structures often consist of more than just the coordination mechanism. For example, if the governance structure is a contract, it should also specify the contract agreements, if the governance structure is a firm, it also includes the legal formal rules concerning legal ownership, corporate status, and tax regimes for the firm.

### 8.4 Four coordination mechanisms
a. Why is a clear distinction between governance structures and coordination mechanisms so important?
b. What four coordination mechanisms can be distinguished?
c. What is the coordination mechanism in the invisible hand?
d. What is the coordination mechanism for contracts?

### Answer 8.4 Four coordination mechanisms
a. A clear distinction between governance structures and coordination mechanisms is key to understanding the different governance structures and the potential possibilities of combining coordination mechanisms into governance structures.

b. The four coordination mechanisms are: the visible hand, the handbook, the invisible hand and the handshake.

c. The coordination mechanism in the invisible hand is the price.

d. The coordination mechanism is not the same for each type of contract. It is often a mix of the handbook, the invisible hand (the price) and sometime also the handshake, depending on the types of contracts.

## 8.5 Coordination in firms and organisations

a. Which group of coordination mechanisms is used in firms and organisations based on hierarchy?

b. How is the coordination carried out in this group of mechanisms and what does that imply?

c. What kind of motivations do we have in a firm or organisation? Does it involve a trade-off problem?

## Answer 8.5 Coordination in firms and organisations

a. The visible hand group.

b. Hierarchy as corresponding governance structure means: the positions in the firm are ranked; higher-order level commands lower level. The coordination will be carried out by authority, direct supervision, or direct order.

c. In a firm or organisation, we also have to deal with two kinds of motivations: one external to the individual concerned, and the other internal. The pressure or desire to do your work well can be created through direct supervision (= external motivation) – as is appropriate in a hierarchical governance structure – and through internal motivation. However, the problem of the trade-off between the two kinds of motivation is present here as well.

## 8.6 Relationship between coordination mechanisms and governance structures, and analysis of hybrids

a. Is there a one-to-one correspondence between coordination mechanisms and governance structures?

b. Which coordination mechanism is predominantly used in spot markets and in firms?

c. What is the effect of a mix of prices, rules, direct supervision and mutual adjustment as coordination mechanisms on the variety of governance structures?

d. What does this mean for the hybrids?

## Answer 8.6 Relationship between coordination mechanisms and governance structures, and analysis of hybrids

a. There is not always a one-to-one correspondence between the two. A given governance structure may, under specific circumstances, use a mix of elements of the four groups of coordination mechanisms.

b. Spot markets are governance structures that predominantly use the price as coordination mechanism. Firms as hierarchies predominantly rely on direct supervision/order as coordination mechanism. However, both firms and markets will often use a mix of 'price-driven incentives' and 'direct supervision constraining behaviour'. The firm's mix will contain a high proportion of 'direct supervision constraining behaviour' relative to price incentives, while the mix in markets will be biased towards 'price-driven incentives'. This means that the application in practice is often a matter of gradation.

c. The mix of prices, rules, direct supervision and mutual adjustment as coordination mechanisms defines a wide variety of governance structures along a continuum which goes from pure spot markets to traditional firms, respectively firms based on vertical integration (= in-house production).

d. There is a great variety of organisational modes – including legally autonomous entities – that do business with each other in a particular way: They mutually adjust with help of the different coordination mechanisms (e.g. mutual adjustment, prices and rules), and they share or exchange means of production, capital, products and services, but still without a unified ownership. A wide range of hybrids is found in the real world, such as: peer groups, cooperatives, contracting, networks, franchising and collective trademarks.

## 8.7 Peer groups

a. What are peer groups and what is an important difference compared with a hierarchy? Please give some examples of both.
b. What is the most important coordination mechanism in a peer group and in a hierarchy?
c. How are the rewards in a peer group and a hierarchy determined?
d. Why do peer groups arise?
e. What are the limitations of a peer group?

## Answer 8.7 Peer groups

a. A peer group is simply a group of people working together without hierarchy; there is no boss. An example of a simple hierarchy is a group of workers with a boss. The boss has the right to adjust the rates of pay, alter the composition of the group, and tell the workers in the group what to do – direct order. Examples of peer groups are small partnerships, such as lawyers, auditors and doctors. Most small manufacturing firms are organised as simple hierarchies.

b. In a peer group, the most important coordination mechanism is mutual adjustment. There is no boss and no direct supervision. In a hierarchy, some people can tell other people what to do, so direct supervision is an important coordination mechanism.

c. The peer group sells its output, the proceeds of which are shared among the members of the peer group according to some sharing rules. In a hierarchy, the boss determines the rates of pay (within the rules of law in a country).

d. Peer groups do arise because of the advantages, for example, over a group of independent self-employed people. Some advantages are:
- Economies of scale in activities may be obtained.
- Economies of scale can be realised for capital goods. Members of a group can share equipment, machines and buildings. Economies of scale may also arise in information gathering.
- A peer group may have risk-bearing advantages over a group of independent self-employed people. Forming a partnership is one way to pool risk.
- A peer group can also be more productive. They can use each other's knowledge. Forms of labour specialisation are also possible. They can also stimulate each other to work hard or create feelings of responsibilities to do their share.

- There are more possibilities for reputation building compared to a single owner, because reputation does not depend on one person.
e.  In a small peer group, shirking may not be a problem. On the contrary, each member may take pride in doing more than his share. In a large peer group, however, shirking can become a severe problem.

## 8.8 Rock band

Suppose you are playing in a professional rock band consisting of six persons and you are doing quite well.
a.  What type of organisational mode would you choose? Explain your answer.
b.  What would be the most important coordination mechanism?
c.  Can we consider the rock band as a form of team production?
d.  Who would bear the risk in such a group?
e.  How would you solve the problems of adverse selection (hidden information), moral hazard (hidden actions) and free-riding of the members in the band?

## Answer 8.8 Rock band

a.  Possible organisational modes are: partnership, partnership firm, and private limited company.
b.  Three groups of coordination mechanisms can be used: the visible hand, the handshake and the visible hand, or a mix of them. For partnership and partnership firm, the handshake will be very important, especially mutual adjustment. In a private limited company, the handshake can also be used, but we often see a form of the visible hand such as authority or direct supervision (as in a hierarchy). The handbook can be used to determine rules for the members of the band. It is interesting to note that rock bands based on a hierarchy approach are better able to survive, for example the Rolling Stones, compared to those in which the handshake prevails.
c.  We can consider the rock band as a form of team production. Problems with team production are: hidden information, hidden actions (and, among others, a lack of credible commitment).
d.  In a partnership or a partnership firm, all the members are involved and in a private limited company it is the firm. The question is here: who owns this firm?
e.  We can make use of the mechanisms described in Figure 7.2 of the book. But we may expect that trustworthiness and the reputation mechanism will be very important.

## 8.9 Continuum of governance structures

According to transaction cost economics, why is a continuum of governance structures needed?

## Answer 8.9 Continuum of governance structures

Transaction cost economics (TCE) shows us why a continuum of governance structures is needed. According to TCE, the **characteristics of human decision-makers** and the **environmental characteristics of the transaction** determine the comparative advantages of a governance structure. Governance structures are a response to various transactional considerations. Transaction cost economics (TCE) tries to explain which institutional arrangement is most efficient for carrying out transactions. The empirical object of TCE is formed by the transactions carried out in governance structures[1]. The variety of ways of organising transactions found in the world reflects the fact that transactions differ in basic attributes. Based on this framework of attributes, we can determine which governance structure or organisational mode is efficient, or able to add value for the parties involved. See also Chapter 5 of the textbook.

## 8.10 Contracts and vertical relationships
a. Why are contracts becoming more and more important?
b. What could be the gain from more coordination and collaboration?
c. Which form can vertical relationships take?

## Answer 8.10 Contracts and vertical relationships
a. Contracts are becoming more and more important because fiercer global competition, rapid technological developments, and more choosy customers are forcing firms to seek more efficient production and distribution structures. In recent years, industries have shown increasing collaboration on issues of product development, quality guarantee systems (certification) and improved logistics. Spot markets are being replaced by contract production and systems of vertical coordination.
b. More coordination and collaboration may lead to improved efficiency in production and distribution channels, and to more product- and market innovations.
c. Vertical relationships can take many forms, like strategic alliances, long-term contracts, licensing, subcontracting, joint ventures, franchising, cooperatives, and networks.

## 8.11 Vertical coordination and vertical integration
a. What is the difference between vertical coordination and vertical integration?
b. Why is vertical coordination becoming more important in, for example, agrifood supply chains?
c. What mechanisms can be used for realising more vertical coordination and what is the final stage?
d. What does a higher level of vertical integration mean for the distribution of the control or decision rights in a chain?
e. What are costs-sharing contracts in terms of vertical integration?

## Answer 8.11 Vertical coordination and vertical integration
a. Vertical coordination refers to the alignment of activities of parties, for example, involved in production and distribution channels or chains. The level and intensity of vertical coordination depends on the types of governance structures used in the channel or chain, the distribution of the control rights, and the presence of a formal organisation in the chain that has an identity distinct from exchange actors, and that is designed to be their joint agent in carrying out coordination activities. Vertical integration is the creation of one organisation that has the coordination over all the transactions.
b. Vertical coordination is becoming more important in, for example, agrifood supply chains for different reasons:

---
[1] The governance structure is the dependent variable, see also Chapter 5.2.

- fiercer global competition, rapid technological developments and more choosy customers are forcing firms to seek more efficient production and distribution structures;
- consumers want higher and more uniform quality;
- private quality guarantee systems are introduced and have to be maintained;
- a greater need for more quality control and information exchange.

c. The mechanism for getting more vertical in agrifood supply chain makes use of contracting. Different types of contracts can be distinguished: classical, neoclassical, and relational contracts. They differ in duration, level of collaboration, intensity of coordination control, and level of vertical integration. The final stage is full vertical integration. Vertical integration is a way to have full direct supervision over all the stages of the production and distribution process in which you want to be involved.

d. The higher the level of vertical integration, the more the control or decision rights are centralised in a chain.

e. They are also a form of vertical integration, depending on the situation, backward or forward integration. See also question 7.27.

## 8.12 Vertical integration

a. What are the two endpoints of the spectrum of options for achieving vertical coordination?
b. What do we mean by in-house production?
c. What is the background of the **make or buy** decision?
d. Which hybrid forms of coordination mechanisms can we distinguish in Figure 8.2 of the textbook?
e. What does vertical integration mean as a process?
f. Can a firm be fully integrated?

## Answer 8.12 Vertical integration

a. The two ends of the spectrum of options for achieving vertical coordination are the spot market and vertical integration.

b. In the **make versus buy** decision, in-house production is called the *making by yourself solution, unified ownership* or the *do-it-yourself* option. It could involve bringing two (or more) separate organisations under unified direction.

c. The background of the **make or buy** decision: the choice available to the firm is whether it should make an intermediate good in-house, or secure it in some market or via contracts.

d. The hybrid forms of governance structures distinguished in Figure 8.2 are: classical, neoclassical, and relational contracts, and equity-based alliances.

e. Vertical integration means moving into the production of previous stages (backward integration) or subsequent stages (forward integration).

f. A firm cannot be fully integrated. For example, for a textbook publisher fully integrated would mean that it would also produce the inputs for producing paper, ink, computers and so on. The question is not whether a firm is fully integrated, but rather in what stages of the production process does the firm want to be involved.

## 8.13 Neoclassical economics and transaction costs view

a. Why does the neoclassical economics assumption that coordination and transaction automatically arises from the operation of the market not always hold?

b.  According to Williamson, what is the alternative?
c.  What do both views say concerning the type of the governance structure?

**Answer 8.13 Neoclassical economics and transaction costs view**

a.  In a world of bounded rationality and opportunistic (strategic) behaviour, the result of neoclassical economics that coordination and transaction automatically arise as a result of the market **does not always hold**. Coordination errors may exist, or transactions will not take place either because:
    *   they are intentionally created through the opportunism and hold-up activities of those with market power; or
    *   they are unintentionally created by the bounded rationality of economic actors who produce too much or too little, given the uncertainties of the market.
b.  Williamson argues that hierarchy (managed coordination) can be a substitute for markets (invisible - hand coordination) and the economic efficiency will thereby be increased.
c.  Both views stress that the type of governance structure does matter.

**8.14 Six governance structures**

a.  Please rank the six governance structures in Figure 8.2 of the text book from left to right according to the coordination role of the invisible and visible hand.
b.  How is 'coordination control' defined? What is the level of 'coordination control' in spot markets?
c.  What do control rights involve in the case of less than pure competition, e.g. monopoly?
d.  Are control rights different for classical, neoclassical and relational contracts?
e.  What characteristics must a relationship or a contract exhibit to be **relation-based**?
f.  Can each strategic alliance be regarded as a relation-based relationship? Please explain your answer.

**Answer 8.14 Six governance structures**

a.  The ranking of the six governance structures in Figure 8.2 of the text book from left to right according to the coordination role of the invisible and visible hand is: spot markets, classical, neoclassical contracts, and relational contracts, equity-based alliances, and vertical integration.
b.  The 'coordination control'[2] is the coordination carried out by the 'handbook' and the 'visible hand' because, going from left to right, this type of coordination is increasing, and in a hierarchy the control rights[3] are carried out by direct order.
c.  The level of coordination control for spot markets is low. In spot markets, the weaker party retains the right to walk away from the exchange, and the availability of substitute products puts external limits on the intensity of control rights that can be exercised as well.
    In cases of less than pure competition, e.g. monopoly, one actor can have a major influence over the establishment of the coordination conditions. To actors with this market power,

---

[2] The coordination carried out by the 'handbook' and the 'visible hand' can be considered as a kind of 'coordination control' because, going from left to right, this type of coordination is increasing and in a hierarchy the control rights are carried out by direct order. At the same time the role of the invisible hand is decreasing.

[3] For a definition of control rights see Chapter 3.6 of the textbook.

it would seem that they have coordination control rights to specify some of the terms of exchanges.

d. The control rights for classical, neoclassical, and relational contracts are different. With the specification of contracts, the intensity of control rights markedly increases from that related to spot markets. As explained, the most important coordination mechanism for contracts is the 'handbook'. However, the emphasis of this coordination mechanism is not the same for the three types of contracts.

- The most important reason is that the classical contract as governance structure is more closely located to the spot markets than neoclassical contracts. It means that the role of the price as coordination mechanism is more important for classical contracts than for neoclassical contracts. For classical contracts, the price is still the most important coordination mechanism and the role of the handbook is moderate.
- For neoclassical contracts, the role of the price decreases and role of the handbook increases. However, detailed handbooks for contracts can easily be interpreted as solidified distrust.
- The role of the price as coordination mechanism in a relational contract is less important than for the neoclassical and classical contracts. More than in the case of classical and neoclassical contracts, the 'handshake' as coordination mechanism can replace the role of the 'handbook' by making use of mutual adjustment, common values and norms, building up credible commitment and reputation.

e. To be **relation-based,** a relationship or a contract must exhibit at least the following characteristics: (1) mutuality in objective identification; (2) mutuality in controlling decision-making processes; as well as (3) mutuality in sharing risk and benefits. If there is a contract at all, it is a less detailed one.

f. Not every strategic alliance can be regarded as a relation-based relationship. It depends on the type of relationship and the type of contract. If strategic alliances are merely limited to the nature of legal classical supplier contracts, neither firm would achieve the broader working relationship that each wants for long-term viability. A neoclassical contract could make a difference; however it depends on the contract specifications and the duration. Therefore, the existence of a contract in an exchange relationship does not necessarily mean that the relationship is a relation-based alliance. To be relation-based, it must fulfil the characteristics specified in (e).

## 8.15 Governance structures
a. What key elements can be used for characterising governance structures?
b. For which governance structure is the personal relationship and restrictions on the choice of the partners less important? Explain why.
c. Which type of enforcement mechanisms can be distinguished?
d. For which type of governance structures is building up and preserving *reputational capital* very important?

## Answer 8.15 Governance structures
a. Key elements that can be used for characterising governance structures are coordination and motivation mechanisms, the identity of partners (personal relation or not), ex-ante restrictions

on the choice of a partner, duration, enforcement mechanism, financial participation (in the form of equity) and the degree of vertical (or horizontal) integration.

b. It is the spot market. The assumption of the anonymity of the market – as used in neoclassical economics – means: the identity of the partners does not matter; it concerns impersonal relations and there are no ex-ante restrictions on the choice of the partner. This can also hold for a classical contract, however to a lesser extent.

c. The type of enforcement mechanisms can be the court of law, the reputation mechanism, or authority.

d. The building up and preserving of *reputational capital* is especially important for relational contracts.

## 8.16 Modes of organisation and business groups

Most people work in an organisation of some kind; a business enterprise or a company, or perhaps a public sector organisation such as a hospital, a university or a government department. Almost everyone grows up in an organisation, called the family. There is a great variety in the groups in which people participate for a variety of reasons. Williamson's original formulation of markets and hierarchies paradigm has been criticised as being too narrow an approach to modern organisations. The criticism pertains to two related points:

- It is too simple to see markets and hierarchies as the only two *governance structures* for transactions: there is a third way of carrying out transactions.
- Markets and hierarchies should not be seen as two mutually exclusive *governance structures,* hybrid forms also exist.

a. Describe a number of organisational forms that fall in between markets and hierarchies. What are important elements of their coordination mechanisms?

b. What are business groups and how can they be characterised?

c. What are the advantages of a business group compared to a group of independent companies cooperating through market transactions?

## Answer 8.16 Modes of organisation and business groups

a. Based on Chapters 3 and 8 of the textbook, we can specify a number of organisational forms that fall in between markets and hierarchies. Important elements of their coordination mechanisms are as follows:

- Classical contract: price is important but less than in the spot market.
- Neoclassical contracts: see scheme in Figure 7.1, Figure 8.2 and Table 8.1 of the textbook.
- Relational contracts: the relationship itself is important. See scheme in Figure 7.1, Figure 8.2 and Table 8.1 of the textbook.
- Network: mutual adjustment, standardisation of norms (through socialisation or selection);
- Clubs: mutual adjustment and standardisation of norms.
- Cooperatives: see scheme in Figure 7.1, Figure 8.2 and Table 8.1 of the text book.
- Joint ventures: Figure 8.2 and Table 8.1 of the text book.
- Vertical integration: see scheme in Figure 7.1, Figure 8.2 and Table 8.1 of the text book.

b. A business group is a group of companies that do business in different markets under a common administration or central control. It consists of a group of legally independent firms, which are nevertheless bound together by one or more formal or informal ties. Formal ties include reciprocal shareholding between members of the group, interlocking directorates, companies owned in part by the same individual shareholders (or group of shareholders), cross-guarantees of bank loan, and trading of parts and supplies between group companies. Informal ties include family ties between managers of group companies, and managers of group companies belonging to the same social or ethnic group

c. The advantages of a business group compared to a group of independent companies cooperating through market transactions are:

- Business groups offer opportunities for reducing transaction costs. When the quality of institutions or the efficiency of the juridical system is poor, transaction costs may be very high. That may occur in capital markets, markets for consumer goods, and for managerial labour. A business group may be able to develop a good reputation. This will help to reduce information asymmetry and lead to a lower cost of capital for that business group's companies. A business group may also build a reputation for quality of consumer products and a common brand name. A company belonging to a business group can use the common brand name. This is a way to overcome the problem of hidden information. When well-trained managers are scarce, business groups may hire young management trainees and educate them through a management development program. For all these reasons, business groups play an important role in developing countries.
- Business groups may possess political influence that facilitates interaction with key government officials, which often leads to preferential access to permits and licences and the preemption of their use by potential entrants.
- Business groups may possess dynamic capabilities in setting up new ventures.

### 8.17 Equity-based alliance

a. To what mode of organisations do equity-based alliances belong?
b. What is characteristic for an equity-based alliance?
c. To which type of mode of organisation or governance structure do agriculture cooperatives and environmental cooperatives belong?
d. What is an important obstruction to walking away from such a mode of coordination mechanism or governance structure? What is this effect called?
e. What is an important key question concerning ownership in such organisations?

### Answer 8.17 Equity-based alliance

a. Equity-based alliances consist of a mixture of organisational forms that include joint ventures, business groups, partial ownership relationships, some forms of franchising, and other organisational forms that involve some level of shared equity capital between the actors in an exchange relationship.
b. An important characteristic of an equity-based alliance is that it involves some level of shared equity capital between the actors in an exchange relationship. Another distinguishing feature between equity-based alliances and relation-based alliances is the presence of a formal organisation that has an identity distinct from the exchange actors and that is designed to be their joint agent in the conducting of the coordination transaction.
c. Agriculture cooperatives belong to the organisational mode or governance structure 'equity-based alliance mode'. They have shared equity capital and a formal organisation. An environmental cooperative is also an equity-based alliance because it has shared equity capital.

d. An important obstruction to walking away from such a mode of organisation or governance structure is the substantial investment in the new independent identity. This is also called the lock-in effect.

e. The control rights in an equity-based alliance concentrate on the property rights of stakeholders in the independent entity created by the parties. In such organisations, an important key question is: who/which party has the residual control rights and who/which party is able to capture the residual income?

## 8.18 Vertical integration

a. What is another term for vertical integration?
b. What is the focus of control in such a single organisation?
c. What is characteristic for the governance structures as we move along the continuum from spot markets to vertical integration?

## Answer 8.18 Vertical integration

a. Vertical integration means the creation of one organisation that has control over the coordination of all the transactions. It is also called *in-house production* and in the make versus buy decision it is the *making by yourself solution*. It is also called *unified ownership* or the *do-it-yourself* option. It could involve bringing two separate organisations under a unified direction.

b. The focus of control rights in such a single organisation is defining property rights of key stakeholders (with the key question: who has the residual control rights and who is able to capture the residual income?). However, in this case the rights are in one surviving entity.

c. Characteristic for governance structures as we move along the continuum from spot markets to vertical integration is that the coordination mechanisms move from the invisible hand in spot markets to the visible hand in vertical integration. In between them we find the 'handbook' for classical, neoclassical and relational contracts and equity-based alliances. The the 'handbook' and 'visible hand' coordination mechanisms can be supported, partially substituted or complemented by the handshake. However, for the spot markets this is less likely, since the anonymity makes the identity of the partners irrelevant. The role of the 'handshake' can be important because it can reduce the coordination costs or, in terms of *quid pro quo,* the transaction costs.

## 8.19 Network and clubs

a. How is the relationship of networks and clubs oriented: vertically or more horizontally?
b. What is an important coordination mechanism for these organisational modes?
c. Why do intermediaries have greater incentives than an individual contract taker to invest in reputation capital?
d. What factors determine the value of reputation for intermediaries and clubs?

## Answer 8.19 Network and clubs

a. Networks, clubs based on self-organisations, and more formal clubs are more horizontal relationships.
b. For these modes of organisation, the handshake is an important coordination mechanism.

c. They have more transactions and the probability of re-transacting with a buyer is greater than the probability of re-contracting between a contract giver and a contract taker.

d. In general, the value of reputation is related to the frequency of similar transactions, the time horizon over which similar transactions are expected to occur, and the profitability of the transactions. For that reason, the incentives to build and maintain a *reputation* are larger:
   - especially for intermediaries, because of the number of transactions;
   - especially for clubs with overlapping generations of members, because of the long time horizon.

## 8.20 Organisational modes
a. What criteria typify the organisational forms of firms such as farms?
b. What stands out if we move from left to right across the spectrum of organisational forms?

## Answer 8.20 Organisational modes
a. The criteria are: ownership (including the separation of ownership and management), corporate status, liability, fiscal aspects, transaction costs, and cost of capital.
b. Moving from left to right across the spectrum, we see:
   - separation of ownership and management will increase as the organisational form shifts from single owner towards a private limited company;
   - co-ownership offers the possibility of building up reputation;
   - separation of ownership and management will increase;
   - who has residual control rights and who is able to capture the residual income becomes less clear;
   - transaction costs increase because of (1) the efforts that are put into reducing the problems of adverse selection and moral hazard and (2) giving incentives, both caused by making use of workers and managers;
   - more possibilities of sharing risk. An important difference between a private limited company and other organisational forms (to the left of the spectrum) is the reduced liability – and therefore risk – which in turn implies a lower cost of capital and possibilities for more large-scale activities;
   - more possibilities for specialisation of work and management;
   - more possibilities to spread fixed costs over more transactions;
   - the governance structure becomes more complex and more robust.

## 8.21 Dominance of the family farm
a. What three groups of arguments are used for explaining the dominance of the family farm?
b. Which factors influence the scale advantages?
c. Which factors refer to transaction costs?
d. Which factors refer to costs of production factors?

## Answer 8.21 Dominance of the family farm
a. The domination of the family farm as organisational mode in agriculture and horticulture is explained by: (1) the nature of the agricultural production process; (2) economic-organisational factors; and (3) costs of production factors.

b. The **nature of the production process** influences the possibilities for economies of scale. First, the economies of scale are limited by the spatial extent of land-bounded agriculture. This rapidly leads to relatively high internal transport costs. A second explanation is the season-bounded character of the different phases of agricultural production processes.

c. The economic-organisational factors refer to transaction costs. High transaction costs arise as a result of (1) technical difficulties in separating the successive phases of the agricultural production process in marketable or contractable transactions; (2) the uncertainty and complexity of the production processes, increasing the level of transactions costs.

d. Farmers (temporarily) bring their own labour, capital and land to their company for a much lower price than the common market price. An explanation for this can be found in: (1) the preference to be a farmer or market grower; (2) mobility-bounded values and norms of the group to which farmers belong; and (3) for an important part, the production factors are asset-specific – the costs of these production factors have become sunk costs, they have low opportunity cost, or a low salvage value. It is also a matter of lock-in effects.

## 8.22 Three organisational modes

The Hanson Clinic is a well-regarded medical centre located in a semi-rural area in the Midwest. One of its specialty areas is treating rare forms of cancer. To support this activity, Hanson wants to construct a new lab. The lab will require highly specialised equipment, a specially-designed building, and skilled staff. The estimated cost of the equipment and building is € 50 million.

The clinic is considering three possible organisational modes. The **first** is vertical integration. The **second** is outsourcing (where another company constructs the building, purchases the equipment and provides contractual services to the clinic). The **third** is to purchase the equipment and a building, and lease them to an independent operator (who would provide contractual services to the clinic).

a. Discuss the positive and negative sides of each of the three alternative structures.

b. What factors do you think are most important in making this choice?

## Answer 8.22 Three organisational modes

a. The table below gives a short overview of the pros and cons.

| Three organisational modes | Pros | Cons |
|---|---|---|
| Integration | Low hold-up problems. Possibility to have more control on the quality of production (independent contractor will have some incentives to shirk on quality). | Low-powered incentives for lab manager to care about costs, etc. |
| Outsourcing | High-powered incentives for the lab manager to cut costs and be efficient. | Hold-up problem. Might shirk on quality. |
| Leasing | Relatively low hold-up problem. High-powered incentives for the lab manager to cut costs and be efficient. | Low incentives for the lab manager to maintain the equipment. Might shirk on quality. |

b.  Relevant factors are: (1) do the firms have incentives to honour contracts and not engage in hold-ups? If so, that will tend to favour outsourcing. (2) Is it easy to observe whether the equipment has been maintained? If not, the leasing option is probably not very good. (3) What is the level of uncertainty? Higher uncertainty makes it more difficult to write complete contracts and makes outsourcing less desirable. (4) How hard is it to measure quality? Ease of monitoring quality will tend to favour outsourcing. (5) How important is it to provide incentives to the lab manager to cut costs? If this is important, outsourcing will be more desirable.

### 8.23 Organisational aspects
a.  Describe three important organisational aspects of a firm.
b.  What is a major difference between organisational aspects of markets and firms?
c.  Discuss the costs and benefits of decentralised decision making relative to centralised decision making.

### Answer 8.23 Organisational aspects
a.  The first is the assignment of control or decision rights; this assignment indicates who has authority to make particular decisions within the organisation. The second is the performance-evaluation system; this system specifies the criteria that will be used to judge the performance of agents within the organisation (for example, employees). The third is the reward system; this system specifies how compensation (and other rewards and punishments) will be distributed among agents within the firm.
b.  The coordination in markets is created spontaneously with little conscious thought or human direction. Through market transactions, property rights are reassigned so that decision making and specific knowledge are linked. Private property rights provide strong incentives for productive actions – they create powerful performance-evaluation and reward systems. Within firms, the coordination is created by management.
c.  The costs of decentralised decision making are agency costs, coordination costs and failures, and less effective use of central information. The benefits of decentralisation are more effective use of local knowledge, more time made available to top management, and training and motivation for local managers.

### 8.24 How to organise?
In a journal we found the following statement: 'Despite the weakness of a free market, the replacing of the market by the government generally makes the problem worse.'
a.  Is this statement not a too simple confrontation between the government and the market? Please give an explanation. What objections do you have?
b.  What modes of organisation should be taken into account?
c.  What does it mean to 'open the black box of the diversity of modes of organisation'?

### Answer 8.24 How to organise?
a.  The market cannot organise everything. Think, for example, of public goods. Public goods will generally not be produced by the market: they have large external benefits compared to private benefits, hence no private party would ever produce them, while society at large obtains large benefits from such goods.

b.  Apart from the 'extreme' cases of a free market and a hierarchy (e.g. government organisations) there are many other 'hybrid' forms for organising things. Think of firms, clubs, etc.
c.  Opening the black box of modes of organisation requires investigating how transactions and arrangements are carried out, for instance with the concepts of coordination mechanisms and market structures.

## 8.25 Separation of ownership and management
a.  What problems arise as a result of the separation of ownership and management?
b.  What theories enable us to analyse these problems?
c.  What are possible solutions?
d.  Compare and contrast the relative strengths and weaknesses of partnership and the private/public limited company.

## Answer 8.25 Separation of ownership and management
a.  The business goals of managers and owners tend to diverge. The managers are likely to act in their own interest, not in that of the owner.
b.  The principle-agent theory, the property rights theory and contract theory are suitable for analysing problems of this kind.
c.  Possible solutions include better means of monitoring for the owners, and providing incentives to the manager to perform her job in the desired way.
d.  For an overview of the relative strengths and weaknesses of various organisational forms, see Table 8.2 in the textbook.

## 8.26 Entry and exit costs
a.  Under what four alternative markets structures can firms operate?
b.  What will the market structure affect?
c.  What is in general the relation between competition and the entry and exit costs?
d.  When is a market said to be perfectly contestable?
e.  What is the relation between exit costs and sunk costs of a firm?

## Answer 8.26 Entry and exit costs
a.  There are four alternative market structures under which firms operate. In ascending order of firms' market power, they are: perfect competition, monopolistic competition, oligopoly, and monopoly.
b.  The market structure under which a firm operates will affect its conduct and its performance.
c.  The lower the entry and exit costs to and from the industry, the greater the threat of competition,
d.  If entry and exit costs are zero, the market is said to be perfectly contestable. Firms can freely enter the market, and sell their produce before a new entrant firm responds to their price.
e.  The lower the sunk costs of the firm, the lower the exit costs.

# 9. Ownership

## 9.1 Concept of ownership
a. Ownership is a well-known concept. However, why is the concept of ownership complicated? Could you give an explanation?
b. How can we interpret 'owning an asset'?
c. Why is 'owning an asset' so difficult to understand and to define?
d. What is often emphasised as marking the economic meaning of ownership?

### Answer 9.1 Concept of ownership
a. The concept of ownership is complicated, even for simple assets. The reason is: on the one hand an asset can be considered as a bundle of rights, and on the other hand an asset is intimately associated with the contractual incompleteness.
b. For economic analysis, it is often useful to interpret 'owning an asset' as having the residual control rights – that is the right to make any decisions concerning the asset's use, return, transfer of an asset that are not explicitly controlled by law or assigned to another by contract – and having the residual income.
c. If ownership means having residual control rights and having residual income, then its importance must derive from the difficulty of writing contracts that specify all the control rights. The difficulties are: what is residual, who has the residual control rights, and who is able to capture the residual income?
d. The income and transfer rights of an asset are often emphasised as marking the economic meaning of ownership.

## 9.2 Ownership as a vague concept and the incentive effects
a. Why is ownership often a vague concept?
b. What is key to the incentive effects of ownership?

### Answer 9.2 Ownership as a vague concept and the incentive effects
a. Ownership can be interpreted as having the residual control rights and the residual income. However, in practice, *residual control rights* and *residual income* can be quite fuzzy and vague concepts. The same holds for the allocation of residual control. In the case of a firm or organisation, where often different stakeholders are involved and different assets are brought in, it is not always simple to indicate who has the *residual control rights* and who can capture the *residual income*. That means that the ownership of a firm, organisation, or within a contractual relationship is often a vague concept.
b. Tying together residual control and residual income is key to the incentive effects of ownership. When it is possible for a single individual to have both the residual control and the residual income, the residual decisions made will tend to be efficient ones. This means that for efficient and effective property, a proper combining of the two aspects of ownership – the **residual control rights** and the **residual income** – is required.

## 9.3 Ownership according to the new property rights theory and old property rights theory
a. How can we define ownership based on new property rights theory and based on old property rights theory?

b.  Why is the question 'Who owns a large corporation' often so difficult to answer?
c.  Why is the concept of ownership considered to be fuzzy in the view of new institutional economics and economic organisation theory?
d.  Suppose we have a public limited company. Do the shareholders have the residual rights?
e.  What role can shareholders have?

**Answer 9.3 Ownership according to the new property rights and old property rights theory**
a.  Ownership can be defined as having the residual contract rights and being able to get the residual income. This definition is more based on the new property rights theory (also often called the incomplete contract theory). Ownership can also be defined as having the full control right, the full income rights, and the full transfer rights over the bundle of property rights of the assets involved. This definition is more based on the old property rights theory.
b.  From an economic perspective, different actors of a large corporation (shareholders, managers, board of directors, employees, etc.) may claim (parts of) ownership. Further, different actors or stakeholders have different interests, different types of information and different rights. A large corporation has also many assets and the following questions arise:
    *   Who has the control rights, i.e. the right to take all the decisions about the use, return and transfer of all the assets? These control rights can be split up in specific and residual control rights;
    *   Who has the residual control rights?
    *   Who has the residual income rights?
    Having both the residual control rights and the residual income rights is considered to be crucial for being the owner.
c.  The specific and residual control rights and the residual income rights are not always clear. It is also not always clear who has these rights. You can have 50% of the residual income (if it can be calculated) without having 50% of the residual control rights (see also question 7.3). So it can be fuzzy.
d.  The shareholders cannot set the dividends that are paid out for them. They have no role in investments or acquisitions decisions. They do not **hire and fire** the managers or set their pay, and have no say in setting prices. They have no rights in deciding on issues that are crucial to running the business. This means the shareholders often do not have the residual rights.
e.  By electing the directors, who are empowered to hire and fire management, they can indirectly affect decisions that are made. If the directors they elect do not follow their wishes, the stockholders can replace them as the opportunities arise. However, the formal definitions of residual rights are in terms of residual control rights and residual income that **are not explicitly** vested by contract or law. The written contracts leave them **few** or no residual rights. It means, shareholders' **rights** are not **residual**; instead, they are strictly delimited and enumerated.

**9.4 Private ownership and efficient agreements**
a.  In our society, ownership creates strong individual incentives. Is a system of private ownership always efficient for the society as a whole? Please give an explanation.
b.  Why is getting the property rights **right** still so important?
c.  What conditions can prevent efficient agreements?

### Answer 9.4 Private ownership

a.  A system of private ownership is not always efficient for the society as a whole. At least the following reasons can be mentioned:

- Pure public goods have the characteristics of non-excludability and non-rivalry. Because of the non-excludability of these goods it is impossible to define and specify private property rights.
- Providing some goods and services involves very high – and often for a large part – fixed costs. This is a result of the non-rivalry or indivisibility of the goods. The consequence can be that the private sector will not provide such goods. Examples of such goods are railways, highways, networks for supplying gas, water and electricity, large irrigation systems, etc.
- Having a single decision maker bearing all the risk in an asset's value may be incompatible with efficient risk sharing and impracticable if the amounts are large.
- Increasing the value of a particular asset often involves undermining competitors, setting monopoly prices, polluting or destroying the environment. These are all activities that cause inefficiencies.

b.  'Getting the property rights **right**' can improve our welfare, since a system of clear, enforceable and tradable private property rights will generate a socially efficient outcome.

c.  Reasons that may prevent efficient agreements are:
    1.  whether there are clear, enforceable property rights that can be transferred easily;
    2.  transaction costs can be high;
    3.  most people are loss-averse, as has been explained in Section 4.6;
    4.  weak institutions at different levels; and
    5.  a weak or bad government.

### 9.5 Ownership theory and efficient ownership

a.  What guidelines can be used to develop an ownership theory that maximises the value of used assets applied in an organisational mode?
b.  Which attributes determine efficient ownership?

### Answer 9.5 Ownership theory and efficient ownership

a.  Two important guidelines are: (1) the residual decisions made will tend to be efficient ones when it is possible for a single individual to have both the residual control rights and to receive the residual income; (2) properly **combining** the two aspects of ownership – **residual control** and **residual returns** – provides strong incentives for the owner to maintain and increase an asset's value.

b.  The attributes of transactions determining efficient ownership are: asset specificity; uncertainty, frequency and duration; difficulty of performance measurement; connectedness and co-specialised assets; non-excludability and non-rivalry of goods; and human capital.

### 9.6 Asset specificity and connected hold-up and lock-in effects

a.  What is the best ownership structure when an asset is specific to a particular use and connected with hold-up and lock-in problems?
b.  In Canada are there huge areas of tar sand with oil. For transporting this oil, special pipelines are necessary. What is the best ownership structure for the oil and pipeline?
c.  What could be a good alternative?

d. What is central in the ownership theory?
e. What elements are crucial for analysing efficient ownership?

**Answer 9.6 Asset specificity and connected hold-up and lock-in effects**
a. Firstly, when an asset is specific to a particular use, hold-up and lock-in problems for that asset can be avoided by having the assets in one organisation. Secondly, when two assets are both highly specific to the same use, the maximising value of assets requires using both together in that use.
b. The best solution is having both assets – oil from the tar sand and the pipeline – in one organisation; the user of the pipeline owns the oil and the pipeline. In general, the user of the asset also owns the asset.
c. A good alternative long-term contract.
d. A central point about ownership theory is that there will be a tendency for specific assets to be owned by those who use them, and for two co-specialised assets both to be **owned by the same person or organisation having both the residual control** rights and **residual income.** This is often called the ownership solution.
e. The hold-up and lock-in analysis is crucial for analysing efficient ownership structure.

**9.7 Uncertainty**
a. What could be a good alternative for full ownership?
b. What is important for such contracts?
c. Why is trust important for a long-term relationship?

**Answer 9.7 Uncertainty**
a. A good alternative could be a long-term contract.
b. Long-term contracts can create incentives to treat each other fairly and subsequently overcome problems of hidden actions and hidden information by way of the repeated relationships between the same parties over a period of years (which means a long-term relationship), trust, and building reputational capital. A good reputation can overcome problems of opportunistic behaviour, while a bad reputation increases the chance of opportunistic behaviour and hold-up problems.
c. Trust is important for a long-term relationship, because the longer the time horizon between performance (quid) and counter performance (quo) of the transaction, the more **trust** is needed.

**9.8 Frequency and duration**
a. Why are short-term (= classical) or mid-term (= neoclassical) contracts less satisfactory for a long period?
b. What role do the costs play for creating a special governance structure for carrying out transactions?

**Answer 9.8 Frequency and duration**
a. The **longer** the time period over which two parties might interact, the more difficult it will be to foresee and contract for all the relevant contingencies. Thus, the less likely it is that a (classical or neoclassical) contracting solution will be satisfactory.

b. When the fixed costs can be spread over more individual transactions, creating a special organisational solution could be preferable, for example, another governance structure including co-ownership.

## 9.9 Difficulty of performance measurements
a. Why does the ownership solution also have some disadvantages?
b. What would be an alternative for ownership if we are concerned that people will neglect certain responsibilities?
c. What is the disadvantage of the use of explicit performance-based pay?
d. When is it useful to base compensation on measured performances?
e. When is ownership a more preferable solution compared to the use of explicit performance-based pay?
f. When the motivation of the person to honour his or her other responsibilities is high, what is the best system?
g. Could you give some examples?

## Answer 9.9 Difficulty of performance measurements
a. **Firstly**, transferring ownership also means transferring the risk of fluctuations in value of the asset to a single individual who may find the risk very costly to bear. **Secondly**, the person who takes care of the asset also has other responsibilities in which performance is sometimes difficult to measure. These other responsibilities will be neglected unless strong enough incentives are established for the asset owner to devote some effort to them. If performance in the other responsibilities is difficult to measure, these incentives are costly and represent an added cost of transferring asset ownership.
b. An alternative could be the use of explicit performance-based pay. This alternative requires attempting to measure the person's performance.
c. The disadvantage is that it incurs an added measurement cost.
d. **Generally**: (1) When it is relatively cheap to measure performance accurately and (2) when the risks associated with asset ownership are relatively large, it is better to base compensation on measured performances than to shift to ownership. These risks could involve a reduction in the non-contractible quality.
e. When care is especially difficult or costly to measure and the risks of asset ownership are not too great, then the ownership solution should be preferred. Examples are medical specialists with their own clinics, or farmers who offer care facilities for disabled persons at their farm.
f. When the motivation of the person to honour his or her other responsibilities is *high*, the best system may be **to avoid** offering any formal **financial performance incentives**.
g. Many doctors, surgeons, teachers and scientific researchers are driven by intrinsic motivation. Knaves are driven by intrinsic motivation and they derive no benefit from the fact that the activity is of use to others. On the other hand, knights are driven by external motivation such as financial incentives[1].

## 9.10 Connectedness
a. What does connectedness of assets mean and what are the effects?

---
[1] See Chapter 4 of the textbook.

b. What is a strong form of connectedness? Could you give some examples?
c. What is a general principle about ownership structure and what does it mean for complementary assets?
d. What can be substitutes for ownership and which costs can be avoided?
e. What is important in that case?

**Answer 9.10 Connectedness**
a. This means that if one transaction has a high level of connectedness, then it will significantly increase the value of the other. Some transactions are largely dependent on others. As explained before, this gives rise to hold-up problems and lock-in effects.
b. When the assets are strongly complementary. For examples, see the textbook.
c. A general principle is that ownership should be structured to minimise distortions in investment decisions caused by **hold-up** and **lock-in** problems. It means that, other things being equal, **strongly complementary assets should be brought under co-ownership**.
d. Sometimes we can make use of substitutes for ownership, and these alternatives may avoid some of the influence costs of ownership. We can think about relational or global contracts, peer groups, partnerships, networks, franchising, joint ventures, and maybe clubs.
e. To be an excellent alternative, components of social capital such as trust, commitment and reputational capital are very important.

**9.11 Non-excludability and non-rivalry**
a. For what types of goods is private ownership impossible?
b. What are characteristics of pure public goods?
c. What kind of problems do we have with non-excludability and non-rivalry?
d. Could you give some examples?

**Answer 9.11 Non-excludability and non-rivalry**
a. Private ownership is impossible for goods which are non-excludable and non-rivalrous.
b. Pure public goods are non-excludable and non-rivalrous.
c. In the case of full non-excludability and non-rivalry, we have to deal with the problem of 'nobody's ownership' and at the same time with 'everyone's ownership'.

**9.12 Human capital**
a. Who can be the owner of a person's set of skills and knowledge?
b. When does non-transferability of human capital become problematic?
c. Does human capital create connectedness of transaction?
d. What is often characteristic for working in a team?
e. Could you give some examples of teams as governance structures?

**Answer 9.12 Human capital**
a. A person's set of skills and knowledge consists of assets that can only be owned by the person concerned.
b. Non-transferability of human capital is problematic when the skills are specific to an organisation or asset.

c. The connectedness of transactions can be a result of the people involved; for example, in the form of human capital.
d. Co-specialised skills and knowledge are often characteristic for working in a team.

## 9.13 Ownership and delegation
a. What is delegation?
b. How is the relationship between the parties governed?
c. What is transferred in a delegation relationship?
d. What does delegation mean for the residual control rights and residual income?
e. Is delegation a widespread phenomenon?
f. Give some examples of delegation by the government.
g. What could be a reason for delegation by the government?
h. What can the role of a third party be?

## Answer 9.13 Ownership and delegation
a. A person, firm or government can delegate certain tasks to another person, firm or organisation. In general, delegation can take place between different types of principals and agents and it occurs when a principal conditionally grants authority to an agent to act on his or her behalf.
b. The delegation relationship is – just like a relationship between a principal and agent – always governed as a contract, even if this contract is implicit (never formally acknowledged or informal; based on unwritten agreement).
c. In a delegation relationship, the principal transfers control rights including decision rights to the agent. In theory, the principal retains authority not delegated to the agent in the contract, including all rights to make decisions in contingencies relevant to principal control not defined in the contract.
d. The delegation relationship is governed by contracts. However, these contracts are mostly incomplete. This means that there are residual control rights and a residual income. The principal can often not avoid the possibility that the agents will receive some of these residual control rights or even a large part of them, and that the agents are able to capture the residual income. The actors – the principal and the agent – are defined only by their relationship.
e. Delegation is a widespread phenomenon. Both governments and firms delegate tasks. Delegation occurs between different types of principals and agents.
f. For example, governments delegate tasks and authority (= transferring control rights) to international organisations. Many countries delegate aid to international aid organisations. The Netherlands is member of the EU. It means that the Dutch government has delegated different tasks and authority to European Commission, the European Central Bank, etc.
g. One of the reasons that governments delegate tasks and authority to an international organisation is to enhance the credibility of its policy commitment. To increase credibility through delegation, two conditions must be met. **First**, the preferences of the agent must be stronger than those of the (national) government itself, so that, left to its own discretion, the agent will adopt a policy that moves the outcome in the direction that the national government knows it 'should' go but cannot implement itself. **Second**, there must be some costs to withdraw authority from the agent. Consequently, in some cases delegation can

be seen as a solution for opportunistic behaviour or **time inconsistency** of the (national) government.

h. Delegation can require monitoring of activities. A very useful form of monitoring the agent can be making use of a third party and this party sends credible signals to the principal (see also textbook section 4.2.6). The advantage of using a third party can be that the principal does not need to expend resources and the reported information is reliable.

**9.14 Pros and cons of delegation**
a. What are possible advantages of delegation?
b. What are possible disadvantages of delegation?
c. What is the optimal trade-off between both?
d. What types of problems can arise in a delegation relationship?

**Answer 9.14 Pros and cons of delegation**
a. Inherent in all forms of delegation is the principle of the division of labour. An advantage of delegation could be that tasks are delegated to a more or less specialised agent with the expertise, time, (superior local) information and resources to perform the tasks more efficiently. Without such gains from specialisation, there is little reason to delegate anything to anybody.
b. Delegation has as a disadvantage the loss of control rights. The principal can often not avoid the possibility that the agents will receive some of these residual control rights or even a large part of them, and that the agents are able to capture the residual income.
c. Therefore, determining the optimal degree of delegation involves a trade-off between the advantages of making use of specialised agents with the expertise, time, (superior local) information and resources to perform the tasks more efficiently and the loss of residual control rights and residual income.
d. The well-known principal-agent problems such as hidden information, hidden actions and the optimal contract can arise.

**9.15 Who 'owns' a project or a firm?**
a. What is crucial for answering the question who owns a project or firm?
b. What is the role of the shareholders? Can they be considered to be the owners of the firm?

**Answer 9.15 Who 'owns' a project or a firm?**
a. Crucial aspects are:
   • What are the returns of a project or a firm? Are they all one-dimensional, for example, are they all expressed in terms of money? Or, in other words, what are the residual elements?
   • Are all the revenues and costs observable to the different groups of people within the project or the firm?
   • Who owns the residuals, who has the residual control rights, and who is able to capture he residual income?
b. The shareholders nominally, and by law, own a public limited company. However, the shareholders cannot set the dividends that are paid out for them. They have no role in investments or acquisitions decisions. They do not **hire and fire** the managers or set their pay, and have no say in setting prices. They have no rights in deciding on issues that are

crucial to running the business. This means the shareholders often do not have the residual rights. In terms of having the residual control rights and the residual income, they are **not the owners** of a firm.

## 9.16 Ownership and property rights

When Henry Ford built his massive motor car assembly plant along the Rouge River in Dearborn Michigan, USA every stage of production was carried out onsite. Moreover, every kind of material required for producing Ford cars, from metals to minerals, was owned by the company. All company decisions were made by Henry Ford himself, the president and founder of Ford Motors.

a. In the case of the Ford Motor Company, who is the owner and what bundle of property rights characterise this ownership according to the 'old approach' and the 'new approach' to property rights theory?
b. What kind of 'good' was being produced at the Ford Motor plant in terms of its characteristics of consumption concerning excludability and rivalry?
c. Suppose the organisational structure of the Ford Motor company changed over time. Ford now sells shares of the company to outside investors and hires a CEO (chief executive officer) for strategic and operational decision-making. How would you explain the ownership of the company now, in terms of the 'new property rights theory'?

## Answer 9.16 Ownership and property rights

a. Henry Ford is the owner of this classical case of the capitalistic firm. As owner, according to the old property rights approach, he has the right: (a) to use the asset; (b) to appropriate the returns from the asset: (c) to change form, substance and location of the asset; (d) to exclude others; and (e) to transfer and sell the asset.

In view of the new property right approach, Henry Ford secured the ownership of his asset by controlling all decision-making rights, including decisions over all the materials he needed to produce the asset in order to prevent the hold-up problem. He was also the president and founder of the company and therefore secured the residual income rights as well.

b. It was a private good, with the characteristics of excludability and rivalry in consumption.
c. Given this new organisational mode, the residual control rights and the residual income rights may be divided between the CEO and the shareholders. In this case, the ownership would be incomplete. However, the possibility exists that the CEO could have more control rights than the shareholders if the CEO has the residual control rights over his own salary level and thus also control over his residual income. If this was the case, then the CEO would be the owner.

## 9.17 Firms financed by a combination of debt and equity

a. Who are the lenders? What do they provide?
b. What is the ultimate measure for the creditors to protect the value of the assets?
c. What does it imply for the directors?

## Answer 9.17 Firms financed by a combination of debt and equity

a. The lenders – banks, the purchasers of the firm's bonds, input suppliers who offer credit – are debt holders. They provide cash in return for a promise to be repaid a fixed amount (perhaps with interest) at a later date.

b. Forcing a firm into bankruptcy is an ultimate measure. Bankruptcy can be seen as an institutional arrangement to protect the value of assets. Once a firm is forced into involuntary bankruptcy, the creditors gain many of the *decision rights* and *control rights* that normally belong to equity holders or the managers.

c. The directors are not free to appropriate the profits for their own use. Because of that, in the case of bankruptcy they will not be able to capture the residual returns.

### 9.18 Financing firms

Many firms are financed by debt and equity. Debt holders are e.g. banks, purchasers of the firm's bonds, and input suppliers who offer credit. The shareholders take care of the equity.

a. Do the different groups of people that contribute to the financing of firms have the same claims on the returns, and the same interest? What are the effects?

b. Which group will favour risky investment and why?

c. What measures can debt holders take to protect themselves against potential moral hazard problems, like risky investments?

d. What is the ultimate protection of the debt holders?

### Answer 9.18 Financing firms

a. The debt holders – banks, purchasers of the firm's bonds, and input suppliers who offer credit – are lenders. They provide cash return for a promise to be repaid a fixed amount (perhaps with interest). The equity holders get to keep whatever profits are left after paying the debt obligations. The effect is that there is a difference in interests between the groups.

b. Equity holders will favour risky investments. They win big if the investments work out well. If the investment loses money, some of the loss may fall on the debt holders or creditors who are not fully repaid.

c. Lenders can do credit checks, monitor the performance, and structure the loans.

d. An ultimate measure is forcing the firm into bankruptcy. The threat of bankruptcy is a check on managerial moral hazard versus shareholders' interests, because managers will lose their jobs, their reputation, their perks, and maybe their pensions.

### 9.19 Whose interests should count?

a. Why is 'whose interests should count?' a difficult question?

b. Do you agree with the statement 'publicly held corporations should **not** be run simply in the interests of their shareholders'?

c. What would be the view of the free market economists?

d. What can happen if managers pursue goals other than maximisation of the value of the firms?

### Answer 9.19 Whose interests should count?

a. The question 'Whose interest should count?' is difficult to answer because different types of stakeholders are involved in a large corporation: shareholders, board of directors, managers, employees, banks, input suppliers, etc, and a large corporation also has many assets. Different stakeholders have different interests, different types and levels of information, and different rights.

b.  One could argue that companies, and especially publicly held corporations, should **not** be run simply in the interests of their shareholders only. People who agree with that, consist of at least two groups:

1.  the managers and employees of the corporations, and maybe other stakeholders such as banks and input suppliers; and
2.  a variety of academics and activists who believe that the pursuit of profits is either socially inappropriate or immoral.

    Both groups may characterise stockholders as uninvolved, absentee owners with no loyalty to the firm and no concerns but their narrow selfish interests in short-term financial gains. They are either unworthy of having their interests predominate or incapable of realising where their long-term interests actually should lie. Instead, the company should pursue **social aims** or should care for **the interests of all the people** who are actually involved in the organisation.

c.  Another opinion is that of investors (both private and institutional) along with the investment funds and stock-brokerage industries, as well as a set of free-market economists. This alliance argues that maximising the value of the firms enhances economic efficiency.

d.  Having managers pursue anything other than maximisation of the value of the firms entrusted to them is to invite calamitous self-serving moral hazard. What results is that the managers will simply pursue their own interests, perhaps adjusted to account for the interests of their allies.

## 9.20 Activist hedge funds

a.  What are activist hedge funds and what do they try to do?
b.  Whose interests count here?
c.  How can we characterise them?

## Answer 9.20 Activist hedge funds

a.  Activist hedge funds take positions in firms quoted on the stock exchange. They try to change the strategies of these firms or to sell important parts of these firms.
b.  These funds aim for high short-term profits for the shareholders. They have completely other interests than the managers or the workers in the firm.
c.  We can characterise these shareholders as uninvolved, absentee owners with no loyalty to the firm and no concerns but their narrow selfish interests in short-term financial gains.

## 9.21 Ownership and vertical integration

a.  What does ownership mean in the old classical capitalistic firm?
b.  What is the difference between ownership rights in a single organisation, for example resulting from vertical integration, and ownership in a classical capitalistic firm?

## Answer 9.21 Ownership and vertical integration

a.  In the classical capitalistic firm, the owner has: (1) full *control rights* (i.e. final authority over all of the policies pursued by the firm); (2) full *income rights* (i.e. the non-restricted right to the firm's residual); and (3) full *transfer rights* (i.e. complete freedom to assign his rights, in whole or in part, to others). The owner of a capitalistic firm has therefore not only the control rights over the bundle property rights but also the right to the residual income. This means that in the case of private property, the bundle of property rights (with all the rights) is completely allocated to one person. This person also has at his disposal the *residual rights of control* and the *residual income*.

b. A firm as single organisation, resulting from vertical integration, could be a firm with more owners, e.g. a public limited company (Plc). A Plc is as an enterprise private property (= property regime). However, in this case, private property does not coincide with individual property. The bundles of property rights of all the assets do not belong to one person after all: different groups of people in the form of shareholders, managers, commissioners, employees, external capital providers, suppliers and buyers are involved. It is an organisation in which various interested parties (also called stakeholders) work together. There is no single person who has the use-right, the right to capture the profits, the right of changing the form, substance and location of assets that are used in the firm and the right to exclude others and the transfer rights.

## 9.22 Family firms

One of the salient characteristics of the history of industry is the transition from family firms to large factory-style corporations. Large corporations dominate the modern economy. Agriculture is one of the sectors which has largely resisted the transition to large corporate firms. However, the family firm is not an univocal concept. It can range from a 'single-owner firm' to a firm in which, for example, four brothers have a private limited company with more than 50 workers. Further, the four brothers can have all the shares and the specific control rights.

a. How can a quasi-rent arise?
b. What are the advantages of the family firms concerning the quasi-rent? Is this different for a firm with a single owner?
c. Which criteria can be used to classify firms as a family firm and as a non-family firm?
d. Which problem arises if ownership and management are separated?
e. Suppose you are the owner of a firm. To whom should you give the control rights, i.e. the right to take any decision about the use of the assets of a firm?

## Answer 9.22 Family firms

a. Quasi-rents arise as a result of asset-specific investments (or sunk costs) and a low salvage value, i.e. a relatively low return of the asset outside the firm.
b. If the family firm creates a quasi-rent, this rent will accrue to the family. It means there are no distribution problems with a third party. Further, it is also an incentive to work hard. In the case of single ownership, there are no distribution problems at all. However, for example, in a family firm with four brothers (e.g. with a private limited company as organisational mode) who have all the shares and the specific control rights also, the distribution of the quasi-rent can be more complex. In a non-family firm such as a public limited company, it is even more complex, because different parties are involved: the managers, shareholders, workers, etc.
c. Criteria which can be used to classify firms in different modes of organisation:
   • The separation of ownership and management;
   • In contrast with large corporations, in family firms there is mostly no separation of ownership of the shares and management;
   • Who has shares? Do they belong to the family?
   • Who has the specific control rights? Do they belong to the family?

- Who has the residual control rights of the firm? Do they belong to the family?
- Who has the residual income of the firm? Do they belong to the family?
- The legal entity;
- The transfer to the new generation. Does the firm stay in the family?

d. If ownership and management are separated, incentive problems will arise.

e. The person with the least benefits (or least incentives) for shirking about the use of assets of the firm.

## 9.23 In-house production

In explaining the recent acquisition of a supplier, an executive made the following argument: 'We purchased the supplier so that we could keep the profit rather than pay it to some other firm'. Evaluate this argument.

## Answer 9.23 In-house production

This argument is dubious. It is in the economic interests of both firms to choose the ownership structure that maximises value. This value can be influenced by adjusting the (purchase) price of the product. If more value is created by outsourcing, the firm can demand a price that yields at least the same profits. It can share in the additional value that is created by choosing an efficient organisational arrangement if it negotiates a lower price. Gains from in-house production can be a result of the avoided hold-up and lock-in effects or, more in general, from incentive effects driven by efficiency arguments to unify both firms into one organisation.

## 9.24 Team owners or club owners and the players

In certain professional sports, team owners or club owners 'own' the players. Owners can sell or trade players to another team. However, players are not free to negotiate with other team owners on their own behalf. The team owners initially obtain the rights to players through an annual draft that is used to allocate new players among the teams in the league. They can also obtain the rights to players by purchasing them from another team. Players do not like this process and often argue that they should be free to negotiate with all teams in the sporting league. In that case, they would be free to play for the team that offers the **most desirable contract**. Owners argue that this change in rights would have a negative effect on the distribution of talent across teams. In particular, they argue that all the good players would end up in rich teams with a lot of media attention such as New York or Los Angeles (because these teams could afford to pay higher salaries) for baseball and for soccer it would be Chelsea or Real Madrid. The inequity of players across teams would make the sport less interesting to fans and thus destroy the league. Do you think the owners' argument is correct? Explain.

## Answer 9.24 Team owners or club owners and the players

In the absence of contracting costs, the assignment of players to teams is not likely to be greatly influenced by who has the property right to decide where the player plays (the Coase theorem). Rather, both the owners and the players will have incentives to have players play at locations where they create the most value. For instance, suppose the Minnesota team has the right to a player who is more highly valued in Los Angeles. The owner of the Minnesota team will have the incentive to sell the player to Los Angeles. If the player can decide where to play, he is likely to choose Los Angeles because they will offer him more money. What does vary between the two ownership systems is the distribution of wealth. The owners are better off under the current system and thus have incentives to argue on its behalf. New York and Los Angeles are likely to have strong teams under either system. However, the argument that they will get 'all the good players' is unlikely to be valid. Once these teams have a sufficient number of stars, the marginal value of additional stars is likely to be lower for the big-market teams than for small-market teams which have fewer star players.

### 9.25 Case about state-owned enterprises in Russia

Since 1992, approximately 70,000 state-owned enterprises in Russia have been privatised. Many of the private buyers were foreign companies and investors, for example from the United States and Western Europe. The idea was to move from a centrally planned economy to a market system. Yet in the late 1990s, a weak economy caused great concern among Russian voters. Politicians, such as Moscow's mayor Yuri M. Luzhkov began promoting 'deprivatisation' or, as the locals put it, *deprivatizatsia*. Under this policy, certain past privatisations would be declared illegal and the transactions would be reversed. The company then either would be run as a state-owned enterprise or sold to another party. For example, in October 1999, a court stripped Wall Street's Kohlberg Kravis Roberts Factory in St. Petersburg. These companies had purchased the factory in 1998, but the courts ruled that the company's initial privatisation five years earlier was illegal. Sources suggested that the company was likely to be resold to Soviet-era managers who were set to lose their jobs when the new investors entered the picture.

Politicians such as Luzhkov vow that not all privatisations will be reversed – only the illegal ones. But the current problem is that privatisation legislation is nebulous about what could be termed a violation. Anything from a missing piece of paper in the original paper tender offer, to investment requirements not being met might be ruled to be a violation. And virtually anyone could file a complaint to trigger an inquiry into a past deal.

### Discussion questions:

a. What impact will the prospect of deprivatisation have on investment by managers of privatised firms?
b. What effect will deprivatisation have on foreign investment in Russia?
c. Do you think that mass deprivatisation is in the long-run best interests of Russia?
d. Who gains from deprivatisation? Who loses?
e. Assuming more people are hurt by deprivatisation than helped, why would a local politician support such a policy?

### Answer 9.25 Case about state-owned enterprises in Russia

a. Managers will be reluctant to make longer-term investments if they think there is a high probability that the company will be deprivatised. In calculating the value of this investment, they must consider the increased possibility that the gains will go to someone else. Short-term investments, where the gains are realised more quickly and can be paid out to the owners (e.g. in dividends), would be affected somewhat less.
b. Foreign investment is likely to decline with an increased threat of deprivatisation. The threat of losing the investment through this governmental action reduces the expected benefits of the investment.

c. Probably not. There will be some immediate transfer of wealth from foreign businesses to some Russian citizens and the government. However, the long-run implications of reduced foreign and company investment are likely to be quite costly.

d. Russian politicians/bureaucrats might gain on the sales of the companies, which provide additional resources to be controlled by governmental bureaucrats. The Soviet-era managers might also gain if they obtain the company at a below-market price. Foreign owners, current managers, and the Russian people (who lose from reduced investment, jobs, etc.) are likely to be hurt.

e. Government officials have incentives to take actions that benefit themselves. To the extent that these officials get additional resources, votes, side payments (from the new buyers), etc., they may support actions that hurt the general population (the general population, for example, does not have enough information or individual incentives to hurt the officials – e.g. by forming a coalition to get someone else elected).

## 9.26 Country club and price membership

Locust Hill Golf Club is a private country club. It charges an initiation fee of $ 32,000. When members quit the club, they receive no refund on their initiation fees. They simply lose their membership. Salt Lake Country Club is also a private golf course. At this club, members join by buying a membership certificate from a member who is leaving the club. The price of the membership is determined by supply and demand. Suppose that both clubs are considering installing a watering system. In each case, the watering system is expected to enhance the quality of the golf course significantly. To finance these systems, members would pay a special assessment of $ 2,000 per year for the next 3 years. The proposals will be voted on by the members. Do you think that the members are more likely to vote in favour of the proposal at Locust Hill or for the one at Salt Lake Country Club? Explain.

## Answer 9.26 Country club and price membership

At Locust Hill the members do not have an alienable property right. If they pay for the improvement they must play the course to get any benefits. Members who expect to leave the club in the near future (older members and people who are more likely to be transferred their jobs) are less likely to support the proposal. They bear the full costs (assuming they will be there three years) and receive limited benefits. At the Salt Lake club, members leaving the club can sell their memberships. They will favour the new investment as long as the increase in the value of the membership is greater than the investment costs (it is a positive net present value project). Thus the members at the Salt Lake Country club are more likely to approve the proposal.

## 9.27 Membership fee

Some tennis clubs charge an up-front fee to join and a per-hour charge for court time. Others do not charge a membership fee but charge a higher per-hour fee for court time. Consider clubs in two different locations. One is located in a suburban area where the residents tend to be of similar age, income, and occupation. The other is in the city with a more diverse population. Which of the locations is more likely to charge a membership fee? Explain.

### Answer 9.27 Membership fee

Two-part pricing is most likely to be optimal when consumers are relatively homogeneous. In this case, the up-front fee will be used to extract the consumer surplus. If demands are heterogeneous, setting a high up-front fee will extract surplus from some customers but discourage potential customers with lower valuations from purchasing the product. Thus, you might expect to see the two-part pricing at the suburban location with a more homogeneous customer base.

# 10. The economics of property rights

## 10.1 Approaches within the property rights theory
a.  What two important approaches can we distinguish in the property rights theory?
b.  What do those terms mean?

## Answer 10.1 Approaches within the property rights theory
a.  There are two important approaches to the property rights theory: the old and the new approach. The **old** approach deals with (1) property as a bundle of property rights and (2) property rights regimes, and the **new one** with property as having residual control over an asset, and having residual income of an asset.
b.  The terms old and new can give some confusion. It does not mean old-fashioned (and therefore not relevant) vis-à-vis modern. Old refers rather to a longer history in the literature. The new property rights approach is strongly linked to the incomplete contract theory. The incomplete contract theory is of a recent date; the new *property rights approach* is also called the incomplete contract theory.

## 10.2 The old property theory
a.  What does the old property right theory deal with?
b.  To what does *property as a bundle of rights* refer?
c.  To what do *property regimes* refer?
d.  What are the differences between property as a bundle of rights and property regimes?

## Answer 10.2 The old property theory
a.  The old approach deals with (1) *property as a bundle of rights* and with (2) *property regimes.* In the case of *property as a bundle of rights,* property is seen as a set of rights. These rights describe what people may and may not do with resources; the extent to which they have them at their disposal, can use, transform, transfer them or exclude others from their property. The old property theory assumes: (1) the rights of the property holder and obligations of the other people in relation to the object are at the forefront; (2) they are instrumental by nature; and (3) they are protected by the government.
b.  *Property as a bundle of rights* refers to the rights of an individual, which include the type of the rights and permitted actions.
c.  *Property regimes* refer to property systems for resources or for firms in a nation or in a region. They consist of government, private, common, or non-property regimes.
d.  Important differences between *property as bundle of rights* and *property regimes* are:
    *   *property regimes* are found at a higher aggregation level than *property as a bundle of rights.* A bundle of certain property rights is used within a certain property regime.
    *   property regimes are not transferable via the market (this is because they are at a higher aggregation level, where the market is not used as a *governance structure*) whereas the rights which make up part of the bundle of property rights are often tradable via the market.

## 10.3 The new property rights theory
a.  What does the new property rights theory deal with?

b. What is another name for the new property rights approach?
c. What does it mean to be an owner according to the new property right theory?

**Answer 10.3 The new property rights theory**
a. The new property rights approach is oriented towards: What does it mean to own an asset? The economic importance of ownership depends on the owner's ability to exercise residual rights of control over the assets. In fact, possession of residual control rights is virtually taken to be the definition of ownership. In many cases, the holder of residual control rights will, to a large extent, also have the residual income rights. Both are often complementary, therefore residual control and residual income often (should) go together. With the approach that property is '*having control over an asset and having the residual income at one's disposal*' the **economic meaning of property** is paramount.
b. The new *property rights approach* is also called the incomplete contract theory.
c. According to the *new property rights approach,* the owner has the *residual control rights* and the right to the *residual income*. In other words, being an owner of an asset means holding control rights and the residual income rights of an asset.

**10.4 Property as a bundle of rights**
a. What types of property rights can be distinguished?
b. What types of rights does the owner of the classical firm have?
c. How can rights be made effective?

**Answer 10.4 Property as a bundle of rights**
a. Rights of the bundle of property rights (Table 10.1).

Table 10.1 Rights of a bundle of property rights.

| | | |
|---|---|---|
| The right to use an asset | *usus* | or user rights |
| The right to appropriate the returns of an asset | *usus fructus* | or income rights |
| The right to change the form, substance and location of the asset | *abusus* | or alteration rights |
| The right to exclude others | | exclusion rights |
| The right to transfer | | Transfer rights |

b. In the classical case of the owner of the capitalistic firm the owner has: (1) full *control rights* (i.e. final authority over all of the policies pursued by the firm); (2) full *income rights* (i.e. the non-restricted right to the firm's residual income), and (3) full *transfer rights* (i.e. complete freedom to assign his rights, in whole or in part, to others) over all the assets.
c. Rights can only be effective if there is an authority in place prepared to protect or enforce the interests of rights holders in certain specific situations. In most countries, it is often the government.

**10.5 Property: having residual control rights and residual income**
a. What does it mean to have residual control rights?
b. What does it mean to have residual income rights? And what is the residual income?
c. What is necessary for an efficient and effective ownership?

## Answer 10.5 Property: having residual control rights and residual income

a. Having the *residual control rights* is the right to make any decision concerning the asset's use, return and transfer that are not explicitly controlled by law or assigned to another person (or organisation) by a contract.

b. The *residual income rights* are related to residual income, which is the amount that remains from the gross return of a company, activity, good or service after all the remaining contractual commitments are fulfilled.

c. For efficient and effective property, properly combining the two aspects of ownership – the residual control rights and the residual income – is required.

## 10.6 Synthesis of old and new property rights approaches

a. Is there a strong contrast between the *old property right approach* and the new one?

b. Give some examples why it is important to make use of both approaches.

## Answer 10.6 Synthesis of old and new property rights approaches

a. These two approaches are not so much a matter of a contrast, but rather, they can be seen as being complementary. They are two sides of the same coin.

b. Some example are:

The **first** example is the old classical capitalistic firm. In such a firm the owner has: (1) full *control rights*; (2) full *income rights*; and (3) full *transfer rights*. The owner of a capitalistic firm therefore not only has the control rights over the property rights but also the right to the residual income. This means that in the case where private property (= property regime) and the bundle of property rights (with all rights) is completely allocated to one person, this person also has the *residual rights of control* and the *residual income* at his disposal.

A **second** example concerns a firm with more owners, such as a Plc. A Plc is as an enterprise private property (= property regime). In this case, private property does not coincide with individual property. The bundles of property rights of all assets do not belong to one person after all: different groups of people in the form of shareholders, managers, commissioners, employees, external capital providers, suppliers and buyers are involved. It is an organisation in which various interested parties (also called stakeholders) work together. There is no single person who has the use-right, the right to capture the profits, the right of changing the form, substance and location of assets that are used in the firm, the right to exclude others, and the right to transfer rights.

The shareholders can not hire and fire people. In modern large firms, the shareholders (= owners in a juridical sense) are no longer the ones who have, or practise, the power of decision-making. This brings up the question of who is the owner of a firm such as a public corporation? It is therefore better to make use of the concepts of having residual control rights and residual income when determining the ownership of such firms or organisations. The ability to have the residual control rights and of capturing the residual income determines *in fact* which people, or groups of people, are the owners.

A **third** example is the leasing of land. In the old capitalist firm approach, the owner of a large farm has the full *control rights* over all the production means, full *income rights* and full *transfer rights*. Leasing to tenant farmers means that the landowner transfers a part of the bundle of the bundle property rights to the tenant. It concerns the control rights over a part of the bundle of property rights and the income rights. Leasing out is a two-sided transaction mechanism: the transfer of (a part of) the bundle of property rights versus the counter performance. The counter performance is the lease price being paid. For land, as well as for many other assets, it is possible to lease the user rights out to another party for a certain period of time, without leasing out the full transfer rights.

### 10.7 Property regimes
a.   What types of property regimes can we distinguish?
b.   What is essential for any property regime?
c.   What problems are related to common property regimes?
d.   What is a major distinction among property regimes?

### Answer 10.7 Property regimes
a.   Bromley[1] distinguishes four possible property regimes:
1.   government property regimes;
2.   private property regimes;
3.   common property regimes;
4.   non-property regimes.
b.   An essential aspect for any property regime is that an authority system is able to ensure that the expectations of rights holders are met. Compliance, protection and enforcement by an authority system are necessary conditions for the viability of any property regime. Private property would be nothing without the requisite of the authority system to make certain that rights and duties are adhered to. The same requirements hold also for common property. If the authority system does not function well or if it breaks down – for whatever reason – then the management, or self-management, of the resource use cannot be carried out any longer. Common property – in that case – degenerates into *'open access'*.
c.   There are two problems related to the *common property regime*. **First,** a breakdown in compliance by co-owners may be difficult to prevent. When, due to developments elsewhere in the economy, the co-owners have hardly any alternatives, maintaining the property regime will lead to loss of opportunities. However, if application of privatisation precludes seasonal adaptation to fluctuating resource conditions, then overuse of a local resource may be necessary for members of the group. **Second**, if the government holds common property in low esteem – that is if the government disregards the interests of those segments of the population largely dependent upon common property resources – then external threats to common property will not receive the same governmental response as would a threat to private property. The willingness of the government to protect and enforce the *common property regime* is less strong than with private property regime.
d.   A major distinction is the decision-making process. In the private property regime, usually the private owner decides what will be done. The common property regime requires consensus among all the co-owners before a specific action can be taken. The transaction costs associated with this, and the required measures to solve the problems of **group size** (e.g. leading to congestion) and **free-riding**, are seen as disadvantages of the common property regime.

---

[1] Bromley, D.W., 1991. Environment and economy. Property rights and public policy. Basil Blackwell, Cambridge, MA, USA, p. 23.

## 10.8 Quality of bundle of property rights
a. What factors are also important for the quality of the bundle of property rights?
b. What can be an effect of a change in the people's preferences?
c. What is the effect of a high level of theft?
d. What is the relationship between quality of the bundle of property rights and transaction costs?

### Answer 10.8 Quality of bundle of property rights
a. Other important aspects for the quality of the bundle of property rights include:
   - the institutional environment, for example, the formal rules about the lease regulation. The informal and formal rules in the society also determine the level of theft. The quality of the property rights is influenced by the level of theft.
   - The way people think about status and the allocation of the property rights. The institutional environment – in which the property rights are embedded – is not a constant factor, nor is the status and the allocation of the property rights. Because of the changes in the institutional environment, these rights are not fixed; they may change from one generation to another. This is revealed in the way that the government recognises and protects property rights.
b. The status and allocation of the property rights can also change as a result of shifting of people's preferences. For example, citizens are feeling that the environmental quality (e.g. greenhouse effects) is going to decline, and they want to prevent this. This is revealed in a shift of people's preferences. Shifting preferences lead to a change in the *optimal level* of environmental quality. This means that by shifting preferences, the *reference level* also changes. Shifting values and changing perceptions, for example, about the role of agriculture, will surely bring about a shift in property rights and policy entitlements.
c. Theft is not only a transfer of an asset, but it also has a direct efficiency consequence, because a high level of theft means weak or insecure property rights. It also brings a society in a hold-up situation. The reluctance to invest when property rights are insecure results in inadequate maintenance and development of assets.
d. A low degree of excludability of a good and a low protection and enforceability of property rights will involve higher transaction costs.

## 10.9 Characteristics of property rights
a. Name a number of characteristics which can be used to describe the quality of a bundle of property rights.
b. Why are these characteristics so important? Please give an example.

### Answer 10.9 Characteristics of property rights
a. Property rights can be described in terms of:
   1. degree of control rights;
   2. division of rights;
   3. protection of the rights;
   4. duration;
   5. flexibility;
   6. enforceability;

7. degree of transferability.

b. These characteristics affect the quality of the bundle of property rights. For example, enforcement of property rights makes it possible to exclude others from the use. Exclusive ownership requires expensive measures for the delineation of resources and enforcement of property rights. The value of exclusive property rights depends, ceteris paribus, on the costs of enforcement of the rights, in this case the cost of excluding others. This ultimately depends on the deployment of force. Individuals as well as the government usually undertake enforcement of exclusive property rights. Enforcement by the government increases the value of privately owned assets and constitutes one of the cornerstones of the market economy. In areas where the government does not help to enforce contracts, or even property rights, this outrightly prohibits possession and exchange, due to high transaction costs. The costs of enforcement of exclusive rights are lower if the population follows the social norms, which coincide with the basic structure of rights that the government attempts to maintain. The disintegration of social norms can have important economic consequences.

## 10.10 First welfare theorem
a. What does the first welfare theorem state?
b. What is a Pareto-efficient situation?
c. What does the first welfare theorem imply for a Pareto-efficient situation?
d. What does the first welfare theorem say about the equity?

## Answer 10.10 First welfare theorem
a. The first welfare theorem states that the allocation of goods and inputs that arise in general competitive equilibrium is economically efficient. That means, given the resources available to the economy, there is no other feasible allocation of goods and inputs that could simultaneously make all consumers better off. Such an equilibrium gives a Pareto optimum for the economy as a whole and is therefore Pareto-efficient.
b. In a Pareto-efficient situation, it is not possible to increase the welfare of one or more individuals without decreasing it for one or more other individuals.
c. The first welfare theorem states that the equilibrium in a set of markets with full competition is Pareto-efficient. This means that given a Pareto-efficient allocation, it is always possible to find a set of prices that offers market equilibrium under a number of specific assumptions. These assumptions are:
   - The preferences of consumers are convex, i.e. the indifference curves are convex (the round side is twisted towards the origin).
   - The production functions are concave.
   These are the usual neoclassical assumptions concerning utility functions and production functions[2]
d. The first welfare theorem says nothing about the equity.

## 10.11 second welfare theorem
a. What does the second welfare theorem state?

---

[2] See also Varian, H.R., 2006. Intermediate microeconomics. A modern approach. Norton & Company, New York, NY, USA, pp. 579-588.

b. What is implied by the second welfare theorem?

c. According to the second welfare theorem, how can a specific income distribution be achieved?

## Answer 10.11 Second welfare theorem

a. The second welfare theorem states that, under certain conditions, every Pareto-efficient allocation can be achieved by some set of competitive prices.

b. The second welfare theorem implies that the issues of efficiency and distributional fairness (= equity) can be separated. If society deems the current distribution of resources to be unfair, it need not interfere with market prices and impair efficiency. Rather, society should transfer resources (including property rights) among people in a way deemed to be fair. The second welfare theorem evaluates the implications of a specific income distribution.

c. A specific income distribution can be attained by the redistribution of purchasing power. This can be achieved by:

1. changing the distribution of the original resources which are at their disposal between these individuals, or by

2. redistributing the purchasing power resulting from the income earned by these resources, by the tax system.

Examples of (1) are:

- Allocating property and user rights of land, water and fishing grounds to certain groups of people.

- Education and extension programmes leading to a more equal distribution of human capital and offering more possibilities to generate income by the (better) use of labour, capital and land.

Examples of (2) are more difficult to find. Imposed taxes must not disrupt the allocated efficiency on markets. This means that taxes must not disturb the pattern of relative prices (and opportunity costs), by which individuals make their choice. Taxes must not shift the use of production factors. They must be as much as possible production-neutral. This means that the excess burden of the taxes should be zero or at least as low as possible.

## 10.12 Basic ideas of the Coase theorem

a. What are the assumptions of the Coase theorem?

b. What does the Coase theorem assume about the assignment of rights?

c. What is an important implication of Coase theorem?

## Answer 10.12 Basic ideas of the Coase theorem

a. In its strong form, the Coase theorem asserts that the initial assignment of property rights makes no difference to efficiency because identical Pareto-optimal allocations will emerge. For realising this interesting outcome, key assumptions are: (1) costless negotiations; (2) fully defined property rights; and (3) the absence of wealth effects. In this special environment, the tranaction costs are zero.

b. The assignment of rights has no effect on (efficient) allocation and has no wealth effects. The Coase theorem only refers to efficiency, and does not evaluate the fairness in the assignment of the rights.

c. By awarding property rights for land, water, fishing and so on, a society can achieve a more equal income distribution. Keeping fairness considerations in mind, property rights can be allocated in such a way as to achieve a more equitable income distribution without adversely affecting allocation efficiency. This fits within the second welfare theorem.

### 10.13 Application of the Coase theorem
a.  What is stated by the Coase theorem concerning external effects? And what does this mean for environmental protection?
b.  What is the start situation in the water case in the textbook, Section 10.3?
c.  How can negative effects for bulb growers, such as the use of water by a factory, be removed?
d.  Does the initial assignment of property rights influence efficient allocation? And what is the effect on income distribution?

### Answer 10.13 Application of the Coase theorem
a.  The Coase theorem states that by giving property rights, negotiation between the parties involved internalises the external effects and leads to a Pareto-efficient situation. Negotiations between the parties involved, without government interference, will lead to efficient allocation or a better protection of the environment.
b.  The start situation is free access of a rivalry good, i.e. water.
c.  Solutions are:
   *   Introducing rules of law through which (1) the bulb growers would eventually be forced to end their activities; or (2) the factory has to get the water from elsewhere.
   *   End free access and assign the property rights to one of the parties. In addition to these all-or-nothing situations (100% water or no water) there are also 'in between' solutions. These situations originate from negotiations. In such cases there is a tendency to reach a Pareto-efficient solution. See Figure 10.1 in the textbook.
d.  The initial assignment of property rights has no influence on efficient allocation. The assignment of property rights to either the injured party or to the party that causes the damage both lead to efficient allocation. The assignment may have major consequences for the incomes of the parties involved. Thus there need not be a conflict between the efficiency criteria and the equity criteria. The property rights can after all be assigned to the party (or individuals) with the lowest incomes.

### 10.14 The assignment of property rights
According to the Coase theorem, in the case of rivalry for the use of a good, it does not matter to which party the property rights of the good are assigned. In all cases, the good will be used in such a way that a Pareto-optimal situation is achieved.
a.  Why is this?
b.  Salt pollution by a foreign company at the source of an international river results in extra costs for a large drinking water company that extracts its water supply from this river. According to the Coase theorem, there is room for a solution whereby salt pollution is reduced to the optimal level. In what context is 'optimal' to be read?

A drinking water company that extracts groundwater would like the owner of a forest in the extraction area to replace his conifers with broad-leaved trees. Broad-leaved trees use less water than conifers, so more groundwater is available for the extraction of drinking water. This would lead to extra net gains of € 1 million for the drinking water company. Because broad-leaved trees grow more slowly than conifers, the owner of the forest would see his net gains decrease by € 0.6 million. The two parties can start to negotiate and both strive to maximise their net benefits. The dilemma in this situation is that if the forest owner keeps the conifers, he causes disadvantages to the drinking water company. If the drinking water company can enforce the replacement of conifers by broad-leaved trees, it causes disadvantages to the forest owner.

c.  Is there a solution to this problem that is Pareto-efficient, whereby the forest owner himself decides to replace the conifers and the drinking water company itself decides about the groundwater extraction?

d.  Can damage caused by environmental pollution, whereby the number of victims is large and the individual environmental damage is small in proportion to the costs required to reduce the pollution, be reduced to an efficient level by the assignment of property rights?

## Answer 10.14 The assignment of property rights

a.  This result is due to the fact that all parties are able to reach an agreement without any costs (transaction costs are zero or negligible).

b.  Optimal means that the sum of the costs of reducing salt pollution and the drinking water company's costs for the extraction of good water are minimal, given the desired amount of water.

c.  One option is the all-or-nothing situations (on the one hand, keeping the conifers and no broad-leaved trees and on the other hand replacing the conifers by broad-leaved trees). Doing nothing leads to lower returns for the drinking water company of € 1 million. Replacing the conifers with broad-leaved trees leads to net benefits of € 1 million for the drinking water company. However, the forest owner has to deal with replanting costs and a lower yearly return of € 0.6 million.

In addition to all-or-nothing situations, there are also solutions by negotiation, which are Pareto-efficient, whereby the forest owner decides on the amount of broad-leaved trees and the drinking company decides on the amount of water extraction.

d.  With a large number of victims, transaction costs will be high. The costs involved by reducing pollution will be too high, certainly when the individual environmental damage is small.

## 10.15 Graphical interpretation of the Coase theorem

Assume there is a winegrower who uses chemical pesticides to protect his vineyards, resulting in pollution of a nearby lake by leaching and erosion. The area where the lake is located belongs to a person who is not only a keen fisherman, but he also has a campsite at the edge of the lake. In the absence of pollution, the lake is a beautiful spot for swimming and other water sport activities. There are no legal regulations against pollution of the lake. Figure 10.1 shows the marginal net benefits of the winegrower by the descending line $(EY^0)$ and the marginal losses of the campsite owner by the ascending line $(0F)$.

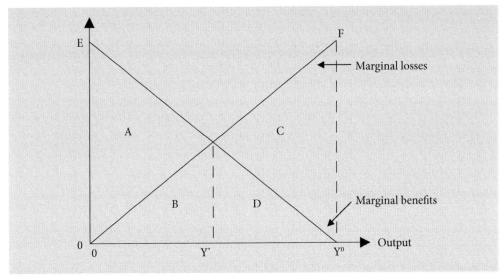

*Figure 10.1 The marginal net benefits of the winegrower (EY⁰) and the marginal losses of the campsite owner (0F).*

a. How much pollution would the winegrower need to produce and how much pollution would the campsite owner want?
b. Assume the winegrower has been given the right to pollute the lake. How much would the campsite owner be prepared to pay to the winegrower to persuade him to reduce pollution to a level that corresponds with $Y^*$?
c. Assume the campsite owner has been given the right to clean water in the lake. How much would the winegrower be prepared to pay to be allowed to pollute the water to point $Y^*$?
d. What will the advantages of negotiation be?

**Answer 10.15 Graphical interpretation of the Coase theorem**
a. The winegrower would want to produce the amount of pollution that corresponds with the output level of $Y^0$ and the campsite owner would want no pollution.
b. The campsite owner would be prepared to pay an amount corresponding to the surface area C+D. The winegrower would be prepared to reduce pollution for any amount greater than the surface area of D.
c. The winegrower would then be prepared to pay an amount corresponding with the surface area of A+B, in order to be allowed to produce an amount of pollution of $Y^*$. The camping owner would then be prepared to accept a pollution level of $Y^*$ for any amount greater than the surface area of B.
d. The advantages of negotiations, if transaction costs are less than the advantages, will result in an equilibrium of pollution of $Y^*$, independent of who has the initial property rights.

**10.16 Transactions costs and the Coase theorem**
a. What are transaction costs if we apply a solution in line with the Coase theorem?
b. What is the mutual relationship between a transaction and transaction costs?

c.  What elements – besides transaction costs – also require attention in applying the Coase theorem?

d.  What is, in general, the most important attribute of a transaction for determining the most suitable governance structure?

### Answer 10.16 Transactions costs and the Coase theorem

a.  Transaction costs of transferring property rights consist of private and public transaction costs. This includes:
    -   the cost of specifying, delineating and establishing the property rights;
    -   the cost of obtaining information and finding a contract partner;
    -   the cost of negotiations, formulating and writing a contract;
    -   monitoring cost and, if necessary, the enforcement costs.

b.  Firstly, whether a transaction takes place or not depends on whether the transaction costs are lower than the net benefits. Secondly, transaction costs also determine the choice of the best governance structure for carrying out the transaction.

c.  The application of the Coase theorem also requires attention to:
    -   property rights will need to be established, protected and maintained;
    -   a need for well-functioning markets;
    -   the number of parties: when the number of parties or individuals involved increases, the incentives for 'free rider behaviour' also increase.

d.  In general, the most important attribute of a transaction for determining the best suited governance structure is the asset-specificity attribute in combination with hold-up and lock-in effects.

### 10.17 Critical points concerning the validity of the Coase theorem

a.  What are critical points concerning the validity of the Coase theorem?

b.  One of the assumptions of the Coase theorem refers to transaction costs. What functions serve the analysing of transaction costs?

c.  Why is the rule 'smoking is forbidden' an efficient solution for the issue of smoking in a public space?

d.  Suppose the government would like to enforce product safety, among others for food products. What would be an effective and efficient solution: (1) producers concluding contracts with consumers; (2) government regulation; (3) self-regulation by the producers? Explain your answer and include also transaction costs arguments.

### Answer 10.17 Critical points concerning the validity of the Coase theorem

a.  **First**, depending on the version, the Coase theorem starts from a free access situation or where private rights already exist. **Second,** one of the key assumptions is that transaction costs are zero. However, each transaction of goods or services involves costs. It means that in practice this assumption does not often correspond with the real world application. **Third**, it is assumed is that a gain in property rights will be valued the same as a loss in property rights. However, most people have loss aversion. **Fourth**, the equity effects of the assignment, trade and final entitlements are ignored.

b.  Analysing the major sources of transaction costs serves at least three functions:
    -   **First**, it helps us to identify where to expect inefficiencies.

- **Second,** it helps us to explain (a) a whole range of practices and formal rules including those that arise to minimise transaction costs and (b) certain government regulations (designed to achieve as much as possible in an institutional environment) where bargaining among individuals would be too difficult, complex, or costly to be a realistic possibility.
  - **Finally,** it lays a foundation for an important part of the institutional economics: *property rights theory*, especially *getting the property rights right*. If the allocation of a bundle of property rights does affect value, then one possible objective is to assign them in a way that creates value.
c. The rule 'smoking is forbidden' is an efficient solution compared to starting a bargaining process between smokers and non-smokers, because the transaction costs are much lower.
d. Private contracting with producers concluding contracts with consumers would involve high transactions costs, especially for controlling and enforcement. It is possible that the target 'product safety' will not be realised. Self-regulation by producers can work, but the results depend on the trustworthiness and the reputation mechanism of the producers. Measures oriented towards reducing hidden information, hidden actions and lack of credible commitment (see Figure 7.2 in the textbook) would involve high transaction costs. Government regulation could be the best solution from the viewpoint of transaction costs, although this solution is not *without* transaction costs.

### 10.18. Role of property rights in a market economy
a. What is a property right?
b. How can we see property rights in historical terms?
c. What role do property rights play in a market economy?
d. Do property rights also have ethical aspects? Please could you give some examples and some major point of conflicts?
e. What is the view of the supporters of the free market system about private property?

### Answer 10.18 Role of property rights in a market economy
a. A property right is a socially-enforced right to select the uses of an economic good. A property right is private when it is assigned to a specific person.
b. In historical terms, property rights may be viewed as a response to scarcity.
c. Property rights are alienable when they can be transferred (sold or given) to other individuals. Since owners bear the wealth effects of their actions, there are strong incentives to rearrange property rights in market transactions to increase efficiency and value.
d. Property rights have – besides economic efficiency and fairness – ethical significance. For examples and some major point of conflicts see the textbook.
e. Supporters of free market systems see private property as a fundamental right, not just a mechanism for generating incentives.

### 10.19 Government and role of property rights
a. Why is role of the government so important?
b. Why should the government protect the holders of patents or copyrights?
c. What are the short-term inefficiency effects of these types of property rights?

**Answer 10.19 Government and role of property rights**

a.  In well-functioning societies, the initial assignment of property rights is typically a task of the government. Governments not only protect property rights, they also create new property rights, for example, through patents, trademarks, copyrights laws, production rights, income rights and property rights for pollution.

b.  The holders of patents or copyrights can use courts to prevent others from using their invention without compensation. Otherwise the incentives for creative and innovative activities would disappear; the long-term impacts would be bad.

c.  These property rights in fact result in short-term inefficiency. Once the idea is created, **it is efficient to have it employed as widely as possible** because there is no opportunity cost to its further exploitation. However, this solution would mean that inventors and developers would receive only a tiny fraction of the returns to investments.

**10.20 The characteristics of goods: excludability, rivalry and property rights**

a.  What are important concepts in the classification of goods and in specifying which type of property rights apply?

b.  What do excludability and non-excludability mean? What does it mean for the provision of these type of goods?

c.  What could be reasons for non-excludability?

d.  What are the effects of non-excludability?

e.  What is the relationship between non-excludability and property rights? What can we do about it?

**Answer 10.20 The characteristics of goods: excludability, rivalry and property rights**

a.  Excludability and rivalry are important concepts in the classification of goods, in specifying which type of property rights apply and what type of governance structures are preferred. Goods, and also natural resources, can be classified on the basis of technical characteristics – excludability and rivalry.

b.  Excludability means that it is possible to exclude individuals from goods, services and natural resources, e.g. persons who do not want to pay for the use of the goods. Non-excludability is the property of a good by which benefits of that good not only can be, but in fact are, made available to all. Once the good is provided, the benefits are available to all[3]. Non-excludability is, due to the lack of property rights, the exclusive factor for deciding which goods must be publicly provided.

c.  Excludability could be impossible for technical or for institutional reasons. In both cases it is not possible to assign property rights.

d.  When exclusion is not possible, problems such as free-riding and the prisoner's dilemma can occur. Free-riding means that individuals (free-riders) can use or consume the good without paying for it.

e.  Non-excludability is a characteristic that arises from a lack of property rights. In order to set a price for a commodity, it must be possible to exclude those who do not pay a price. For some goods, exclusion is possible but costly. The metering of water use, tolls for routes and bridges, introduction of production quotas and $CO_2$ emission quotas, etc. are examples of

---

[3] This can not only refer to positive goods but also to negative things.

costly, and not always universally adopted, exclusion devices. Exclusion might be possible at a cost in a situation involving environmental pollution or congestion. There are, however, other goods for which exclusion is intrinsically impossible. National defence is a commonly quoted example of a good from which exclusion is not possible. If exclusion is impossible or too costly to be privately profitable, an essential precondition for the establishment of effective property rights is lacking.

### 10.21 Rivalry and non-rivalry
a. What does rivalry mean? What do we assume in the ideal typical situation of a market with perfect competition in all markets?
b. What does non-rivalry mean for the use of a good?
c. What is an important measure for the level of non-rivalry?

### Answer 10.21 Rivalry and non-rivalry
a. Rivalry relates to the possibility that a good can be used only by an individual and not, at the same time, by other persons. With divisible goods, i.e. goods which can be technically divided into marketable units, rivalry is clearly present. In the ideal typical situation of a market with perfect competition in all markets, all goods, factors of production and natural resources are completely rivalrous. One person's right to the good is always at the cost of the other person.
b. In the case of a non-rivalry good, several individuals can use a good at the same time. Multiple use, i.e. use by several persons simultaneously, is then possible.
c. An important measure of rivalry is the marginal cost. For non-rival goods, the marginal costs of use are nil.

### 10.22 Public, quasi-public good and club goods
a. What is the difference between pure public goods and quasi or impure public goods?
b. What is the difference between a pure public good and a common good?
c. What is the difference between a quasi-public good and a club good?
d. How can the government regulate the use of a common good?

### Answer 10.22 Public quasi-public good and club goods
a. A pure public good is non-rival and non-excludable, whereas a quasi or impure public good is non-rival but is excludable.
b. A pure public good is non-rival and non-excludable whereas a common good is rival and non-excludable.
c. A quasi-public good is non-rival and excludable whereas a club good is partially non-rival and excludable.
d. The government can regulate the use of common goods by introducing user rights, quota, pollution rights (e.g. $CO_2$ emission rights) and licences.

### 10.23 Spectrum of goods
a. Why are *rivalry* and *excludability* useful concepts?
b. What are pure public goods?
c. What are impure or quasi-public goods and what are common goods?
d. What is characteristic for club goods?

e. What is the essential difference between club goods and pure public goods? What is a club?

## Answer 10.23 Spectrum of goods

a. Once the characteristics *rivalry* and *excludability* of goods are defined, the so-called spectrum of goods can be distinguished, ranging from pure public goods to pure private goods. Based on that we indicate the most suitable governance structure.
b. Pure public goods have the properties of *non-rivalry* and *non-excludability*
c. Goods whose benefits are non-rival and (partially) excludable are called impure public goods. Common goods are goods and services whose benefits are (partially) rival and non-excludable.
d. The benefits of club goods are excludable but partially non-rival.
e. The essential difference between club goods and pure public goods depends on the existence of an exclusion mechanism. For the characteristics of clubs, see Section 3.7 of the textbook and question 3.18.

## 10.24 Externality

a. What is an externality?
b. What is the relationship between property rights and externalities?
c. Why might externalities lead a firm to discharge too much pollution into a river?
d. The Congress in the USA has passed a law that limits the level of cotton dust within textile factories. Why might a textile firm reduce too much cotton dust (i.e. below the level set by the Congress) within its workplace?

## Answer 10.24 Externality

a. An externality arises if one party's action has unintended side effects on the utility or profits of another party. Externalities might be positive or negative.
b. The failure of property rights to be well-defined is an important ingredient of many externality situations.
c. Some of the costs of the pollution are borne by others (there is an externality), and so the firm does not consider these costs as part of its decision making (unless the costs are low for negotiating with the harmed parties, in which case the firm faces an opportunity cost of not being paid to lower the pollution level).
d. Since the firm must hire the workers who would be exposed to the air pollution within the factory, there is no externality. Lower air quality makes the job less attractive and thus raises the wage the firm has to pay its employees. Thus, there are private incentives for the firm to choose the efficient level of air quality within the factory.

## 10.25 Property rights

a. Suppose you are working as an economist at the FAO. The FAO has worked out the idea that group ownership (i.e. common property rights) would be the solution to overfishing in the oceans and seas. Please name some critical points of this property regime.
b. What does a high level of theft in a country mean for the quality of the property rights? What will the effects be on investments, maintaining and developing of assets?

# 11. The economic theory of takings

## 11.1 Takings
a. What are takings?
b. Under what conditions are takings allowed?
c. Which two types of takings can be distinguished?
d. Do compensated and uncompensated takings have different incentive effects?
e. Why should the government be careful with compensation in the case of takings?

## Answer 11.1 Takings
a. Takings means removing or taking away of property rights, mostly by the government.
b. In many countries, the constitution circumscribes the power of the government to take private property. Such power may only be used under two conditions: (1) the private property is taken for a public use, and (2) the owner is compensated.
c. Two types of takings can be distinguished:
   - Titular takings. In this case, all the property rights are taken away. The government takes land from many owners in order to provide some public goods, such as schools, highways, dams, airports, military bases and nature areas.
   - Regulatory takings. This is a restriction on the use of the property without taking the title from the owners. This involves a loss of a part of the property rights.

   Regulatory takings are less far-reaching than titular takings. The owner keeps the title, only a part of his property rights is taken away, and the regulation causes a fall in the value of the asset. Strong direct regulation for realising e.g. environmentally-friendly farming practices is a form of takings which involves a loss of a part of the property rights.
d. Compensated and uncompensated takings have different incentive effects. If the government does not have to compensate for titular takings and regulatory takings, then it will impose too many of them. In the case of regulatory takings, if there are too many restrictions, resources will be incompletely utilised. Thus, uncompensated restrictions result in inefficient use. Another strong argument for compensation besides efficiency is that of equity.
e. Compensation should take into account:
   - Compensation means that the risks for private persons are lower or even zero. In this case, their investment level will be higher.
   - Full compensation might even provide incentives for strong private efforts or investments.
   - Non-compensation for takings gives government officials an incentive to take too much, whereas compensation for takings makes government officials internalise the full cost of expropriating private property rights.
   - Non-compensation for restrictions gives government officials an incentive to overregulate, whereas compensation makes government officials more careful because of the cost of losing part of private property rights.
   - The income distribution or the equity effects demand a careful policy on the part of the government.
   - Loss aversion of the people involved. This has consequences for the level of compensation. A compensation 'equal to the market value of the property' does not often compensate the loss aversion as a result of the taking.

## 11.2 Takings versus taxes
a. Why does the government need resources?
b. What ways can the government use to obtain resources?
c. What is the excess burden of taxes?
d. If the government needs resources for carrying out its tasks, what is preferable: takings or taxes?

## Answer 11.2 Taking versus taxation
a. The government needs resources for preparing and carrying out her tasks and has to regulate activities of people, such as producing public goods, expenditures for the poor, social security, etc.
b. The forming and functioning of the government requires a transfer of resources from private to public hands. Private property must be transformed for public use. There are two ways for having the required resources at its disposal: (1) imposing taxes and using the taxes for buying resources and hiring people for fulfilling the tasks of the government; (2) making use of takings. In the last case, the government has access to resources and labour directly.
c. The distortion from taxes is termed as *excess burden*. For consumers, it is a loss in their consumer surplus (i.e. a loss in utility) and for the producers it is a loss in their producer surplus. Together, this is called the *excess burden* or *dead weight loss* of the taxes.
d. If we balance takings against taxation:
   - Taxation gives less distortions, is less inequitable, has less negative incentives and less uncertainties, resulting in less hold-up problems.
   - In the case of takings, the person whose property has been taken has bad luck. Taxation gives a better risk-spreading than takings of properties. The risks are shared by all the tax payers.
   - Taxation is based on income, wealth, returns or inheritance. Each person is confronted with the same tax tariffs. If the government needs resources for carrying out its tasks, taxation is by far preferable to takings.

## 11.3 Compensation of takings and compensation paradox
The government should only make use of takings if (1) the owner is compensated; (2) the use of private property is restricted to a public purpose.
a. Why does the owner have to be compensated?
b. Why does the use of private property have to be restricted to public purpose?
c. What is the link between these rules, and efficiency and equity arguments?
d. Do uncompensated and compensated takings have different incentive effects? Explain why.
e. What is the compensation paradox about no compensation and full compensation?

## Answer 11.3 Compensation of takings and compensation paradox
a. The government should only make use of takings if the owner is compensated:
   - to prevent misuse;
   - otherwise the government would end up with too many public goods;
   - for avoiding the problem '*who is the person who has bad luck?*'
b. The government should only make use of takings if the use of private property is restricted to a public purpose. The reasons for this are:

- prevention of misuse;
- preventing the transfer of property from one private person to another (e.g. land from farmers to the son of a (corrupt) president);
- the public purpose requirement prohibits the use of takings (1) which avoid the market and (2) which includes a transfer of property from one private person to another.

c. The link between these rules and efficiency and equity arguments is that both rules are necessary for realising efficiency and equity.

d. Uncompensated- and compensated takings have different incentive effects:
- No compensation means no costs for the government, and this is an incentive to take too much.
- No compensation also creates hold-up effects in the society.
- In the case of uncompensated- and compensated takings, the person who is the victim has 'bad luck'. However, this is more an equity argument.
- Fully compensated takings can lead to useless investments or wasteful improvements in assets.

e. The compensation paradox confronts the effects of no compensation and full compensation. This is described above.

## 11.4 The Coase theorem, takings and land reform

a. What criteria can be used for comparing the application of the Coase theorem, takings and land reform?

b. What is the crucial difference between the application of the Coase theorem, takings and land reform?

c. What is the 'assumption' about the valuation of the losses and gains for the Coase theorem, takings and land reform? What do you think about this assumption?

d. What does the compensation rule 'equal to the market value of the property' mean for the valuation of the losses and gains?

## Answer 11.4 The Coase theorem, takings and land reform

a. The start situation, purpose, transfer in property rights, transaction mechanism, economic basis, compensation, valuation of gains and losses, income distribution and the applied theory; theory of firm or theory of the state can all be used as criteria.

b. The purpose of the Coase theorem is to realise a more efficient situation, as explained in Chapter 10 of the textbook. For takings, the purpose is to produce public goods, and for land reform the purpose is often to maintain political power.

c. The valuation of the gains and losses are assumed to be equal in the Coase theorem. For takings, the valuation of the gains and losses is not clear. For land reform, the valuation of gains and losses does not matter for the political ruler. The assumption about the valuation of the gains and losses – all things being equal – is often doubtful, given the loss aversion of people.

d. The compensation rule 'equal to the market value of the property' assumes that gains and losses are considered to be equal.

## 11.5 Zoning of land

'When I bought this land, it was zoned only for farming. But the longer I live here, the more I resent the wealth transfer I'm paying to other landowners without such restrictions.' Please give some comments.

### Answer 11.5 Zoning of land

You aren't paying any wealth transfer. Presumably you paid less for the property because of these restrictions. Hence, you were compensated for the restriction in the form of lower land prices. The owner of the land when the restriction was added bore the cost. Nonetheless, such comments frequently come from individuals lobbying to get a law changed in order to transfer wealth back to themselves.

## 11.6 Restrictions on the number of pubs

Dubliners often complain that there are too few pubs in their city. At night, pubs can be quite crowded and prospective customers are often turned away. Some Dubliners blame this pub 'shortage' on the English who originally enacted laws restricting pubs centuries ago when they ruled Ireland. Is it appropriate to blame the English? Explain.

### Answer 11.6 Restrictions on the number of pubs

The English originally might have enacted the restrictions on the number of pubs, but it is the current Dubliners who maintain the restrictions. They could have overturned them. It is most likely the case that existing pub owners, along with temperance groups, are maintaining the existing limitations. The existing pub owners don't want to see the monopoly rents competed away.

## 11.7 Nature areas and takings

A few years ago, it was decided in the Netherlands that several areas that are now in use as cultivated land, should be 'given back to the sea', or reformed into nature areas (some of these areas were created by drying parts of the water areas directly adjacent to land, the famous Dutch 'polders'). Because the cultivated land is (in most cases) private property now, the areas have to be 'taken' by the government first, the current owners are expropriated, they will lose their complete bundle of property rights.
a. Dutch farmers often heavily oppose these plans. How could you explain this from economic theory?
b. What should the compensation schedule for these takings look like?
c. Do you think that this is a typically Dutch problem?

### Answers 11.7 Nature areas and takings
a. This can be explained based on a combination of loss aversion of people and the economic theory of *takings*. First, the farmers will have loss aversion. They will lose their land, their job, the cultural environment into which they were born. The farmers have often had the land in use and in ownership for generations. The concept of loss aversion (developed in the prospect theory of Kahneman and Tversky[1]) is that losses are valued much higher than gains, even if

---

[1] Kahneman, D. and A. Tversky, 1979. Prospect theory: an analysis of decisions under risk. Econometrica 47: 263-292.

the market price of both is exactly identical. A compensation based on the market price does not take into account the loss aversion of people.

Second, the economic theory of *takings* describes the requirements which should be fulfilled to apply an efficient use of takings by the government. In short, these requirements are:

- Full compensation for the owners and users of land, and in this case taking into account the loss aversion of people.
- A government should only take private goods if this is necessary to create public goods. In the case of the removal of polders, dispute is possible if this indeed creates public goods or only private goods in favour of some private persons or interest groups.

Summarising the opposition can be explained by a combination of the loss aversion of people and the economic theory of takings. In practice, the offered compensation is often based on the estimated market value of the land as reference level. This ignores the loss aversion that people experience.

In addition, there are of course arguments that are not directly linked to economic theory (e.g. the idea that many farmers feel that their own plots are the best ones).

b. The compensation schedule should fully compensate the current owners and users of the land. This should be based on a reference level that takes into account the issues mentioned above (in practice, even an appropriate estimation of the market value of agricultural land may already be difficult as the quality of soils differs widely).

c. This also occurs in many other countries. In many cases the land will be not used to 'give back to the sea', or converted into nature areas, but for infrastructure projects such as roads, railways and airports, dam projects for generating energy and water storage for irrigation, e.g. in Spain and China.